FEMINIST FANTASIES

Also by Phyllis Schlafly

ON POLITICS

A Choice Not an Echo

ON FAMILY AND FEMINISM

The Power of the Positive Woman
The Power of the Christian Woman
Who Will Rock the Cradle?
Equal Pay for Unequal Work
Stronger Families or Bigger Government?
Meddlesome Mandate
Pornography's Victims

ON NATIONAL SECURITY

The Gravediggers
Strike from Space
The Betrayers
Kissinger on the Couch
Ambush at Vladivostok

ON HISTORY

Mindszenty the Man
Safe Not Sorry

ON EDUCATION

First Reader
First Reader Workbook
Turbo Reader
Child Abuse in the Classroom

FEMINIST
FANTASIES

Phyllis Schlafly

Foreword by Ann Coulter

SPENCE PUBLISHING COMPANY • DALLAS

2003

Published in the United States by
Spence Publishing Company
111 Cole Street
Dallas, Texas 75207

Library of Congress Control Number: 2002114581

Printed in the United States of America

To my mother,
Odile Dodge Stewart,
and
to my grandmother
Bertha Layton Dodge
who taught me strength and survival
in an uncertain world
based on Christian faith,
hard work, and perseverance

Pause awhile,
And let my counsel sway you in this case.

Much Ado About Nothing

Contents

II
The Media:
Mirror or Maker of Trends?

III
Questioning a Woman's Place

IV

A Gender-Neutral Military?

V
Marriage and Motherhood

Foreword

WRITING THE FOREWORD to a book by Phyllis Schlafly is like being the warm-up band for the Rolling Stones. Though conservative women in my generation are often compared to Schlafly, all of us combined could never match the titanic accomplishments of this remarkable woman. Schlafly is unquestionably one of the most important people of the twentieth century. Among her sex, she is rivaled only by Margaret Thatcher.

That Phyllis Schlafly is the mortal enemy of a movement that claims to promote women tells you all you need to know about feminism. That many people alive today are unaware of Schlafly's achievements tells you all you need to know about the major media.

Schlafly is brilliant, beautiful, principled, articulate, tireless, and most important, absolutely fearless. And, as this book demonstrates, she is always right. She has always been right. She will always be right.

No, wait: Correction! One time she was wrong. In 1977, while being harangued by Dr. Joyce Brothers on the *Merv Griffin Show*, Schlafly claimed Harvard Law School had been admitting women since at least 1945. In fact, Harvard Law School did not begin admitting women for several more years. But in 1945 it may have been prepared to make an exception for Phyllis Schlafly.

This Phi Beta Kappa had already earned her master's degree in political science from Harvard in a brief eight months—getting As in constitutional law, international law, and public administration, and an A-minus in modern political theory, long before grade inflation. Though Harvard Law School did not admit women, Schlafly's professors urged her to stay and attend law school or, alternatively, earn her doctorate. (Imagine the Harvard faculty meetings today had she stayed on and become a professor there!)

Consider that this was back when Harvard was a serious place, so it meant something. Schlafly's Harvard professors—whose specialties were things like constitutional law, not cutting rap CDs—deemed her "brilliant." The professor who intervened on her behalf, Benjamin Wright, was a distinguished constitutional historian—the sort of legitimate scholar who wouldn't have a chance of being hired at today's Harvard.

Years later, when Schlafly was testifying against the Equal Rights Amendment (ERA), she was often ridiculed by media feminists for not being a lawyer. So while writing her syndicated column, raising six highly accomplished children, and defeating the ERA, Schlafly went to Washington University Law School in St. Louis. She graduated near the top of her class, winning the prize in administrative law.

Though Schlafly is most famously associated with her stunning, nearly miraculous defeat of ERA, she has played a pivotal role in a broad range of political controversies for four decades.

In 1964, she wrote *A Choice Not An Echo*, which sold an astounding three million copies. (The average nonfiction book sells five thousand copies.) The book changed the Republican Party forever. In this respect, it was not unlike many battles Schlafly would wage: first she would have to conquer the Republicans and then she could conquer the nation.

A Choice Not An Echo is widely credited with handing Barry Goldwater the Republican nomination for president. Goldwater lost badly in the general election, but the Republican Party would never be the same. His nomination began the retreat of sellout, northeastern

Rockefeller Republicans (who wanted to wreck the country with only slightly less alacrity than the Democrats). Without Schlafly, without that book, without Goldwater's candidacy, it is unlikely that Ronald Reagan would ever have been elected president.

Later in 1964, she collaborated with Admiral Chester Ward on another book, *The Gravediggers*. This book accused the elite foreign policy establishment of cheerfully selling out our nation's military superiority to the Soviet Union. It sold a whopping two million copies.

Also with Ward, Schlafly co-authored the extremely influential (and extremely long, at over eight hundred pages) *Kissinger on the Couch*, methodically assailing Kissinger's foreign policy. As with her crusade against the ERA—which she waged simultaneously—*Kissinger on the Couch* would turn conventional wisdom upside down.

Until then, attacking Kissinger's beloved Strategic Arms Limitations Treaty (SALT) was the secular version of challenging the Pope on Christ's divinity—or, I suppose, challenging a constitutional amendment that purported to give women "equal rights." But she was right, she was persuasive, and she overturned popular opinion.

Indeed, Schlafly has written prolifically about American foreign policy and military affairs. She was an early and vigorous proponent of a missile defense shield. For many years she was national defense chairman of the Daughters of the American Revolution. She has written extensively about ICBMs and defense treaties. Meanwhile, feminists engaged in cliffhanger debates about whether to wear lipstick.

It was fortuitous that Schlafly was lured away from national defense and became the feminists' worst nightmare. In the early 1970s, the Source Library in Darien staged monthly political debates that were broadcast on radio. Every program featured two debaters and a panel of student questioners—of which, I note, my oldest brother, in high school at the time, was the head.

In December 1971, they wanted a debate on the Equal Rights Amendment but couldn't find anyone to oppose it. Finally, a friend of

Schlafly's gave her a try. Schlafly declined. She explained she had little interest in the ERA, but to give her a call if they ever wanted a debate on national defense. The friend implored Schlafly simply to read the amendment.

She did, was duly appalled, and came to debate. Thus was a crusade born. The Source Library's decision to ask Schlafly to debate the ERA was the most historically significant fluke since a little girl wrote to Abraham Lincoln telling him he should grow a beard.

Almost no one remembers this now, but when Schlafly turned her attention to the ERA, any reasonable person would have said it was unstoppable. The Senate had passed it 84 to 8. The House passed it 354 to 23. Thirty states approved it in the first year after it was sent to the states for ratification. Only eight more states were needed. There was little question that the ERA was about to become our next constitutional amendment.

But the ERA had not yet faced Phyllis Schlafly. Over the next nine years, thanks to Schlafly and her Eagle Forum, only five states ratified it. In the same time, five states rescinded their earlier ratifications, for a net total of zero ratifications.

Not surprisingly, given her background, one of Schlafly's most devastating arguments against the ERA was that it would end the female exemption from the draft. Though the amendment's proponents sneered at this, she was right. Law professors were making the same point in the likes of the *Yale Law Journal*. Beyond this, I will not attempt to summarize Schlafly's case against the ERA. It is in this book. Any argument that could stop the ERA steamroller dead in its tracks manifestly can speak for itself.

Suffice it to say that Schlafly's arguments trumped the political platforms of both parties, both Republican and Democratic presidents and their wives, and a slew of Hollywood celebrities including Alan Alda, Carol Burnett, Marlo Thomas, Phil Donahue, and Jean Stapleton. As Schlafly said, they have the movie star money and we have the voters.

To a Gen-Xer like me, the most unfathomable aspect of Schlafly's success is that she mobilized a vast army of women without the internet. Not without reason she has been called the greatest pamphleteer since Thomas Paine. (But unlike Paine, she never went bad.)

The story behind Phyllis Schlafly's biography, *Phyllis Schlafly: The Sweetheart of the Silent Majority*, provides a good snapshot of Schlafly's power to inspire. The book's author, Carol Felsenthal, explained how she came to write Schlafly's biography after attacking Schlafly in print in 1977.

An ERA supporter and feminist, Felsenthal had written a column for the *Chicago Tribune* ridiculing Schlafly's ninth book, *The Power of the Positive Woman*. She said it was irrational, contradictory, and simple-minded. And then something extraordinary happened: "Two days later, the letters of protest started coming, and they kept coming— from people who were enraged that I had insulted 'Our Savior,' as one letter writer called Schlafly, or 'Our Wonder Woman,' as another called her. . . . [T]he *Tribune* book editor does not run a regular 'letters' column. These people were writing for one reason only—to convert me, to make me see the light."

Though Felsenthal had written hundreds of columns before this, she said she could "count on one hand the number of letters they provoked." Thus, she became fascinated with the woman who could arouse such passionate support. Felsenthal's meticulously researched, definitive biography of Phyllis Schlafly is the result. Charmingly, the toughest part of Felsenthal's project was overcoming Schlafly's humble resistance to the very idea of a biography.

I have my own story about Schlafly's vast influence. When I worked for the U.S. Senate from 1995 to 1997, Republicans had just taken Congress for the first time in forty years. It was a busy time: this was the beginning of the (failed, as it turned out) "Republican revolution." (Don't blame me—the "Republican" majority consisted of many of the same liberal Republicans Schlafly has battled throughout her career.)

There was a lot of energy and activity on all fronts. But over time, a peculiar phenomenon occurred, heartwarming and comedic at the same time. Letters began pouring in to every Senate office vehemently opposing the United Nations Treaty on the Rights of the Child.

It was a preposterous treaty, it goes without saying, providing children with such "rights" under international law as refusing to do household chores. The Clinton administration had sent the treaty to Congress for ratification, where, mercifully, it promptly went to the bottom of Senator Jesse Helms's "In" box.

There was little chance Helms would take it up. But, on the other hand, crazier things have become law. Only the overwhelming public opposition ensured that this treaty would not become law.

Letters adamantly opposed to the treaty streamed in, day after day, month after month, piling up in Senate offices. Most letters that come to congressional offices are written out of pure self interest. (People who live on government grants tend to be strongly opposed to any efforts to relieve the taxpayer of paying their salaries.) Yet here were boxes and boxes of letters from well-informed people seeking no government favor, but rather opposed, on principle, to a proposed international treaty. How did they know? It turned out, of course, that Phyllis Schlafly had written a column about the treaty. The letters followed.

There is no major national debate in the past four decades in which Schlafly's powerful, salubrious influence is not manifest. Schlafly could have rested on her laurels after writing *A Choice Not an Echo*. She could have rested on her laurels after defeating the ERA. Indeed, she could have rested on her laurels on any number of occasions, and America can be thankful that she did not.

The sheer breadth of the issues Schlafly takes on is astonishing. It is impossible to think of anyone alive today who addresses such a range of topics in any depth. Most public figures focus on one or two issues and stick with those. Not Schlafly—and with no detriment to her always incisive analysis. (If anyone on the left did this with Schlafly's skill, we'd never hear the end of it.)

In this book, Schlafly writes about a number of legal issues I count among my specialties, such as the Violence Against Women Act and sexual harassment law. Time and again she goes like a heat-seeking missile to the heart of the matter and shreds legal monstrosities with blinding clarity. Don't be fooled by how easy she makes it look! Like an Olympic athlete, her talent is to make it seem easy.

It's almost unfair for Schlafly to train her analytical mind on the feminists. But what the feminists lack in truth, morals, and linear thinking, they make up for in their hegemonic control over the major media.

No matter. Throughout her career, Schlafly refused to be intimidated by mediocre opinion makers decreeing what "everyone" is supposed to think. She would read up on an issue and then take a position that almost no academic would defend simply because it was so contrary to accepted opinion.

She relentlessly pressed points that polite people thought it bad taste to talk about. They preferred to approve the general sentiment and not think about any messy details or facts. Thus, for example, Schlafly questioned how ERA would affect separate male-female locker rooms, gays, abortion, adoption, widow's benefits, divorce law, and the military. She has an knack for pulling the string that unravels complicated left-wing nonsense.

In this book are some of the arguments that changed the world. Among my favorites is "Going Around with the Wrong Crowd." I always knew it was true: liberal women think men are pigs because liberal men *are* pigs. Schlafly cites chapter and verse on the private lives of such liberal luminaries as Marx, Sartre, Rousseau, Picasso, Ibsen, and Hemingway. Love of totalitarianism and misogyny go hand in hand.

It is impossible to resist mentioning that Schlafly came up with the only clever remark the feminists have ever had. When Schlafly ran for

Congress in 1970, her opponent ceaselessly browbeat her for being a woman, complaining that she should be home raising her children. Schlafly responded: "My opponent says a woman's place is in the home. But my husband replies, a woman's place is in the House—the U.S. House of Representatives."

Be sure to mention this to the next feminist you see wearing a T-shirt that says, "A Woman's Place is in the House . . . and Senate."

A fitting summary of Schlafly's approach to the feminists is in the last line of her profile. You know she means it, and yet you also suspect she takes devilish pleasure knowing that it drives feminists crazy. After an abbreviated summary of her many accomplishments, Schlafly's profile concludes: "The mother of six children, she was named 1992 Illinois Mother of the Year."

ANN COULTER

I

The Revolution Is Over

O, these deliberate fools, when they do choose,
They have the wisdom by their wit to lose.

The Merchant of Venice

All I Want Is a Husband

In mid-1982, the women's liberation movement, or feminism as it prefers to be called, suddenly became passé. The movement was born in the mid-1960s with the publication of Betty Friedan's *The Feminine Mystique* and was fashionable in the media, in colleges, and in women's magazines from 1972 to 1982.

In 1982, the tide turned, even in pro-feminist newspapers and magazines. An op-ed piece written by a feminist in the *Chicago Tribune* in October 1982 started out, "Let's face it. The Revolution is over. I just turned 31 and all I want is a husband."

Feminists in their thirties began to admit candidly that they have "baby hunger." That's the emotional trauma that comes over today's liberated woman when she turns age thirty and realizes that the clock is ticking and her years of possible motherhood are slipping away.

The *New York Times Magazine* published a cover story written by a feminist on October 17, 1982, called "Voices From the Post-Feminist Generation." She told how one of her male friends asked her to get him a date with "a woman who's not a feminist." She replied that she didn't know any. He told her she was wrong and suggested that she inquire among younger women.

So this feminist writer in her thirties started interviewing smart young women in their twenties, and she learned quite a lot. She discovered that, among women in their twenties, "feminism has become a dirty word." She discovered that young women in their twenties have concluded that feminists are "unhappy," "bitter," "angry," "tired," and "bored," and that the happy, enthusiastic, relaxed women are not feminists. The writer found that young women are especially turned off by feminism because of its "incredible bitterness." She admitted that "feminism had come to be strongly identified with lesbianism."

The *Wall Street Journal* ran a series of news stories about the disruption in corporations and law firms caused by the wave of pregnancies at the managerial and professional levels. Since more women hold high-level jobs, their time off for pregnancy has caused serious problems. In the past eight years, the number of women over thirty having a child has almost doubled.

A study by the advertising firm of Batten, Barton, Durstine & Osborne discovered that "the professional homemaker is a happy woman who feels good about herself and her ability to stick to her decision to remain at home, even under strong societal pressure to find an outside job." She is feminine and traditional; she is not feminist.

The ideology of feminism teaches that women have been mistreated since time began and that even in America women are discriminated against by an oppressive male-dominated society. As a political movement, feminism teaches that a just society must mandate identical treatment for men and women in every phase of our lives, no matter how reasonable it is to treat them differently, and that gender must never be used as the criterion for any decision.

As an economic movement, feminism teaches that true fulfillment and liberation for women are in a paying job rather than in the confining, repetitive drudgery of the home, and that child care must not be allowed to interfere with a woman's career. Feminism's psychological outlook on life is basically negative; it teaches women that the odds are stacked so severely against them that they probably cannot succeed in whatever they attempt.

Feminism has nothing at all to do with being "feminine." Feminine means accentuating the womanly attributes that make women deliciously different from men. The feminine woman enjoys her right to be a woman. She has a positive outlook on life. She knows that she is a person with her own identity and that she can seek fulfillment in the career of her choice, including that of traditional wife and mother.

1982

Female Emancipation?

"Love and Success: Can We Have It All?" was the headline over an article in *Glamour* magazine. The subhead proclaimed the feminist answer to that question in large type: "Yes, say today's high-powered young women. Reining in your ambition is no longer an acceptable price to pay for love."

The article starts off with enthusiastic examples of highly paid professional or business women who are successful in their careers, just like men. One is a lawyer, one a doctor (license plate MS MD 1), one a vice president of a large corporation.

It all sounds so perfect—until the fine print on the back page reveals the costs. One survey shows that, among women who earn $50,000 a year or more, the divorce rate is four times the national average. Another survey shows that, among women who earn $25,000 a year or more, the divorce rate is more than twice the average for all women. A third survey shows that, among professional and managerial women whose median income is $20,000 to $25,000 a year, 46 percent are single, 19 percent are divorced or separated, and 58 percent are childless, all figures much higher than the national average. A fourth survey shows that women who go on to graduate school divorce more often than those who stop after four years of college.

The November 1982 issue of *Psychology Today* carried an article called "Real Men Don't Earn Less Than Their Wives," which frankly reports that research shows that the rate of divorce for women who hold non-traditional jobs is twice as high as for those who hold traditional jobs. It concludes that the "risks to marriage are serious but not insuperable."

The real answer to the love-and-success question is: anything's possible, but a woman who tries for both at the same time should know in advance that it is a high-risk lifestyle and be prepared to pay the price.

Until the twentieth century, women always participated in the labor force just like men, whether on the farm or in the craftsman's shop. It required the productive labor of both husband and wife, and often their children, to make ends meet. When the Industrial Revolution swept across America in the nineteenth century, women worked in the factories just like men.

One of the greatest achievements of the American economic system is that, by the end of World War I, our productivity had increased so much that the average working man was able to bring home a sufficient wage so his wife did not have to labor in the factories, mines, or fields. "Female emancipation" meant freeing women from the harness of the labor force so that they could have a better quality of life at home.

Over the last ten years, inflation and high taxes have cut so deeply into the take-home pay of the average working man that women by the millions are being pushed out of the home into the factories, and even into the mines. Almost half of all American wives are now in the labor force. Feminists call this liberation. They brag about the higher and higher percentage of women in the labor force.

The rationale behind the push for affirmative action for women is that an oppressive society, business discrimination, and the outdated stereotype of woman in the home are to blame when a given category of employment includes fewer than 50 percent women. Affirmative action programs are designed to force employers, through federal and financial penalties, to increase artificially the percentage of women employed in each job classification, especially the "nontraditional."

The fourth annual *American Family Report*, a national survey conducted by Louis Harris and Associates for General Mills, has plenty of evidence to indicate that most women have not chosen full-time labor force participation as their life's goal. The survey results show that 39 percent of women prefer to work only at home, and another 14 percent prefer to do only volunteer work, making a total of 53 percent who do not want to be in the labor force at all. Another 32 percent want only part-time work, leaving only 12 percent of all American women who want full-time employment in the labor force.

In response to the question "Do you think the trend toward both parents working outside the home has had a generally positive, a generally negative, or no effect at all on families?", 52 percent of Americans answered "generally negative."

In the days before the federal government took such an active role in regulating employment, one man's wage could support a wife and family. Now, with high taxes and high inflation, it seems to take eighty hours of work a week to support a family. Instead of progress, this just might be regression to a nineteenth-century economic system.

1982

Phyllis Schlafly's National Anthem

One of the top ten rock records of 1982 was "I've Never Been To Me," sung by "Charlene" and issued by Motown Records. Thereby hangs an amazing tale of ideology, timing, social trends, and censorship.

The song was first released in 1976. Its timing was wrong, and it didn't catch on. Then, in early 1982, a disc jockey played it one night, and all his phone lines immediately lit up with enthusiastic callers. The song became an overnight sensation.

In the first two stanzas, Charlene sings about her exotic life enjoying sexual encounters all over the world. She was living in a liberated "paradise" on earth. When she "ran out of places and friendly faces" in the United States, she continued her travels to Greece and Monte Carlo because she "had to be free." As she sings it, "I've been undressed by kings, and I've seen some things that a woman ain't s'posed to see."

But all that sexually liberated "paradise" didn't make her happy. She's alone now, and she's "crying for unborn children that might have made me complete." Hence the refrain of the song, "I've been to paradise, but I've never been to me."

The song gives Charlene's advice to the "discontented mother and the regimented wife" who fantasizes about the exciting life she doesn't have. Charlene wishes someone had told her the truth about real love before she wasted her youth on "lies."

Anyone who has been watching the lifestyle sections of metropolitan newspapers and national magazines knows that stay-at-home motherhood now is "in"—especially for women in their thirties and forties who have discovered that the calendar is catching up with them and there is more to life than just having a well-paying career.

But this rock tune delivers an even more powerful message. It implies that having a baby is necessary to make a woman "complete." Even more remarkable, it says that real "truth" is not only in having a baby, but in loving and living with only one man.

For years, teenage girls have been taught the opposite. Through a combination of peer pressure, classroom sex courses, x- and r-rated movies, suggestive television programs, soft porn literature, and rock music, they've been taught that sex with any partner is ok if you feel good about it, that housewives lead dull and unrewarding lives and that fulfillment for women means liberation from home, husband, family, and children. Now, at last, young women are hearing about the joys of a husband and children from a rock record. Times surely have changed.

But, wait a minute; there's more to this story. As soon as "I've Never Been To Me" became a hit song, liberals and feminists felt threatened by its clear pro-family message, and they set out to silence it.

Columnist Richard Cohen waxed indignant about it in the *Washington Post*. He was upset because "the pendulum is swinging back" to motherhood. He said the song ought to be called "the Phyllis Schlafly national anthem," concluding that the song's popularity proves that a "reaction has set in" to the feminist movement, which he supports because it "shattered stereotypes" and "liberated women."

Now comes the most interesting part of this story about this "motherhood song." After it became so popular and its message so clear, Motown Records accommodated liberals by issuing a censored version of "I've Never Been To Me." Of course, Motown and the radio stations didn't use the word "censored"; they called it the "edited version."

Anyone who tuned in on adult rock radio stations during the first half of 1982 could hear the song within a couple of hours of listening. Some stations played the original version and some played the censored version. Censored was the middle part where Charlene interrupts her singing to talk straight to the housewife who thinks she is missing out on liberated living: "Hey, you know what paradise is? It's a lie, a fantasy we create about people and places as we like them to be. But you know what truth is? It's that little baby you're holding, and it's that man you fought with this morning—the same one you're going to make love with tonight. That's truth; that's love."

"Censorship" is the current chic slogan of liberals who are trying to intimidate pro-family activists who object to obscenity, profanity, blasphemy, immorality, and violence in textbooks and television programming. The liberals are like the thief who tries to conceal his crime by pointing to someone else and crying "stop, thief." The pressure groups against motherhood are the most ruthless censors of all.

1982

Does Mom Have to Work?

ABC-TV and Barbara Walters are lobbying for government, instead of parents, to assume the responsibility of taking care of babies. That's the conclusion we can draw when ABC's *20/20* aired *When Mom Has To Work*, on February 6, 1986.

Barbara solemnly announced that a debate about "whether mothers should work is no longer relevant" because most mothers "have" to take a paid job. She said that only 10 percent of moms stay home any more, and that most families need two paychecks. Barbara didn't check her facts carefully enough. The latest figures show that only half of mothers with children under age two have paid jobs. The other half are full-time homemakers, but Barbara pretended they don't exist.

The ABC program showed three employed couples, each with two preschool children. Barbara commiserated with them over their problems with hired child care, the guilt the mothers feel (she called it the "pain" of a deeply felt emotional conflict), the way the husbands feel neglected, the long hours of hard work, and the strains on marriage.

The program showed how the parents must wake up the children at 5:30 or 6:00 AM so they can be fed and dropped off at a daycare center before the mothers report to their jobs. The little children looked woefully unhappy at being forced to accept this unnatural schedule. The program was obviously designed to arouse sympathy for the "mom who has to work," but it evoked more sympathy for the preschool children who were dropped off and picked up each day like a bag of laundry. One pathetic youngster said, "Mommy, I wish you didn't have to work. You're always so tired."

Women's lib has been telling us for years that fathers should be supportive of their wives' careers and willing to do half the housework and baby tending. Indeed, these three husbands were supportive and caring. But when Barbara added up the hours, the wives were putting in a seven-hour day of domestic work on top of their full-time jobs, while the husbands were doing only four hours a day of domestic work.

The wives felt put upon because they had too little sleep and too much stress. Yet the husbands still felt neglected because their wives were always so tired and flopped into bed exhausted at 8:00 PM. The husbands discreetly shared their complaint with the nationwide television audience that their wives had no time or energy for romance.

After these probing invasions of the privacy of three young families, Barbara told us what we are supposed to think about all this. First, she berated the United States for being "the only industrial nation without a daycare policy." Then she proposed an ambitious action program.

Barbara told us that we should make helping these couples "a national priority." And who are the "we"? Well, she wants the taxpayers to provide good all-day care for preschoolers, presumably beginning in infancy, and she wants the schools to provide babysitting services for schoolchildren until their parents can collect them in the evening. In addition, she wants the government to force employers to guarantee paid maternity leave and give mothers "flexible" hours. That means choosing their hours to accommodate themselves rather than their employer.

There is one thing Barbara Walters didn't tell ABC viewers. Each of the three couples has an annual income between $50,000 and $57,000. This important fact blows the whole argument that the mothers "have" to work and that taxpayers or employers "should" subsidize child care.

It is unfortunate that the feminist movement has taught young women that they should put their own career above every other value including caring for their own children, and that their time is too valuable to waste on being a full-time mother. These mothers have made their choice, as they have a right to do in a free society. But they have no right to ask taxpayers or their fellow employees to finance that choice.

1986

Boys Just Want to Have Guns

A recent article by a left-handed writer summarized the centuries-old, unreasonable and unfeeling discrimination that society imposed on left-handed persons. He told how growing up in the New York public schools in the 1930s and 1940s meant repeated whacks from teachers who tried to force him to write with his right hand.

This writer reminded us that anti–left-handed bias is enshrined even in the language of Western civilization. The Latin word for left, *sinister*, translates to "evil" in English. The French word for left, *gauche*, means "crude" or "awkward" in English.

When the mistaken belief that schools should endeavor to correct left-handedness was finally relegated to the junk heap of quack psychology, a remarkable fact emerged in U.S. statistical annals. Between 1932 and 1970, the recorded percentage of left-handed people rose from 2 to 10 percent of our population. Since it is incredible that the percentage actually increased so dramatically, the statistics could reflect a new willingness of southpaws to admit they are different, or the anonymous bureaucrats' willingness to admit that left-handedness is just as normal as right-handedness, or both.

Modern scientific, medical, and psychological opinion now teaches that it is wrong—physically and psychologically—for teachers to try to force left-handers to be right-handers. I wonder if, a few decades hence, writers will comment as condescendingly on the peculiar pedagogical passion of feminists to force boys to abandon their boyishness and girls to abandon their girlishness.

Those who have not kept up with trends in the classroom will be surprised to learn how pervasive is this passion. Operating like a censorship gestapo, the feminist movement has combed primary grade readers, school textbooks, and career-guidance materials to eliminate any mention of the natural gender traits of youngsters.

In the late 1970s, the major textbook publishers, such as Macmillan and McGraw-Hill, published "guidelines for the elimination of sexism," which listed the words, illustrations, and concepts that would henceforth be censored out of all textbooks. This impudent intolerance galloped unchecked through school materials.

Yet despite all the attempts to blur gender identity by, for example, showing pictures of girls playing with snakes and boys using hair spray, and even to pervert the English language by forcing schoolchildren to use such annoying pronouns as he/she or s/he, there is no evidence that human nature is changing. The attempt to change it confuses youth and frustrates adults.

A case in point is a hilarious article in the *Washington Post* called "Boys Just Want to Have Guns." The *Post* writer admitted that her three-year-old son, and the sons of all her pacifist-feminist-yuppie friends, despite their parents' persistent efforts to bring them up sex-neutral (without toy guns or television except *Sesame Street*), nevertheless are naturally, irrepressibly male: boyish, aggressive, and fascinated by guns.

In addition, she moaned, the daughters of "what used to be the Berkeley left," given trucks and airplanes, still go for dolls and dress up with jewelry. "The boys slug each other and the girls paint their fingernails. Where are they getting this stuff?", she asks.

It's not just little girls and little boys who rebel at the blurring of gender identity. The magazine *Working Woman* featured an article called "Does the New Woman Really Want the New Man?" The consensus in this feminist magazine was a frustrated No. The author complained that, while the New Man is no longer possessive, he's also no longer committed. So, warns the author, the New Woman won't find "the classic knight on the white charger" and may have to settle for a man who just benefits from her energy and follows her lead. But, the author ruefully concludes, "her heaviest liability is a likelihood of winding up alone."

Even the greeting card industry has discovered this. A current card in the stores shows a picture of a woman reciting the lyrics of a favorite feminist theme song: "I am woman—strong, invincible. . ." Inside the card was the rest of the sentence: "and lonely."

1986

A Night at the Opera

My first and only visit to the Metropolitan Opera in New York City was to hear Bizet's *Carmen*. It was an experience I looked forward to— and one I shall never forget.

The most memorable part of the long evening wasn't any of the famous arias. It was the curtain calls that came close to midnight. It was quite remarkable to see and hear that elegantly attired audience of beautiful people booing like angry fans at a baseball game.

They booed Maria Ewing's Carmen. Most of all they booed the director and the others responsible for this new production of one of the most popular of all grand operas. Half the audience in the less expensive seats had long since voted with their feet and gone home. But the people in the one- and two-hundred-dollar seats stayed to the bitter end to enjoy the pleasure of audibly manifesting their displeasure.

It costs the Met at least $500,000 to put on a new production, either a new opera or a newly staged and newly costumed old opera. The music of Bizet's *Carmen* is a perennial favorite; the orchestra was perfect; the sets were stunning and appropriate; the singers were adequate.

But the audience didn't just say "ho-hum" or "we've heard that song before." They were revved up to a frenzy of booing. With a century of experience in operas, showmanship, and audiences, how could the Met stage such a fiasco? The only explanation I can come up with is that this production of *Carmen* was directed and costumed by men and women who don't understand human nature. They don't understand what attracts a man to a woman and the chemistry that happens between them.

Carmen is the story of a saucy tart who attracts men as honey attracts flies. Full of song and dance, she flirts with the soldiers, plays around with Don José, who falls passionately in love with her, and then dumps him in favor of a handsome toreador. Bizet's plot is realistic and true to human nature. Carmen knows how to attract a man, any man, all men. But she herself goes not for a pliable lover who can be manipulated like a marionette on a string, but for a real man. In her society in Seville, Spain, a real man was a bullfighter.

The director of the Met's 1986 *Carmen*, Sir Peter Hall, transformed this flashy dame into a woman who was tough and sullen, depressing and dowdy. The man behind me mumbled, "She acts like a manic-depressive."

Carmen's body language was wrong: she hung her head, slouched, turned her back to everybody, and assumed masculine and contrived positions of body, arms, and legs. Carmen's costumes were wrong: somber, slovenly, and eccentric. In one act, she wore a hat so only a few in the front rows could see her face. She portrayed a personality that the *New York Times* called "a pouty teenager, determined not to ingratiate herself with us in any way," and she surely succeeded. By her death scene, the *Times* added, "it was hard to care whether she lived or died."

There's nothing the matter with innovation applied to theater or opera if it is an improvement or even if it makes a good show. There is nothing wrong with portraying a female character who is nasty, sullen, and mannish. But you can't show such a character as irresistible to men, because she isn't.

As I travel the college lecture circuit, I meet hundreds of young men and women who want to have a mature relationship with someone of the opposite sex, but they don't understand how to do that. Many young women have not cultivated a feminine personality that can make a man feel like a man. Many young men are so confused about women, uncertain about how to behave, and unable to make decisions, that they can't make a woman feel like a woman.

Androgynous trends in literature, entertainment, and education have disadvantaged a significant segment of young Americans in their twenties and thirties so that they don't know how to attract a spouse and cultivate a mutual and enduring commitment to marriage and family. That's too bad, because they are missing out on the greatest joys of life.

1986

Ms. Discovers Human Nature

I must confess that I never would have read the magazine if the airline hadn't provided free copies as I boarded the shuttle at LaGuardia Airport. But as I thumbed the pages of Gloria Steinem's *Ms.* magazine, waiting for my plane to take off, I was fascinated at the changes in this magazine since I last read it.

Fourteen years ago, the magazine featured pre-marriage contracts obliging husbands to do half the dishes and the diapers, and housewives' declarations of independence from essential housework. Today, there aren't any husbands or babies to complain about.

The first article that caught my eye, "Learning to Flirt at 37," was the confession of a mature feminist with a good job and an apartment of her own, who grew up in the 1960s believing that flirting was "Victorian in the midst of the sexual revolution." After all those years of buying her own flowers, opening her own doors, and cooking dinner for herself after going to the movies alone, she actually answered an ad in the local newspaper headlined "Learn to Flirt."

She called the number listed, and the flirting teacher convinced her that even a feminist can flirt if she uses time-tested arts. The teacher taught this feminist such simple techniques as: do cross, uncross, and recross your legs but don't cross your arms, and do imitate the seductive glances on soap operas but don't initiate conversations on toxic waste removal.

Next there was a tear-jerker article by a female author commiserating with a friend who was still mourning a break-up with her live-in boyfriend a year after it happened. As he told her when he casually signed off a two-year relationship, he "wasn't looking, it just happened; so don't take it personally."

The author then interviewed eighty-seven victims of breakups with live-in lovers. She found that the average duration of these extramarital relationships was two years. The typical break-up occurs when the man wants out; but instead of saying so, he makes signals that the thrill is gone and leaves it to the woman to define the relationship as ended.

I turned to an article called "Star Wars" but, alas, it wasn't about Ronald Reagan's anti-missile system. It was about how men feel threatened when women's careers move faster and higher than their own. The illustration showed the man with a vacuum sweeper while the woman goes out with her briefcase; the unhappy look on the man's face was a sure sign that he won't be sticking around that household very long.

Another article confessed that the main topic of conversation among brainy, successful women is the "man shortage." The author acknowledged painfully that "after 15-plus years of consciousness-raising and general feminist hell-raising, most middle-class women who are single and heterosexual still confine their search for mates to men who are well upscale of them in income and status."

Feminists since the 1970s have been trying to force us into a gender-neutral society and bring about sex-role reversals. Their ideology is based on the notion that gender differences are caused by stereotyped education and an oppressive male-dominated society.

So it was fascinating to read the article called "Designer Genes" which admits that men and women are naturally, biologically different. It proposes that "a committee of reputable biologists" engage in "genetic manipulation" to change human nature so that men and women will have an equal motivation, desire, and enjoyment of the sex act.

There were even, mirabile dictu, ads for diamond engagement rings, make-up, and sheer pantyhose. It looks like "voices from the post-feminist generation," proclaimed three years ago by the *New York Times Magazine*, have even invaded *Ms.* magazine.

1986

Losers in the Sexual Revolution

Whew! After watching ABC-TV's marathon documentary called *After the Sexual Revolution* on July 30, 1986, I'm glad I'm not part of the Sexual Revolution! ABC-TV showed three dreadfully dreary hours of unhappy women, working harder but enjoying life less because their personal relationships with men and children are so unsatisfactory.

One after another, they cried their complaints into the camera. We saw successful career women who made business their first priority and now have discovered that their biological clock has ticked on, and they have passed up the chance to have a family. One woman coped with her dilemma by deliberately bearing a child whose father is married to another woman. Another was bearing a fatherless child via artificial insemination. A third chose a twice-divorced husband with his ready-made family.

We saw the woman in her late thirties, fighting back tears, saying "the women's revolution was wonderful—but I want someone to love and be loved by." We heard about the "fear of being alone" and the five thousand dating services that have profited from the problems of loneliness and isolation.

We saw what is supposed to be the prototype post-feminist blue-collar couple: a woman who is a subway maintenance worker and a man who is her househusband. Sorry, ABC, your provincialism is showing; that lifestyle will never play in Peoria.

Even the woman who has a successful business plus a husband and one child (who she admitted came second in her life) was griping because she had to fight for what she had achieved and had to keep her emotions under control. It hadn't occurred to her that successful men do those things, too. Then there was the woman who didn't want a promotion because it would mean working longer hours and no lunch break.

We saw the victims of the easy divorce laws so eagerly promoted by the feminist movement in the 1970s. In truth, those easy divorce laws liberated husbands to trade in a faithful wife of twenty years and enjoy a younger woman.

We saw the middle-aged woman who returned to the labor force and was trying to cajole or shame her husband into sharing the housework because she is so tired at the end of the day. Poor guy—he tried to bake the frozen dinner in its paper box, and the dials on the automatic washer were beyond his grasp.

We heard the Stanford professor say that women are not better off than in 1959 because women are now working longer and harder. "The more women achieve in their career," we were told, "the higher their chance of divorce."

ABC couldn't resist the opportunity to sermonize. Peter Jennings started off with the false feminist dogma that, prior to the women's lib movement, American society was "predicated on women's inferior status." Betsy Aaron's preaching for the Sexual Revolution was particularly obnoxious. She proclaimed that "the age-old idea of virginity" is out, that "divorce is no longer a dirty word," and that "the stay-at-home housewife is becoming part of our history." She observed that "instead of one lifelong marriage, now it's often a merry-go-round of marriage and divorce." That's called "serial marriages."

ABC's solution for these emotionally confused women is for our government to imitate the policies of countries that have warehoused children in tax-funded institutions in order to keep their mothers employed in the labor force. ABC scrolled the list of countries whose policies we are advised to copy: the Soviet Union, East Germany, Rumania, Hungary, Bulgaria, China, and Nicaragua.

ABC's documentary reminded us again and again that the Sexual Revolution is "here to stay." But if enough women see the program, the Revolution's days can be numbered. The personal testimonies of so many unhappy women cry out that the price they paid to join the Sexual Revolution was too high.

1986

Post-Feminist Career Women

Although we hear a daily drumbeat from the national media telling us that the American social structure is now permanently stratified with mothers in the labor force and children in daycare centers, a careful monitoring of newspapers reveals plenty of evidence that this is not a satisfactory pattern. There are two reasons: mothers don't like it and children don't like it.

Take, for one example, a feature story in a Chicago newspaper about Susan Anderson, a successful television anchor who chucked her job in order to stay home with her two children. In her own byline article, she described how she agonized between career and children, and how she made the choice she did.

Susan Anderson had invested fifteen years in a smashingly glamorous career at one of the largest television stations in one of the largest markets in the country. She would face a significant drop in her living standards if she gave up her six-figure salary. She knew that broadcasting is a very competitive, youth-oriented business. It had been hard enough to get hired in her mid-twenties, but it would be lots tougher if she dropped out and tried to go back in her mid-forties.

She even had a supportive husband who was willing to cut back his legal practice so he could spend more time at home. He was quite willing to live with any decision Susan made. But then, she looked ahead into the future and thought of the many who have wished they had spent more time with their children. Has anyone ever lamented on his deathbed, "I wish I'd spent more time on business?"

The punch line of her article was, "I just could not shake an almost primal feeling. It wasn't so much that I thought my kids needed me more than the job allowed, but that I needed them more."

Now, for a contrast, look at a "piece of my mind" article from the *Journal of the American Medical Association*. It was written by a woman surgeon who made the opposite decision—to stick with her career. But she wasn't happy with her choice.

Dr. Margaret Levy wrote, "When I was a medical student, I was naive enough to believe that I could do everything I wanted to do." She tried to have a rewarding career in medicine, which she loves, and at the same time raise a family. "Let me tell you, once and for all," writes Dr. Levy, "that this is neither physically nor psychologically possible. Take my word for it." Whatever arrangement the career woman makes for her children, she says, "call it anything but Mom."

Dr. Levy has two young sons. When she looked at her friends' "daycare kids," whom she described as "absolutely pathetic, no matter how good the daycare is," she knew she had to have another alternative. Since her career track as a surgeon offered a better lifestyle, financially speaking, than her husband's, he gallantly stayed home for eight years to provide parental care.

But Dr. Levy still isn't happy. Like most employed mothers, she admits to being in a constant state of exhaustion and frustration. Most of all, she admits to being "envious" of all the time her husband has had with the children. Here's how Dr. Levy describes her current situation: "I am not a liberated woman. I am incarcerated in a world and lifestyle far more complex and complicated than my great-grandmother, raising her eleven children in an apartment in the Bronx, could have imagined."

The *Wall Street Journal*, usually a booster of feminist ideology, reported that "as more working parents entrust their infants to daycare, some researchers are warning that daycare at too early an age may psychologically harm a child."

The *Journal* interviewed Professor Jay Belsky, a Pennsylvania State University psychologist, whose recent research shows that infant daycare undermines a child's "sense of trust, of security, of order in the world." What makes Belsky more newsworthy than the millions of mothers who have always known that fact is that, in the 1970s, he helped forge an academic consensus that daycare generally benefits a child.

Professor Belsky announced his change of mind at an American Academy of Pediatrics meeting in 1985. He now says that various studies show toddlers in daycare to be insecure, more anxious, aggressive, hyperactive, and more likely to cry and misbehave at ages nine and ten.

1987

Making Heroes out of Rapists

Twenty years ago, the feminists developed the theory that rape has nothing to do with sex, that it is instead an act of violence, evidence of male hatred and aggressiveness toward women. Maybe this strange notion is the reason why we haven't heard any outcry from feminists about the genre of rapist-heroes on television soap operas.

I'll admit I didn't discover this problem myself, as I am no watcher of soaps. It was discovered by *TV Guide*. The magazine caught my eye as I went through the checkout counter at the supermarket. At first I thought the article called "Let's Stop Turning Rapists into Heroes" would be some kind of *National Enquirer* sensationalism. But alas, the article was for real. It described a series of television soaps in which rapists became heroes soon after their crimes. Let me recite the specifics so you will know I didn't make this up.

The first rapist listed showed his face ten years ago on ABC's *General Hospital* when Luke raped Laura, who eventually fell in love with and married him. The only other time I ever heard of such a disgusting scenario was years ago in Ayn Rand's *Fountainhead*, and I stopped reading that novel when I figured out how the plot was unfolding. Whereas rape is (or should be) judged a crime, *General Hospital* made it look like an act of love. Laura even referred to the incident as "the first time we made love." There apparently was some flap from women when this sequence aired several years ago, but there has been no particular opposition to the rape-romances of recent years.

On ABC's *Dynasty*, Adam raped Kirby in one season and proposed to her in the next. The idea that a woman would marry her rapist is not only absurd, it is downright dangerous. It gives docudrama authenticity to what has been called the "rape myth," namely, the notion that women secretly want to be raped. On ABC's now defunct *Ryan's Hope*, Roger unsuccessfully tried to force Maggie into bed, and two years later they were married.

ABC's *All My Children* has a character named Ross who, in a drunken rage, raped his father's fiancee, Natalie. For this crime, he went to prison; so much, so good. But he immediately broke out of jail and then became a hero, starring in all sorts of heroic escapades. CBS's *As the World Turns* presents Josh, another character who turns from rapist to hero, very sympathetically. No, he doesn't marry his victim; instead his victim's sister falls in love with Josh, and the victim and their mother both accept the relationship.

All these story lines have desensitized viewers to the crime of rape. They present rape as the route to success and good sex. A campaign to get the soaps to cease and desist from such anti-woman garbage would be a good project for the feminists. It's not only insultingly sexist but socially repugnant. But I'm not holding my breath because the feminists have such a warped idea of what "sexism" is. They would prefer to continue attacking as "sexist" a husband who puts his wife on a pedestal and treats her like a queen.

1989

∞

Fortune Favors the Trophy Wife

Fortune magazine joined the cabal trying to make no-fault divorce a social good by publishing a cover story called "The CEO's Second Wife." The article proves what George Gilder wrote in his landmark book *Men and Marriage*, namely, that "the only undeniable winners in the sexual revolution are powerful men. Under a regime of sexual liberation, some men can fulfill the paramount dream of most men everywhere; they can have the nubile years of more than one young woman."

The *Fortune* article presents a long succession of CEOs of major corporations who divorced their wives of several decades and married flashy, trim babes who help them spend their money while consorting with the other rich and powerful. The article conveniently includes a list of names and ages of some forty CEOs and their second (or third or fourth) wives. The essential requirements, according to *Fortune*, are to be thin, expensively groomed, and have your own career.

Fortune's article is certainly not unbiased reporting. It reeks with the editorial message that in the 1980s "divorce is fully respectable," and the CEO "with the old, nice, matronly wife is looked down on. He's seen as not keeping up appearances. Why can't he do better for himself?" The up-and-coming CEO not only does not have to feel guilty; taking a second wife as a "trophy" is the "in" thing to do.

Nowhere does the article ask the question, If the CEO doesn't live up to his marriage contract, why should anybody believe his word on anything else? Nowhere does the article criticize the untrustworthiness of a man who treats his wife like his automobile, that is, when he tires of her, he trades her in for a younger model. No, instead, *Fortune* justifies the practice of powerful CEOs indulging their desires with "trophy wives." It's one of the perks of success, like a company jet.

Fortune even helps the faithless husband to salve his conscience. Sometimes, *Fortune* says in extra large type, dumping his wife and marrying a younger woman "even results in his becoming a more considerate manager."

The *Fortune* writers apparently had no difficulty interviewing a long series of second wives and photographing them in their expensive clothes as they teach another woman's husband how to "build a new life" without children. Some of the second wives even revealed how they connived to get the married CEO to succumb to their wiles.

In his essay on the consequences of such a social system, George Gilder accurately says that the rich and powerful man who does this "is no less effectively a polygamist than if he had maintained a harem." Our easy divorce laws, adopted under pressure from the women's liberation movement during the 1970s, have enabled one spouse—without the consent of the other—to say "I divorce thee" three times (as Islamic law allows) and then be free to live with a new partner.

The victims of this system are the cast-off wives who grow old alone when their husbands leave and remarry. Between the ages of thirty-five and sixty-five, there are 50 percent more divorced or separated women than divorced or separated men. Middle-aged and older women do not often marry young men.

Gilder says that "a society is essentially an organism," and we cannot simply expel a few million women from the fabric of families, remarry their husbands to younger women, and quietly return to our business as if nothing had happened. "What has happened," he says, "is a major rupture in the social system, felt everywhere."

1990

Working Girl Explodes a Feminist Myth

To the anguished moans and groans of feminists, the movie scriptwriters have struck again. Even if television news departments, editorial writers, and congressmen haven't discovered it, screenwriters (who are on the cutting edge of cultural trends because they must lure customers into the theaters) know that we are in the post-feminist era.

In 1987 they gave us *Fatal Attraction*, in which the heroine was the full-time homemaker, a beautiful package of fulfillment and emotional serenity, while the villain was the fortyish career woman, violently desperate to possess a man. That was followed the same year by *Baby Boom*, in which a high-powered female executive abandoned success on the fast track in favor of life in the country with a man, a baby, and home-based, kitchen-oriented work.

Working Girl in 1988 dashed other feminist dreams and delusions. It shows that women in business are just as cutthroat as men and that some successful women executives treat their female subordinates just as ruthlessly and oppressively as men have been alleged to do.

Feminist ideology teaches that the business and professional world is a male enclave whose borders are guarded by sexist men protecting their territory by discriminatory security as impenetrable as the Berlin Wall once was. Even if talented and able women somehow make it onto the playing field, the theory goes, they are oppressed and kept from rising to the top by a "glass ceiling" (a new concept invented by feminist ideologues for semantic warfare).

But that isn't all. Feminist mythology also teaches that, "come the revolution," when women rise to positions of power and importance in the professional world, the entire business environment will be different. Women executives will be compassionate, caring, cooperative, and will change the workaday world from power seeking to pleasantries.

Working Girl shows that 'tain't so, after all. When the Ivy League business school graduate, with her expensive clothes and aristocratic ways, makes it into the office with a view over Manhattan, she is just as dictatorial, dishonest, and downright horrid to her female underlings as the archetypical male in feminist fairy tales.

To add insult to injury, those who lend a helping hand to the poor little working girl from the wrong side of the tracks, who is trying to lift herself up by her own bootstraps by attending a lowbrow budget college at night, are successful men! They are the ones who give her the big chance to rise out of the secretarial pool, where she would otherwise be doomed to suffer the daily indignity of being expected to make coffee for her boss.

Working Girl thus confirmed a revealing article published in the *New York Times Magazine* of June 26, 1988, called "Why Feminism Failed." Feminist journalist Mary Anne Dolan, who rose to become editor of a then major metropolitan newspaper, the *Los Angeles Herald-Examiner*, described the feminist dream that "female" qualities would produce a new management environment which would "make mincemeat of the male business model." Under her direction, the *Herald-Examiner* soon boasted the first 50-50 male-female masthead in the country. Women got most of the coveted positions, including editor of the editorial page and sports columnist.

Ms. Dolan, whose own perspective is revealed by her admission that she was an enthusiast of Geraldine Ferraro's vice presidential campaign, was vivid in her description of what happened. Ms. Dolan regretfully admitted that five years later those women had taken on "the worst aspects of the stereotypical corporate ladder-climbing male. As soon as masthead status was achieved, the power grab began." She said that the supposedly "wise and mature" women she hired turned out to be "brittle, conniving, power-hungry and unyielding."

Ms. Dolan is not particularly optimistic that this situation will change soon. She noted that, when one of her woman journalist friends died young from cancer and they all gathered at the funeral, the most power-grabbing feminist of the bunch sat in the pew "with the current and former publishers of the newspaper, both men, one at each elbow."

'Twas ever thus. Feminism is doomed to failure because it is based on an attempt to repeal and restructure human nature.

1990

Busybodies and Crybabies

Maybe it was just a coincidence in a slow news week. *Time* magazine came out with a cover story in 1992 headlined "Busybodies & Crybabies: What's Happening to the American Character?", and the same week the feminists launched a media initiative called the Glass Ceiling.

Time described how the busybodies, those self-appointed, overbearing wardens of behavior and political correctness, are infecting American society with a nasty intolerance. Pitted against the busybodies, according to *Time*, are the crybabies, those who position themselves as victims, blaming everybody except themselves for their problems.

The peddlers of this new industry called victimology argue that every plight, condition, or momentary setback is not a matter to be solved by individual effort, but is a social problem. The victims' "greatest talent," according to *Time*, is the ability to hand out guilt, and indeed they are adept at using every tool of modern communication and courts of law to dump the blame on others.

A good example of the crybabies was a recent op-ed piece in the *New York Times* written by a young woman complaining that, although she is "young, urban, professional, literate, respectable, intelligent and charming," she is unemployed. She realizes that plenty of jobs are available, but she thinks it is "absurd" that she should take a job (such as typist) beneath her expectations, so she and her unemployed peers have "bounced checks to keep ourselves in oxford shirts and Ann Taylor dresses." She adds, "We expect rewards and recognition."

Busybodies and crybabies cooperate with each other to achieve their goals. The bureaucratic busybodies who want to use the power of government to direct our lives always need new groups of victims in order to rationalize expanding their regulatory turf and spending more of the taxpayers' money, and the crybabies are always glad to have government anoint them victims.

The Glass Ceiling initiative is a good example of how busybodies and crybabies work in tandem. The crybabies are the feminists who think they should, at the very least, be vice presidents of Fortune 500 corporations, and the busybodies are their pals in media and government who want to use affirmative action to place them there.

The feminists are forever crying about how "artificial barriers" interfere with their success in the labor force. But the chief barrier is not artificial but the result of women's own choices. The Yankelovich survey found that a majority of women (56 percent) would quit their jobs permanently if money were not a factor—a dramatic shift in opinion from the previous year.

The typical 1990s woman wants the mommy track, not the fast track. That's why we are having a boom in home-based employment and in births to women in their thirties and forties. Reaching the top echelons of big corporations requires twenty to thirty years of sixty- to eighty-

hour work weeks, extraordinary motivation, and commitment to a lifetime in the labor force. The majority of women do not make that choice.

1992

The Feminist Identity Crisis

The feminist movement defined itself in November 1977 at the federally financed National Conference of the Commission on International
Women's Year (IWY). Gracing the platform were three first ladies:
Rosalynn Carter, Betty Ford, and Lady Bird Johnson. Participating were
all the leaders of the women's liberation movement. These included Bella
Abzug as chairman, Gloria Steinem, the head of the National Organization for Women (NOW), the head of the Women's Political Caucus,
the head of ERAmerica (the lobbying group for the Equal Rights
Amendment), the head of the Gay Task Force, the sponsor of the ERA
in the Senate, and the sponsor of the ERA in the House of Representatives. The political button most frequently worn by the delegates read
"A woman without a man is like a fish without a bicycle."

With five million dollars of federal funds to spend, the conference
passed twenty-five action-oriented resolutions. The four "hot button"
issues (*Newsweek*'s term) were ratification of the Equal Rights Amendment, government-funded abortion, lesbian privileges to be recognized
with the same dignity as husbands and wives, and universal federal
daycare, which *Time* magazine estimated would cost twenty-five billion
dollars a year.

The publicity that the national media gave this feminist extrava-
ganza proved counterproductive: the more the public saw of the feminists and heard of their demands, the less they liked them. The feminists
never won another ERA victory after IWY, though ERA was subsequently
voted on at least twenty-five times in legislatures and in referenda.

The feminists tried to redefine themselves in 1992 under the banner "The Year of the Woman," with Hillary Rodham Clinton extolling the "politics of meaning." But in the 1994 elections, feminist candidates of both parties were trounced while a half dozen attractive, conservative, pro-life Republican women were newly elected to Congress.

The steady rise of the pro-family movement over the last two decades has given feminism a terrible identity crisis. Feminism has no happy role models. Its ideology is sterile and its spokespersons are bitter. In a special issue dated Fall 1990 entitled "Women: The Road Ahead," *Time* magazine conceded that "The feminist label is viewed with disdain and alarm; the name of Gloria Steinem is uttered as an epithet."

Newspapers during the 1990s were full of stories with headlines such as "Superwoman goes home," "Working mothers jilt their jobs for home and family," "Young women trade jobs for marriage," and "Return of the sole breadwinner as fastest-growing family unit." One-third of preschool children now live in an Ozzie-and-Harriet family.

The very notion of a "mommy track" was denounced by feminists when it was suggested by Felice Schwartz in a 1989 *Harvard Management Review*, but it has now become a respectable career option for smart women. The Robert Half employment agency reported that 82 percent of professional women prefer a career with flexible hours and slower career advancement. Whereas 52 percent of mothers are employed, only 13 percent want to be.

Demographers are speculating about the causes of these changes: lower interest rates on homes, increased income taxes, the high costs of maintaining a second job (car, wardrobe, restaurants, and the like), daycare diseases, and the opportunities for telecommunication in the home.

Human nature just might be a factor, too. Except for the unfortunate women who were caught up in the feminist foolishness of the 1970s, most women don't want to be liberated from home, husband, family, and children.

The *Providence Journal* published a three-page analysis called "The Fading of a Movement." It quoted the consensus of Rhode Island feminists that today they have "not many women, not much movement." The aging feminists complain bitterly that young career women refuse to be called "feminists." They won't accept what they call the "F-word" because it "has come to stand for strident, argumentative, angry, humorless." They say, "It's your fault I can't have babies because I waited too long or took birth control too long or whatever. You told us we could have it all. Now we see we can't."

The feminists launched their movement in the early 1970s by proclaiming women as victims, laying a guilt trip on men, and demanding retribution. They built their ranks by a technique called the consciousness-raising session, in which feminists would come together and exchange horror stories about how badly men had treated them. Grievances are like weeds: if you water them, they will grow. With feminist nurturing, little grievances quickly grow into big grievances.

But you can't fool all the people all the time, and in the process, the American people have had their own consciousness raised. They discovered that the feminist movement is both socially destructive and personally disappointing. A *Time*-CNN poll confirmed that 64 percent of women do not want to call themselves feminist.

If you watch the media closely, you can see indications that some now have the courage to comment on feminism's mistake. A cartoon in the *New Yorker* showed a modern young woman standing at a cocktail party, coyly saying to her male companion, "It's all right, now, to call me a girl."

Despite the feminists' identity crisis, don't expect them to quietly fade away, because so many of them hold taxpayer-funded perches from which they continue to promote their agenda. You'll find them in well-paying jobs in government, in the media, and in academia, where a handful of determined activists can do a lot of mischief.

1994

Lord of the White House Plantation

When former Senator Bill Bradley was asked his current opinion of Bill Clinton, he used the most appropriate word in the English language. Bradley called Clinton's behavior "disgusting."

Monica Lewinsky's plaintive words quoted in the Starr report—"I feel disposable, used and insignificant"—display Bill Clinton's attitude toward women. He is typical of men who push for feminist laws and policies, pretending that mistreatment of women is a societal problem. It's not. The treatment of women as second class or subservient is a personal offense by individual men such as Bill Clinton who look upon women as things rather than persons.

The star-struck, ambitious girl, who had stalked Clinton, desperately wanted him to treat her like "a person." It was not to be. He used her to service him sexually while he conducted his business by phone with congressmen and with his famous adviser, Dick Morris. Monica was insignificant to Clinton. After all, he told her he had had hundreds of adulterous liaisons, so she was just as disposable as all the others.

The way Clinton used his secretary Betty Currie was almost as degrading. Acting like the lord of the White House plantation, Clinton required Betty Currie to serve as an enabler for his sexual encounters. She guided Clinton's bimbos into the Oval office, told him how much time he had before his next appointment, and protected him from sudden discovery. She, too, was disposable, used, and insignificant.

Contrary to the whines of Clinton's defenders, Monicagate was not "just about sex," nor was he entitled to shield it as "his private life." It was a workplace offense for which any corporate or military boss would have been fired. The acts took place in a taxpayer-financed office, with a taxpayer-salaried, very subordinate employee, with a taxpayer-salaried secretary as facilitator, with a taxpayer-salaried Secret Service protecting his trysts, with taxpayer-salaried surrogates sent out to lie about it to the media and to the grand jury, and with taxpayer-salaried lawyers defending his illicit acts.

Clinton didn't treat any women as equals or with respect. He humiliated his wife, used vulnerable women (Monica Lewinsky, Paula Jones, Kathleen Willey) to gratify his sexual wants, used his secretary (Betty Currie) as a facilitator, and used the few strong women around him (Madeleine Albright, Donna Shalala, Ann Lewis) to spread his lies.

One good result of Monicagate is that it discredited the feminists and exposed them as part of the radical left wing of the Democratic Party. The entire media, including the liberals, laughed at their hypocrisy and double standards. Their pretense of being advocates for women's rights was blown away, revealing them as a mean-spirited bunch whose affections are for sale. Feminist Erica Jong explained why the feminists continue to support Clinton on CNBC on September 29: he vetoed the ban on partial-birth abortion, and he appointed feminist Ruth Bader Ginsburg to the U.S. Supreme Court.

1998

Hillary: Feminist Heroine?

Hillary Rodham Clinton is a feminist heroine because she saw to it that her husband never betrayed the feminists. He betrayed everybody else, including his wife. He betrayed doctrinaire liberals when he approved welfare reform, he betrayed his gay rights constituency when he signed the Defense of Marriage Act, he betrayed his civil rights constituency by restricting the rights of criminals, he betrayed members of his own cabinet by sending them out to lie for him, but he never crossed the feminists even when it was in his interest to do so, such as on partial-birth abortion. He used a pro-abortion litmus test for Supreme Court nominations and staffed his administration with radical feminists.

For all that and more, the feminists can thank Hillary.

Hillary's most famous soundbites were calculated to reassure the feminists that she is their soul sister. On the famous CBS *60 Minutes* interview in 1992 when she "covered" for Clinton's liaison with Gennifer Flowers, Hillary defiantly said, "I'm not some little woman standing by her man like Tammy Wynette." Hillary was willing to alienate millions of country music lovers in order to broadcast her feminist message even as she was playing the role of the long suffering wife in denial.

During the year when we suffered through the Monica soap opera, Hillary proved in spades that she was exactly what she denied: "some little woman standing by her man." That wasn't feminist behavior, but the end (keeping Clinton in office) justified even non-feminist means.

Hillary's personality and ideology came through even clearer during the 1992 campaign with her calculated comment about "baking cookies." Instead of responding to a reporter's question about the conflict of interest between her law firm and Governor Bill Clinton's office, she replied: "I suppose I could have stayed home and baked cookies and had teas." That wasn't a slip of the tongue; it was perfectly descriptive of the feminist worldview, which is based on a cultural and economic put-down of full-time homemakers.

Hillary's views on marriage were spelled out back in 1974 in the *Harvard Educational Review* (43:4): "The basic rationale for depriving people of rights in a dependency relationship [i.e., wives] is that certain individuals are incapable or undeserving of the right to take care of themselves and consequently need social institutions specifically designed to safeguard their position. Along with the family, past and present examples of such arrangements include marriage, slavery, and the Indian reservation system."

That's vintage 1970s feminism, the ideology that wives dependent on their husbands are second-class citizens, that marriage treats wives like servants bogged down in dirty diapers and dirty dishes, and that women need out-of-the-home careers to achieve real fulfillment.

Hillary displayed this same mindset when she sounded off on her notion that children should be raised and regulated by the "village" rather than by their own mothers, who are presumably not educated enough to do anything more stimulating than baking cookies.

So, a feminist heroine Hillary truly is, but a feminist role model she is not. In fact, she is—pardon the expression—just a housewife. She became a national figure only because she is the wife of Bill Clinton. She made her money and built her so-called career the old-fashioned way: she married it. She didn't have an independent career like, for example, the self-made careers of Elizabeth Dole, Wendy Gramm, Jeane Kirkpatrick, Kay Bailey Hutchinson, Dianne Feinstein, Donna Shalala, Madeleine Albright, or Geraldine Ferraro. Hillary's career and income from the Rose law firm were built on the political fact that her husband was governor of Arkansas, appointing judges and regulators who would rule on her cases.

She tried hard to pretend she is a feminist career woman. Campaigning in 1992, she promised us a "co-presidency." As she put it, "If you vote for my husband, you get me; it's a two-for-one, blue plate special."

When Hillary moved into the White House in January 1993, the feminist claque in the media demanded that we accept her as the prototype of the modern wife who has an independent career and makes more money than her husband. She made it clear she would not play the role of First Lady, but would be Presidential Partner, with her own identity, policy-making authority, and White House staff. We were told that she represented the changing of the guard from old-generation wives like Barbara Bush, whose lifestyle is now presumably obsolete.

Hillary started her adult life sputtering the campus drivel of the 1960s. In her graduation speech at Wellesley College in 1969, Hillary Rodham said she was searching for "more immediate, ecstatic and penetrating modes of living," so she could come "to terms with our humanness" and "talk about reality, authentic reality, inauthentic reality."

She still had not come "to terms with reality" by the time she made a speech as First Lady at the University of Texas on April 6, 1993. Hillary's rambling discourse there sounded like an all-night bull session in a coed college dorm. "We are in a crisis of meaning," she declaimed. "What do our governmental institutions mean? What do our lives in today's world mean? . . .What does it mean in today's world . . . to be human?"

We're inclined to respond, Speak for yourself, Hillary. Lacking meaning in life is an individual, not a societal, problem, since plenty of us have no trouble finding meaning, and it would seem she should have discovered it by the time she moved into the White House. In that Texas speech, she called for "a new politics of meaning," but that may have been a slip. She probably meant to call for a new meaning of politics.

Despite her inability to cope with life's meaning, Hillary has never outgrown the adolescent arrogance of the campus radicals of the 1960s and the bra-burning feminists of the 1970s who believed they had the mission "to remold society by redefining what it means to be a human being in the twentieth century." That's the arrogance that led her in 1993 to try to redesign and take over the $850 billion U.S. healthcare industry. She handled that project so badly that it became a major factor in electing a Republican Congress in 1994.

After Hillary assumed control of the healthcare issue, we saw typical feminist behavior in action. She accepted deference and chivalry from the middle-aged congressmen who refrained from asking her any tough questions, and then she used her position as First Lady to flout the law. The lawsuit filed by the Association of American Physicians and Surgeons proved that she deliberately violated federal law by running her Health Care Task Force and Working Group in secret in order to conceal the identity of persons who had provable conflicts of interest. If she hadn't had the President to hide behind, she would have followed Webster Hubbell and others out of Washington.

When the Monica Lewinsky scandal broke, Hillary affected the role of victim while at the same time quarterbacking the cover-up, manning the battle stations, and manufacturing the spin about a "vast right-wing conspiracy." In feminist lingo, she became a macho feminist—that curious combination of victimology, toughness, and lust for revenge.

There's just one thing about Hillary I haven't been able to figure out. When she denounced the "vast right-wing conspiracy," why did she wear a pin that incorporated the same eagle that I and my friends have been wearing as an insignia since 1967?

2000

Terrorism Meets Feminism

One of the unintended consequences of the terrorist attack on the World Trade Center on September 11, 2001, was the dashing of feminist hopes to make America a gender-neutral or androgynous society. New York City's fire*men* dared to charge up the stairs of the burning World Trade Center. The firefighters' death tally was: men 343, women zero.

It is a testament to their courage and skill that many thousands of people were successfully evacuated despite mass confusion. The fewer than three thousand officeworkers who died were mostly trapped above the explosions and could not have been evacuated under any circumstances.

The feminists had made repeated attempts to sex-integrate New York's fire department through litigation, even though the women couldn't pass the physical tests. They even persuaded a judge to rule that upper body strength is largely irrelevant to firefighting. When ABC-TV aired its 1991 documentary *Boys and Girls Are Different*, host John Stossel showed film clips of women failing their tryouts for the Los Angeles fire department. On-camera interviews with Gloria Steinem and Bella Abzug mouthing feminist demands that women be hired as firefighters regardless look rather silly today.

September 11th called for all the masculine strength that strong men could muster. Firefighting is clearly a job for real men to do the heavy lifting, not affirmative-action women.

President George W. Bush sent our special forces to the rugged and remote Afghan hills and caves to get the terrorists, dead or alive. Fighting the Taliban is a job for real men. When the national media interviewed some of our marines, one of our guys said, "There's no place I'd rather be than here." America is fortunate that the warrior culture has survived thirty years of feminist fantasies and that some men are still macho enough to relish the opportunity to engage and kill the bad guys of the world.

Watching the war pictures on television, we almost expected to see *High Noon* sheriff Gary Cooper or John Wayne riding across the plains. Feminists should go to see the movie *Black Hawk Down* and reflect on the fact that women could not have done what our men did in Somalia.

For several decades, the feminists have been demanding that we terminate the discrimination that excludes women from "career advancement" in every section of the U.S. Armed Forces, assuring us that hand-to-hand combat is a relic of the past and that all our wars will now involve only pulling triggers and pushing buttons. Tell that to our troops who trudged over land mines and jagged rocks where there aren't any roads.

In the 1980s and 1990s, the feminist assault on the right to be a man who is masculine became increasingly intense. It wasn't just a semantic game when they insisted that the words *gentleman, masculine,* and *manly* be excised from our vocabulary. Feminists are playing for keeps.

They attacked the right to be a masculine man in the U.S. Armed Services, the kind of man who would rush into a burning building to save a woman or search Afghan caves for Osama bin Laden. Feminists have intimidated our military into using a training system based on gender norming the tests, rewarding *effort* rather than achievement, and trying to assure that females are not "underrepresented" in officer ranks. It's bad enough that men are forbidden to question the double standards or preferential treatment given to women: it is dishonorable to induce them to lie about it.

Feminists used the government and the courts to feminize that citadel of masculinity, Virginia Military Institute. In the name of equality, they first sought to end the policy against the admission of women, then to dilute the training to accommodate females. The school still requires a monthly fitness test, but cadets are not required to pass it. No one should have been surprised when a Brother Rat turned up pregnant.

The feminists have used the courts to try to criminalize masculinity. Feminist lawyers first created judge-made law to expand the statutory definition of sex discrimination to include sexual harassment, and they now prosecute sexual harassment on the basis of how a woman feels rather than what a man does.

The feminists' attack on the right to be masculine is in full swing at colleges and universities. Feminism is a major tenet of political correctness, and the female faculty are the watchdogs of speech codes. Subservience to feminist orthodoxy on campuses is not only mandatory, it is nondebatable. Women's studies courses and many sociology courses are tools to indoctrinate college women in feminist ideology and lay a guilt trip on all men, collectively and individually. The thought police have wiped out any pretense of academic freedom—feminist foolishness may not be criticized.

The feminists use Title IX, not as a vehicle to ensure equal educational opportunity for women, but as a machete to destroy the sports at which men excel. In the 1981-82 academic year, 428 colleges supported varsity wrestling teams; in 1998-99 that number was reduced to 257. In the same period, the number of men's gymnastics programs dropped from eighty-two to twenty-six.

The feminist battalions are even on the warpath against the right to be a boy. In elementary schools across America, recess is rapidly being eliminated, shocking numbers of little boys are "medicated" with psychotropic drugs to force them to behave like little girls, and zero-tolerance idiocies are punishing boys for indulging in games of normal boyhood such as cops and robbers.

Of course, when you wipe out masculine men, you also eliminate gentlemen, the kind of men who would defend and protect a lady—like the gentlemen who remained on the *Titanic*. Of the ship's survivors, 94 percent of those in first-class and 81 percent of those in second-class were women.

2001

Still Not Happy at the Top

By the end of the century, women executives had made it to the top of the corporate world. As Hewlett-Packard's CEO Ms. Carleton Fiorina proclaimed, "There is not a glass ceiling," and she proved it by her eighty-million-dollar contract. Other female CEOs included Ellen M. Hancock of Exodus Communications and Andrea Jung of Avon Products.

But the pro-feminist press still complains that life isn't fair to women. A four-column *New York Times* headline on June 24, 2001, whined, "So Where Are the Corporate Husbands?" The situation that provoked this long news article was that "more than three decades into the women's movement, seventeen years after *Fortune* magazine predicted the demise of the corporate wife, a vast majority of chief executives of the nation's top corporations are not only men, but married men with stay-at-home wives."

Continuing this feminist whine, the *Times* reported, "When the top executive is a man, he still usually makes use of a corporate wife." Note the feminist snarl that oozes from the words "makes use of." The *Times* cries out, "But when a woman runs a business, she does many of the 'wife chores' herself. And the rest fall by the wayside, perhaps to the detriment of her career." When corporate husbands emerge, "they don't play their roles with quite the verve of a full-blown corporate wife."

Feminists who set the revolution in motion were not only intent on propelling women to the top of the ladder; they planned to redesign the ladder itself (including causing "the demise of the corporate wife"). But that turned out to be just another fantasy that faded in the glare of reality. Dashing more dreams of the feminists, the Census Bureau reported in the year 2000 that the percent of women in the labor force with infants under age one dropped from 59 percent to 55 percent.

When the women's liberation movement burst onto the media in the 1970s, their public message was a demand to end sex discrimination, particularly in employment. But equal pay for equal work had become the law of the land in 1963, years before the feminist movement got under way. When Ruth Bader Ginsburg wrote her analysis of federal laws that allegedly discriminated against women in 1977, *Sex Bias in the U.S. Code*, she could not cite a single law that discriminated against women in employment.

Whining about equal pay for equal work was just a cover for the feminists' real goals in the workplace. They ran to Big Brother Government to provide the reverse discrimination called affirmative action, wage control by feminist-directed "comparable worth" commissions, and the forced hiring of feminists in highly-paid jobs which a "glass ceiling" supposedly denies them.

All during the 1970s and 1980s, feminists waged a vicious assault against the right to be a woman who is not a feminist. The feminist catalogue of rights did not include the right to be exempt from conscription or military combat or the right of a wife to be supported by her husband.

Feminists strove to eliminate the role of stay-at-home wife by making it socially disdained, economically disadvantaged, and legally shorn of traditional protections. Feminist allies in the media carried on an unrelenting attack against traditional marriage, peddling the notion that the Ozzie-and-Harriet lifestyle is out and that serial marriages are in.

The goal of the feminists is the complete restructuring of our society, changing attitudes as well as behavior, abolishing gender roles, and repositioning gender relationships. But even with the active assistance of Big Media, changing human nature is still beyond their grasp.

2001

II

The Media:
Mirror or Maker of Trends?

More of your conversation would infect my brain.

Coriolanus

Kramer v. Kramer

The movie *Kramer v. Kramer* dramatizes how feminism destroys marriage and how everybody, especially children, ends up as losers. Since the plot is so dreary and uninspiring, the movie's success must be laid principally to the fact that it touches one of the most sensitive nerves of today's society.

Mr. and Mrs. Kramer's marriage had none of the usual marital problems. There was no adultery, no alcohol, no financial worry, no physical indignity. The only problem was feminism. Mrs. Kramer began to think she wasn't a "whole person," and that she was "only" a wife and mother. She lost her self-esteem. She decided to abandon her husband and child in order to be liberated to seek her own self-identity. So she walked out on her husband and child.

After she was liberated from marriage and landed a job making more money than her husband, she realized she wanted her child again. So she used the weapon of the court's traditional bias in favor of mothers. The middle-aged judge awarded her the child even though she was the one who had walked out on the marriage. The audience "court" would have opted for Mr. Kramer.

At the end of the movie, Mr. Kramer was unhappy, Mrs. Kramer was unhappy, and the child was the unhappiest of all because he was left with only one parent and he loved them both. The marriage was destroyed, and the only cause was the psychological problems created by feminism.

Kramer v. Kramer is a most instructive movie. It shows that feminism is anti-family and a cause of divorce. It proves that the real victim of women's lib is the child. It also shows that women's lib doesn't always look like Bella Abzug: it can also have the face of Meryl Streep.

1982

Can Babies and Husbands Cope?

The NBC news "white paper" called *Women, Work and Babies* put an important subject on the agenda for national discussion. Jane Pauley, then America's most famous employed mother of twins, posed the question, "Can America cope" with the phenomenon of mothers who have full-time jobs?

The program was not about single parents trying to support themselves and their children. The program was about two-earner couples in which the wife (a) wants a professional career for her own self-fulfillment, (b) simply likes the extra money (to go on vacations, etc.), or (c) admits she can't stand being at home with her children and would rather be anywhere else.

Any successful lawyer knows that, if he can frame the question, he can often get the verdict he wants from judge or jury. The question really is not "Can America cope?" but "Can babies cope?" or "Can husbands cope?"

NBC presented the problem from the feminist point of view and, true to form, offered the solution from the liberals' point of view. The *New York Times* review of the show, commenting on the ideological bias of the White Paper, called it "a plea for free lunch." The message was that "society" should provide more taxpayer-financed daycare centers and employer-financed special benefits and job security for mothers. The *Times* concluded, that's the way to "solve" the "problem" of the kids so we can all shout "hooray for the two-income couple and self-realization in the marketplace!"

Let's be blunt about this demand. Any plan for society, or government, or corporations to assume the direct and indirect costs of caring for babies means imposing the real costs on the taxpayers and the general public, which, in turn, means on the singles, the couples who have already raised their families, and the couples who are living on a lower single income. It's hard to think of anything more unjust.

Non-mother care of babies is very expensive. This is true even at the minimum wage rates paid to workers in most daycare centers, and even with inadequate conditions and supervision.

But cost is the adults' problem. From the babies' point of view, daycare diseases are more serious. Anyone who has watched flu bugs and other contagious diseases go through a family of several children at home must recoil in horror at the thought of thirty toddlers in diapers, all ill and screaming for their mothers. The NBC program admitted that daycare babies are twelve times more likely to get the flu than home-care babies.

Another major problem from the babies' point of view is the constant change of personnel. Babies don't adapt well to the high turnover rate of hired care providers.

While babies are the biggest losers in any system of non-mother care, it was clear from the NBC program that husbands lose, too. When a woman has a baby and a career, the husband ranks third on her scale of priorities, and a poor third at that, because she's simply too exhausted for anything else even if she has any extra time, which she usually doesn't.

The lifestyle sections of newspapers have had many articles in recent months about how men in their twenties and thirties are rejecting or avoiding marriage. Is it any wonder? What man wants to risk a financial and emotional commitment, buy a ring, and assume a mortgage on a house, when he will rank only number three in the heart of the woman he loves?

All that talk about egalitarian marriages in which the husbands share 50-50 in child care simply doesn't happen in practice, as Jane Pauley complained bitterly. The NBC program maintained that only 13 percent of husbands share baby care as the feminists say they should.

Jane Pauley tried to tell us that it is "the rule, not the exception" for mothers of small babies to be in the labor force, and she predicted that the traditional Mom "seems headed for extinction." That was a self-serving slur to try to justify her own lifestyle. Fourteen million mothers have made the commitment to give their babies full-time care at home, and they are staggering under an income tax burden that is unfair to families with children.

1985

Madison Avenue and Motherhood

I feel sorry for the advertising agencies that must produce the thirty- and sixty-second commercial spots costing hundreds of thousands of dollars on prime-time television. They have the task of making their product irresistible to a market they don't understand. Women buy most of the consumer goods, so the pitch must appeal to women. But how do you create a television ad featuring a woman without alienating some of the women you want as customers?

Highly paid ad men are discovering what Walter Mondale didn't seem to know when he chose Geraldine Ferraro as his running mate in 1984. Women are simply not a uniform bloc with the same attitudes (commercial or political) who can be appealed to as a group.

The feminist movement has carried on a running criticism for the last decade against advertisements that show mothers taking pride in clean households, good cooking, and other evidences of a homemaker's domestic skills. In the feminist view, women should be liberated from the stereotype that homemaking is a fulfilling career. Yet marketing research shows that mothers constitute 60 percent of the prime-time audience, and they are the target of 75 percent of prime-time advertising dollars. The percentages are even higher during daytime television.

A 1978 Enjoli perfume television ad showed a mother saying to her husband, "I can bring home the bacon, fry it up in a pan and never, never, never let you forget you're a man." In 1984, the Enjoli woman has changed her tune, saying, "I can bring home the bacon, fry it up in a pan, but once in a while you've got to give me a hand."

The *Wall Street Journal* calls this change "Madison Avenue trying to keep up with motherhood." But is Enjoli selling perfume or selling changing lifestyles and women's lib? It seems obvious that the smell of the bacon would smother the delicate fragrance of perfume no matter what the words in the woman's mouth.

Some advertisers have succumbed to feminist demands by domesticating Dad. Dads now cook Aunt Jemima's waffles, change diapers with Johnson & Johnson baby powder, and shop at supermarkets for Kraft cheese. Is this the way life is, or the way the avant garde wants it to be? Such advertising may be raising false hopes in career-oriented young women.

Many advertising agencies are coping with conflicting social trends by censoring mothers out of their commercials altogether. A survey of 250 recent television spots found that only nine showed women as mothers. A large percentage didn't show women at all, using men or only the products themselves.

Recently there has been a significant increase in commercials that use employed women to peddle a product. United Airlines shows a mother looking at a family picture in her briefcase while on a business trip, while Pour-a-Quiche shows mother and dad driving home together from their jobs.

Statistics show that 53 percent of women are employed outside the home and 47 percent are not. If companies want to sell their products, their ads can't afford to omit empathy for nearly half of the market just for the sake of being trendy.

The artificial world of prime-time television programming, by contrast with advertising spots, seems to have abandoned the traditional family and plunged into a world where there are almost no mothers. June Cleaver, Harriet Nelson, Lucy Ricardo, and other stay-at-home moms have vanished. They've been replaced by single women, divorced women sharing homes, and female detectives with unemployed husbands. Some mothers appear, but they are usually widowed, divorced, or unwed, or their children are peripheral to the plot.

In the real world, however, the tide is going against feminism and toward motherhood. Every woman doesn't need a baby, but every baby still needs a mother.

1985

Doing the Dirty Work

Art Buchwald's particular brand of humor has made him a social commentator on current cultural and political trends just as Will Rogers's humor delighted an earlier generation. A Buchwald column entitled "Liberation and the Self-Maid Woman," like many of his Capitol Punishment columns, was truth hiding behind humor.

After talking with a liberated lawyer named Lila, Buchwald concluded that "behind every liberated woman, there is another woman who has to do the dirty work for her." (We will overlook Buchwald's bias that it is "dirtier" to take care of children and cook family meals than it is to outwit, outmaneuver, and outlitigate an opponent in a lawsuit.)

Buchwald made the amazing discovery that Lila's career in a Washington law firm absolutely depends on a Latin American domestic named Juanita who takes care of Lila's children, cooks the meals, cleans the house, and tends to Lila's husband's shirts. Juanita's wages consume half of Lila's salary, but, even so, job turnover is high. Lila has to hunt up a new "Juanita" about every eight months.

Playing the straight man in this conversation, Buchwald asked Lila about all those magazines that show husbands sharing the household duties. Lila explains that those husbands exist only in magazines. Husbands, she says, are more than willing for a wife to be liberated, just as long as she takes care of the house and children, too.

In his own inimitable style, Buchwald caricatures the conversation, and one can infer that he sympathizes with Lila's dilemma. He had thought Lila was the shining example of a liberated woman who had the best of both worlds. He is shocked to find that, without Juanita mopping floors, Lila wouldn't be liberated at all. As he put it in his exquisite hyperbole, "in order to be free, a woman must find another slave to replace her."

In all the gallons of ink that have poured over the subject of women's roles in the last decade, it took a humorist to lift the curtain on this sensitive subject. Equal employment opportunity has been the law of the land since 1963; that's not controversial anymore. But even if we build a society in which women have absolutely guaranteed equal opportunity in hiring, pay, and promotions—even if modern young women have a single-minded dedication to a business or professional career, and put in as many overtime hours and lifetime effort as their male competitors—the average woman still will not achieve the heights of career and financial success that the average man does.

That is because men have one great asset over their female competitors—men have wives. And, in the world we know, there are not very many persons who want to be the wife of a woman. Wives are a tremendous asset to career-oriented men. Wives provide the nurturing of the children, the keeping of the house, the emotional security of a nest to come home to, and most important, the incentive for a man to work hard and succeed.

One attractive, liberated career woman who was recently divorced stated the problem frankly. She admitted that the divorce was caused because "neither one of us wanted to be a wife."

What Buchwald and Lila discovered, feminist ideologues have known for some time. That is why they work so hard to eliminate the economic rights of wives and mothers. The feminist legislative agenda includes such anti-wife proposals as eliminating the dependent wife's benefit in Social Security and repealing all state laws that spell out the wife's right to be supported by her husband.

Taking away rights from wives doesn't put one thin dime in the pockets of any unmarried employed woman. What lurks behind these anti-wife proposals is the resentment of career women like Lila that her male competitors in the business world have the advantage of wives, whereas her children are taken care of by a hired, temporary "Juanita."

The Me generation, which seeks only its own fulfillment, will probably say that sex-role stereotypes aren't fair and that we must use the strong arm of government to abolish them. But those who believe that it is a social good for children to be cared for by their own mothers in a family environment are not about to acquiesce in the elimination of the traditional rights of wives.

1986

Who Invented Free Love?

The lifestyle or women's sections of metropolitan newspapers certainly have very different features from those they had fifteen years ago. Gone are the days when a couple of pages were filled with brides in wedding dresses and engagements of young women and men who pledged to live together in traditional marriage. Now the brides are relegated to small pictures on back pages, while the headlines and the friendly photos are given to those who live what is euphemistically called "alternative lifestyles." Readers are treated to a steady succession of features about different living arrangements, such as lesbian mothers, or women who decide to have a child but refuse to allow the child to have a father.

A typical example of these offbeat features was the flattering lifestyle article about Linda LeClair and Peter Behr. These two anti–Vietnam War college students from the late 1960s, we are told, deserve their niche in history as the standard-bearers of the New Morality.

No, Linda didn't do something constructive based on personal achievement like Dr. Sally Ride. No, Linda wasn't elected or appointed to high office. No, she didn't succeed in business or a profession, or distinguish herself by volunteer service. What she did, as a sophomore at Barnard College, was to live unmarried with her lover in 1968 and be the first to flaunt her immoral behavior on a college campus.

The female author of this newspaper feature apparently believes that this makes Linda something of a folk hero who opened up new worlds for women. "She really liberated things." The article credits her for the shift to coed dorms on college campuses.

A few small details toward the end of the story, however, blemished Linda as a role model. Linda and Peter broke up soon after their extra-marital liaison became known. She dropped out of college and, fifteen years later, is a single working mother still seeking a college degree. Peter owns a massage therapy clinic in Canada and is married to a woman he met at a massage therapy convention.

TV Guide featured an article by Marlo Thomas talking frankly about her roles in television dramas. Fifteen years ago, she pointed out, the girl she played in a television series never slept with her boyfriend; the script made that very clear. When she kissed him, they were never in a bedroom; he was always at the door on his way out.

In the mid-1980s, Thomas continues, she started a new series about a woman who has a lover, not a boyfriend. She says it is now okay for a television heroine to have an adulterous relationship. According to

Marlo Thomas, this means that women have "grown up." In her view, this is liberation, and television reflects the advances women have made.

Why are so many media sources constantly selling the message that "sexual liberation" is part of "women's liberation"? The sexual revolution forced women to take most of the risks while accommodating the promiscuous playboy lifestyle.

Most of the media refer to abortion as the preeminent women's right. The sex act involves two people, yet the woman is expected to assume the risk for the "mistake"—the physical risk plus the emotional trauma of killing her own baby. The woman is left with the bitterness of being exploited. Contraceptives are usually touted as another manifestation of women's liberation. Again, the responsibility for the worry, the inconvenience, and the physical risk from side effects falls on the woman.

Disease? The woman suffers more. She bears the high risk of cervical cancer from promiscuity. Women's sores from incurable herpes are more painful, and they last longer. Beyond that is the danger that her venereal disease poses to her unborn children, even later in life.

Easy, no-fault divorce has come about over the last fifteen years as part of "women's liberation." The result has been economic devastation for women; divorce is the chief cause of the feminization of poverty. The ex-husband's standard of living goes up after divorce, and he can look for a younger wife; the ex-wife's standard of living goes down dramatically, and she is unlikely to find a younger husband.

Sexual liberation is just a snow job to con women into taking the risks so that men can reap the rewards of the playboy lifestyle. Sexual liberation imposes most of the financial, physical, and psychological costs on women. As Bette Midler said, "Free love, who invented that? Guys invented that, because the women have all the burden of free love."

1986

Statutory Rape and Date Rape

Statutory rape is the crime committed by a man who has sexual intercourse with a minor girl under the age of consent (which varies in different states from ten to eighteen years of age). It is based on the assumption that, since young girls can be taken advantage of by sexually experienced men, whether or not the girl consents to the intimacy is irrelevant because the man (presumably since he is older and an authority figure) has the wherewithal to induce her consent.

In 1981 the U.S. Supreme Court upheld the constitutionality of statutory rape laws against a challenge that they are sex discriminatory. The Court upheld a California law making it a felony for a man to have sexual intercourse with a woman under age eighteen who is not his wife. This decision was much criticized by the feminists as upholding a sex-discriminatory law based on what they call "outmoded" sexual stereotypes.

The feminist movement has tried to eliminate laws against statutory rape for two reasons. First, these laws constitute impediments to their goal of a totally sex-neutral legal system: only a male can be prosecuted for this crime, and only a female can be his victim. Second, as explained by Ruth Bader Ginsburg in her 1977 report on *Sex Bias in the U.S. Code* published by the U.S. Commission on Civil Rights, a law designed to "protect weak women from bad men" is "offensive because of the image of women it perpetuates."

Now let's look at how prime-time television entertainment editorializes for the feminist movement. The title of ABC-TV's two-hour movie called *When She Says No* was a deception. The woman named Rose said "yes" in a hundred ways over several hours; she invited three men into her hotel room for what they thought was recreational sex engaged in by consenting adults, and then two days later she initiated a criminal prosecution of the three for rape.

While the dramatization presented the issue from both male and female viewpoints, the movie came off as an editorial in behalf of the woman. The audience was led to believe that the men should be convicted of rape because they should not have relied on her consent, even though she pursued and flirted with them all evening, led them on, freely invited them into her hotel room, and voluntarily undressed herself.

The feminists, who for ten years have opposed the laws designed to protect girls under age eighteen from predatory Don Juans, now want the law to protect women like Rose from what is colloquially known as "date rape." Yet Rose was no child; she was a thirty-year-old divorcee and university instructor with a PH.D.

The feminists' double standard is fascinating. They want a girl of twelve or thirteen years to be able to consent so her seducer can go scot-free. But they want a professional woman of thirty to be able to consent at midnight and then change her mind two days later and prosecute her erstwhile friends for criminal rape.

Rose claimed that her apparent consent was forced and therefore shouldn't be recognized in law as a "yes." But how was she forced since there was no physical violence? After coaching by her feminist lawyer, she claimed that the intercourse wasn't her fault because society had conditioned her to take orders from men—first her father, then her husband, then the male professor who headed her department.

But didn't the feminists tell us that such notions of the weaker sex are really old-fashioned stereotypes from which the modern woman has been freed? Certainly a woman who has spent ten years in the feminist atmosphere of a university campus should be totally liberated from any need to have society protect her from what Rose conceded was her own "stupidity."

The ABC-TV movie dramatized and defended the false feminist ideology that women are the helpless victims of a power structure in which men have the power and the authority, while women are psychologically trained to obey. In truth, Rose was just a lonely thirty-year-old woman who craved male attention at any price, even from three men whose unattractiveness was matched only by their lack of affection.

1986

Male Wimps

Time magazine gave a cover and seven pages to promote Shere Hite's diatribe against men called *Women and Love: A Cultural Revolution in Progress*. Shere Hite is an ex-model who posed nude for *Playboy* and *Oui*. She then proclaimed herself a "sexologist" (a sort of female Kinsey) and made several million dollars on two books (in 1976 and 1981) allegedly revealing inside information about women's sexuality. Naturally, this made her a darling of the media, who accorded her the free publicity that sold enough books to enable her to live in a million-dollar Fifth Avenue apartment decorated like an Italian palace.

Women and Love is built on the thesis that men are to blame for all women's problems. Specifically, she accuses men of committing "emotional and psychological harassment" and of failing to cultivate "verbal closeness" with women.

The men who manage the news magazines and the network talk shows, and who decided to give Hite's book extravagant free advertising, must like to be insulted and kicked around by the feminists. What except masochism can explain why they feature such feminist furies?

Hite's book is a compendium of the views of 4,500 frustrated and disillusioned women who blame their emotional troubles on men and now announce they are "fed up with men." Hite elevates their personal sob stories to the status of a societal problem and calls their cumulative complaint a "large-scale cultural revolution."

Hite is sure men should be blamed because they are treacherous troglodytes and women are socially conditioned to serve them. "It's men's

attitudes toward women that are causing the problem," according to
Hite, because men have "condescending, judgmental attitudes." In com-
menting on *Time*'s article, one letter to the editor suggested that Shere
Hite's name should be pronounced Sheer Hate.

Wasn't the women's liberation movement of the 1970s supposed to
cure that condescension and promote equality of men and women in
factory, office, kitchen, and bed? Hite says it hasn't worked out that way.
She asserts that, in spite of women's liberation and the sexual revolution, women remain oppressed and are expected to play the traditional
nurturing, love-giving roles while sharing the breadwinner role, too.

Since Betty Friedan's opening blast two decades ago, the feminist
propagandists have preached the notion that we must redesign society
to become gender neutral and that men must shed their macho image
and remake themselves to become househusbands at least half the time.
Men must learn to cry, cook, and accept women who are career oriented,
competitive, and unfaithful.

So, the feminists succeeded in making a large percentage of the new
generation of men into a bunch of wimps who have a guilt complex and
acquiesce in a daily diet of male bashing. The New Man is unsure of
his role, his mission in life, and even himself.

These New Men now feel no responsibility to provide their wives
with a home and financial support (they expect their wives to have jobs
and share the mortgage payments, as well as do the dishes and the diapers), and they feel no obligation to remain faithful or stick around for
a lifetime. Employers are tongue-lashed into indulging their female
employees with special privileges that would never be accorded to men,
and preachers are intimidated into rewriting Scripture and hymns to
suit the strident feminists.

Shere Hite, the paradigm of women's liberation and sexual liberation, now proves out of her own mouth that feminism is a failed ideology that produces women who are burned out and bitter. Men who
accept the blame for this result are, indeed, wimps.

Maybe the Hite book will be the proverbial straw that breaks the camel's back and will encourage men to say *they* are fed up with the foolish feminists. Maybe then we will start to hear from some real men.

1987

Carving the Joint

Hard times have hit the feminists. The more successful their favorites become, the more visible they are when they don't behave like ideological feminists.

Congressperson Pat Schroeder (D-CO) was the feminists' best hope for a female on a national ticket in 1988. She campaigned in fifty cities and thirty states and raised the respectable sum of $800,000, with the National Organization for Women chanting "Run, Pat, Run!"

It wasn't pulling out of the race that demoralized the feminists. It was that Schroeder cried and fell apart in her husband's embrace when she announced her withdrawal from the race. The feminists were acutely embarrassed because Schroeder's emotional performance confirmed the fears that many people have about a woman being president, namely, that she isn't "man" enough for the job. "What happens when she sits down at a table with Gorbachev and he won't give up his missiles?" asked one Democratic consultant.

The Schroeder exit came hard on the heels of the resignation of Secretary of Transportation Elizabeth Dole, the highest-ranking woman in Republican officialdom, in order to campaign for her husband Bob Dole for president. The feminists can't accept that a successful woman would put her own career second to her husband's.

Just how bitter the feminists are on this point was dramatically brought home to me several years ago when I debated before the student body at West Point. When I suggested that a male cadet select a wife who would put her career second to his, twenty-five female cadets got up, slammed their seats, and noisily stomped out of the auditorium in a discourteous display of protest.

But the Schroeder and Dole setbacks were doubled in spades by the success of two movies: *Fatal Attraction* and *Baby Boom*. The feminists must be burning the midnight oil trying to figure out how to cope with the dilemmas posed by these box-office wonders.

The resident male feminist at the *Washington Post*, Richard Cohen, manifested his frustration in a column headlined "A New Stereotype: The Crazy Career Woman." He is beside himself with anger that audiences lining up to see *Fatal Attraction*'s steamy sex scenes find themselves watching a movie that shows a career woman who is a psychopath while the wife is "bright, educated, and totally fulfilled" as a full-time homemaker and whose character exhibits serenity and "formidable strength."

In a cover story, *Time* magazine also reported the feminists' rage about the film, predicting that *Fatal Attraction* "will linger in the American central nervous system."

Diane Keaton's movie, *Baby Boom*, poses another challenge for the feminists. It is the tale of a female Yale undergraduate–Harvard MBA, high-pressure management consultant, earning six figures at a top corporation, wearing designer fashions and enjoying a live-in lover, who abandons it all to live with a baby and husband in a small town and develop a cottage industry making baby food.

The ideas of baby displacing briefcase and home work displacing the board room at a Fortune 500 corporation are anathema to the feminists, so they feel compelled to engage in social commentary complaining that *Baby Boom* is based on an improbable theme from the 1950s.

Diane Keaton's own life is the archetypical feminist success story: she is sophisticated, never married, childless, has a career that earns her a million dollars per movie, and has famous lovers like Woody Allen and Warren Beatty. It is unlikely that she ever spent evenings in front of the fireplace reading Dr. Spock.

Now, approaching age forty with neither husband nor baby, she took on a movie script that makes a statement that there is a lot more to life for a woman than a successful business career. Keaton admitted off camera that "the movie says you can't have everything—everybody has to compromise," and when a baby comes into the picture, "everything gets out of control, but her life gets a lot better." *USA Today* quoted Keaton as admitting in an interview that she herself would like to have a baby.

If the feminist movement were truly a "women's rights" movement, British Prime Minister Margaret Thatcher would be hailed as the prime example of women's ability to achieve and win in competition with men. If the feminist movement were truly working for "women in politics," Mrs. Thatcher would be their role model of success.

But the silence from the "women's rights" crowd is deafening. Feminists show the same non-support of Jeane Kirkpatrick, a truly talented woman who was an eloquent voice for our country as ambassador in the anti-American forum misnamed the United Nations.

Margaret Thatcher proved that the route to success for a woman is not the clenched fist, the whimper of a victim, or even affirmative action. It is the same route as for a man: hard work, perseverance, and sticking to sound, conservative principles. In a 1982 interview, she remarked, "I owe nothing to women's lib." Later, when asked if she would be a "butcher" after her third election, Mrs. Thatcher (a grocer's daughter who grew up in a home without an inside toilet or hot water) replied, "I'm not a good butcher, but I've learned how to carve the joint."

We can thank Margaret Thatcher for showing us how to carve the feminist joint out of the subject of role models for women.

1987

A Non-Feminist Novel

Gone With the Wind's (GWTW) fiftieth anniversary inspired much commentary and nostalgia, but the usually garrulous feminist spokespersons were conspicuous by their silence. GWTW is not a book for feminists. Feminist ideology teaches that women were helpless and oppressed prior to the women's lib movement of the 1970s. They can't accept the role model of a woman who faces life's challenges without government help.

Women didn't don uniforms and ride to battle during the Civil War, but the women in GWTW exhibited the strength of the South. When the Union soldiers invaded their home, not only the spunky Scarlett but even the sickly Melanie grabbed a weapon to protect their virtue and their home.

GWTW was real life to those who read it and saw the movie in the late 1930s. Scarlett and Rhett, Melanie and Ashley were real people. Tara was a place we hoped to see some day. Indeed, visitors in Atlanta still ask directions to Tara more often than any other tourist attractions, not realizing that Tara exists only in the minds of GWTW readers.

Gone With the Wind came to an American people devastated by six years of the Great Depression—an economic and social crisis of immense proportions. President Franklin D. Roosevelt said "the only thing we have to fear is fear itself," but that was just empty rhetoric to the unemployed. Our problem wasn't fear: it was despair.

Gone With the Wind is the story of those who repudiated defeat in the face of defeat all around them. GWTW tells the history (omitted from most history books) of what the Civil War did to the South, including the hunger caused by destruction of crops, the desolation of burned out homes, the pain of war wounds and amputations without anesthetics, and the deaths of a generation of young men.

History books record the heroism of the Civil War's battles, but GWTW recorded the heroism in the daily lives of women and men who had to cope with the war that came to civilians in the cities and the countryside from circumstances beyond their control.

After the French Revolution, one day a friend asked a writer, "What did you do during the Revolution?" To which the writer replied simply, "I survived." Indeed, there are times when survival is the supreme achievement, and the Old South during and after the Civil War was such a time. GWTW tells about those who survived and rebuilt what they lost, by sheer will and hard labor—without disaster relief, disability payments, welfare, Social Security, veteran's benefits, unemployment compensation, food stamps, or housing allowances, indeed, at a time when government was the enemy.

Communist regimes have banned GWTW. That's because its theme is contrary to the Marxist dogma that the individual must be submerged in the all-powerful state. As Margaret Mitchell explained in her published letters, the communists suppressed GWTW in their countries because the novel is "a glorification of individual courage and individual enterprise (both qualities being highly obnoxious to communists)" and because it reveres what the communists call a *bourgeois* love that free people have for their land and home.

GWTW is absent from most high school reading lists. Maybe that's because television-reared youngsters haven't the intellectual stamina to tackle a one-thousand-page book. Maybe it's because the majority of high school students are too vocabulary poor to read books written prior to the era of the dumbed-down classics. Maybe it's because those who select school reading lists are too eager to assign stories of defeatism and despair and have no time for tales of heroism and hope.

When one of the television networks aired an expensive mid-1980s remake of Arthur Miller's *Death of a Salesman*, the critics lauded it as a dramatic triumph, but it bombed in the Nielsen ratings. People are not willingly entertained by tales of failure. Most of us prefer to hear about heroism in the face of great odds, about the strong-willed who survive when their world is blown away with the wind, about people's determination to rise again from the ruins.

That's why *Gone With the Wind* is a saga for all seasons. GWTW's sales of twenty-five million books are second only to the Bible's, and its shared and deeply felt emotions have not been equaled by any other book in this country. No one is a truly educated American who has not read *Gone With the Wind*. It is the great American novel.

1987

Going Around with the Wrong Crowd

Ever since the feminist ideologues burst into our national consciousness in the mid-1960s, I have wondered where they got their peculiar notions about men. Feminist ideology according to Simone de Beauvoir, Gloria Steinem, Betty Friedan, Kate Millett, and Germaine Greer teaches that men, especially husbands, are awful creatures and that a wife is just an unpaid servant mistress. Simone de Beauvoir, whose 1949 book *The Second Sex* made her the acknowledged founder of the modern women's liberation movement, described marriage as an "obscene bourgeois institution." Her book, which has become a staple of university women's studies courses, is full of such nonsense as "one is not born, but rather becomes, a woman."

I thought all this bitter commentary was a creation of their weird imaginations, because it is so at variance with the men I know. Most American men are decent and honorable, working long hours (often moonlighting) to provide for a wife and children.

Now, at last, through the meticulous research of one of the twentieth century's premier historians, Paul Johnson, I have discovered where these feminists got their nutty notions. His book *Intellectuals* makes it clear that the left-wing intellectuals of the last two centuries really did treat their wives and mistresses like unpaid servants and usually treated their children even worse.

The intellectuals about whom Johnson reports were not just artsy celebrities who could assume the public would accept an immoral bohemian lifestyle. They were writers who arrogantly presumed to diagnose the ills of society, to prescribe cures, and to tell mankind how we should all live our lives and how society and the economy should be structured.

So how did they run their own lives? They were typically selfish and self-centered, cruel and violent, dirty (many of them seldom bathed), and never treated any women as equals. They built a reputation on the falsehood that their theories would help the working class, but they never knew any of the working class except as mistresses.

Jean-Jacques Rousseau, the French philosopher who wrote prolifically about "truth" and "virtue," kept an illiterate laundress as his mistress for thirty-three years, treating her like an unpaid servant, while he continued his affairs with many other women. He wrote that he "never felt the least glimmering of love for her . . . the sensual needs I satisfied with her were purely sexual and were nothing to do with her as an individual." Rousseau was known for his theories about raising children— a subject he knew nothing about because he forced his mistress to abandon their five babies at birth on the doorstep of a foundling home. He never saw them again because, he wrote, children were "an inconvenience," and their noise would interfere with his writing. His only concern for his parents was to get cash from them, and he let his foster mother, who rescued him from destitution at least four times, die indigent, possibly from malnutrition.

The poet Percy Bysshe Shelley saw himself first of all as one who tried to define the social purpose of literature and use poetry to stir social action. He was wildly promiscuous, drove his first wife to suicide, treated his wives and mistresses shabbily, did not support his own children, and falsely accused his mother of adultery.

Karl Marx, who had more impact on actual events than any other intellectual in modern times, made his wife's life a nightmare. He kept her and their children destitute while he disdained work and seldom bathed. He denied his daughters an education and vetoed their careers because he thought women were suitable only to be clerical assistants. He kept a female slave in his household from the age of eight, never paid her a wage, used her as his mistress, and refused to acknowledge their child. She was the only member of the working class Marx ever knew well, and his alleged research about the so-called proletariat was a fabrication.

Henrik Ibsen, whose play *A Doll's House* is a feminist favorite today, allowed his first mistress and their child to die destitute. He treated his wife shabbily (far worse than the wife in his famous play) and had a long succession of affairs with other women, who got younger as he got older until they were down to age fifteen and even ten, whom he exploited as models for characters in his plays.

Leo Tolstoy, who had the effrontery to think he was some kind of messiah destined to remake society, used and abused his wife and forced her to read torrid accounts of all his sexual exploits in brothels and with a succession of whores, gypsies, and peasant girls. He wrote that prostitution is "necessary for the maintenance of the family." He refused to acknowledge his illegitimate offspring, and he refused to admit that a woman could be a serious, adult, intelligent human being.

Ernest Hemingway was abusive and alcoholic, publicly humiliated his four wives, had numerous affairs with younger and younger women, and could not form any kind of civilized relationship with a woman except one based on her complete subservience. One complained, with justification, that she was leading "a slave's life with a brute for a slave-owner." A notorious liar, he was one of the most enthusiastic defenders of the communists in the Spanish Civil War.

Bertrand Russell, who ground out a steady stream of advice on almost every political and social issue from disarmament to religion, was one of the leading names in the twentieth-century movement to "emancipate" women from Victorian morality through "free love." He portrayed women as victims of an antiquated system of morality, while hiring lawyers to give his ex-wives as little support as possible. He had three wives and seduced almost any woman who was available, including chambermaids, governesses, and daughters of friends he happened to be visiting.

Jean-Paul Sartre, a professional philosopher who presumed to preach to a mass audience, aligned himself with the communists. When he seduced Simone de Beauvoir, he said his credo was "travel, polygamy, transparency." Sartre used her as his mistress, cook, laundress, seamstress, and housekeeper, all the while boasting of affairs with younger and younger women until he got to teenagers. He treated her like a slave and didn't even leave her any money. Simone de Beauvoir was an educated and able feminist and she didn't have to live like a servant-mistress unless she chose that lifestyle.

Edmund Wilson, another adulterous literary notable, had four wives whom he abused. He voted communist or socialist in every election. He was forever demanding big government spending for welfare, but he refused to file his own income tax returns.

Victor Gollancz, the Englishman who became wealthy publishing pro-communist books, hired women employees because he could pay them lower wages, impose harsher working conditions, and use them as his mistresses. He treated his wife like a slave, using her as housekeeper, chauffeur, barber, and valet, and forced her to put up with his frequent adultery and his disagreeable habit of pawing other women in public. Like many of the other pro-communist intellectuals of his time, he had no contact with working people. He refused to publish the most brilliant author whose books were offered to him, the anti-communist George Orwell.

Paul Johnson's *Intellectuals* proves that the public posture of famous left-wing intellectuals cannot be separated from their private lives. The one explains the other. Women were "loved" only insofar as they were servile and acquiesced in being treated like man's property. Fortunately, the bizarre feminist theories about men and marriage are true only of the crowd they choose to associate with—the left-wing intellectuals.

I would not want anyone to get the impression that the substance of this important book is to recount sexual relationships. Paul Johnson's primary thesis is that the leftist intellectuals were liars who had no regard for the truth and falsified "evidence" for their communist or socialist economic theories. That's not surprising, since a man who spends his life lying to women will probably lie about everything else, too. For that story, you'll have to read *Intellectuals*.

1989

The Monster behind the Myth

What a loathsome, depraved, and vicious monster! That's the conclusion one is forced to accept after reading the definitive exposé, *Picasso: Creator and Destroyer*, by Arianna Stassinopoulos Huffington.

The biographer stripped off Pablo Picasso's phony mask of art and showed him to the world as a sadist who started in brothels and spent a ninety-year lifetime abusing, beating, and deliberately humiliating a long succession of women who loved him. Along the way, he betrayed his friends and calculated the destruction of everyone who crossed his path.

The truth about Picasso has been a long time emerging. Fortunately, it fell into the hands of an author whose descriptive skills, powerful vocabulary, empathy with victims, and sense of drama were equal to the task of relating this sordid story.

Picasso has long been acclaimed as the greatest artist of the twentieth century. Picasso himself orchestrated that adulation by an expert manipulation of public attitudes and venalities in a way that Madison Avenue advertising companies might envy. As Mrs. Huffington reports, "Picasso had mastered the publicity game before the world knew that such a game existed."

Picasso stands in a class by himself as having milked the public during his own lifetime for more cash than any other artist in history. The more than ten thousand works he had produced by 1961 were then estimated to have a commercial value of $100,000,000.

Picasso treated his customers with the same contempt as he treated his mistresses, wives, and friends. In 1912, Picasso denounced beauty as "crap" and set himself on his path of deliberate ugliness. "Museums are just a lot of lies," Picasso said in the 1930s, "and people who make art their business are mostly impostors." He should know, since he was himself the chief charlatan. In a 1952 interview with the Italian writer Giovanni Papini, Picasso confessed how he exploited the indolent wealthy who "desire only the peculiar, the sensational, the eccentric, the scandalous in today's art." "Through amusing myself with all these farces," Picasso admitted, "I became a celebrity. . . . But when I am alone, I do not have the effrontery to consider myself an artist at all, in the grand old meaning of the word. I am only a public clown, a mountebank. I have understood my time and have exploited the imbecility, the vanity, the greed of my contemporaries."

Upon joining the Communist Party after World War II, he said doing so was "the logical conclusion of my whole life, my whole work." The Soviet Union awarded him the Lenin Peace Prize in 1962 and adopted his peace dove painting as a communist symbol.

Picasso was cruelly domineering and morbidly possessive of his mistresses, even while he was faithless to them all. He was vindictively jealous of every contemporary man or woman who displayed talent. Picasso seduced an underage girl at a children's camp, inflicting on her the exotic sexual experimentation he had learned in thirty years of sexual experiences. He painted his violent *Guernica* as two of his mistresses were engaged in a fistfight alongside of him in his studio.

Picasso brutally beat his mistress Dora and many times left her lying unconscious on the floor. He burned his mistress Françoise's cheek with a cigarette and told her, "There's nothing so similar to one poodle dog as another poodle dog, and that goes for women, too." Picasso callously refused to inconvenience himself by driving a few blocks out of his way to take Françoise to the hospital to have her baby, telling her to find her own way because he needed the chauffeur to drive him to the 1949 World Peace Congress.

Picasso's disordered paintings were mirrors of his deep and universal hatred of women and his attitude that a woman is a servile animal. Women with distorted and deformed faces and bodies filled his paintings that purported to portray the modernist world. Picasso's last self-portrait, painted in 1972 a year before his death, depicts the final anguish and despair of this egomaniac, even then still fueled by hatred. His widow, his longtime mistress, and his grandson all committed suicide after his death.

Mrs. Huffington has performed an international service to humanity by exposing the hypocrisy of Picasso: his sadistic abuse of women concealed behind his so-called charisma, his violence concealed behind his dove of peace, and his life pattern as a destroyer (of women, friends, values, and traditional beauty) concealed behind his pretensions of art.

1989

Reinventing the Family

When *Newsweek* devoted an entire issue of one hundred pages (less ads) to "The 21st Century Family" in November 1989, the lead sentence was

"The American family does not exist." In case you are a member of this time-honored institution which *Newsweek* relegated to the age of the 1950s (in the eyes of the authors, just as remote as the age of the dinosaur), perhaps you should do your own "hard thinking about what a family is for" instead of relying on the thinking of writers of undisclosed family status and sexual or marital preferences. *Newsweek* pontificated that it was "inevitable" that "we" would "reinvent" the family. "We," it seems, means the dozen or so writers who contributed to this issue.

This redefinition of the family, according to *Newsweek*, includes families of divorced parents and stepchildren, unmarried couples living together, single women deliberately having babies by donor insemination, gay and lesbian couples with or without children, grandparents raising children, and genetically made-to-order babies. Proclaiming that "most scholars now consider the 'breadwinner-homemaker' model unusual, applicable in limited circumstances for a limited time," *Newsweek* didn't include this model among the current family "varieties."

Newsweek seems to think that the Ozzie-and-Harriet lifestyle was created and validated by television and that the media can now play God and design a different version for the 1990s.

But is the new family described in *Newsweek* an improvement? Does it serve our goals of providing a base from which to face life's challenges, a safe haven to care for our young, a nest where love and companionship can grow, and an encouragement to nurture each other through life's many stages of aging? One searches the pages in vain to find positive answers to these questions.

If you stick with the issue to the bitter end, you will find that *Newsweek* reported the new evidence that infants in daycare for twenty or more hours a week are at risk and that the high turnover rate among paid caregivers and the high disease rate of institutionalized children make daycare a very uncertain and unhappy place for children.

Back on page ninety-two, *Newsweek* ruefully admits: "Despite the compelling evidence about the dark side of daycare, many experts say there's a great reluctance to discuss these problems publicly." Why? "Because they're afraid the right wing will use this to say that only mothers can care for babies, so women should stay home."

What the liberals and the feminists are really afraid of is not the right wing but the eternal truth that the traditional family is still the best way to live, and that babies still need mothers in the home.

1990

War of the Roses

The movie *War of the Roses* is, surprisingly, an old-fashioned morality play lurking behind an R-rated movie with bad words and embarrassingly explicit sexual scenes. The moral of this 1990 black comedy is that, of all the options a married couple can choose, divorce is the worst. Lesson-master Danny DeVito gives it to us straight and unvarnished at the end of a couple of exhausting hours.

The plot is as simple as the special effects are improbable and convoluted. Boy meets girl; they marry and have two children; husband is a successful lawyer and makes lots of money; they buy and furnish the house of her dreams. They have eighteen years of a good marriage: good sex, good income, good children, no adultery, no alcoholism, no poverty, no abuse, and no worries. Their biggest problem is making house-decorating choices.

Then one day, out of the blue in the middle of the night, Mrs. Rose announces that she wants a divorce: she just doesn't want to live with Mr. Rose anymore. There was no provocation, no fault; she didn't even deign to offer a reason. Although she certainly was no lady, she expected him to play the stereotypical gentleman and get out, leaving her to enjoy the house that they had built. To her surprise and dismay, he fought to keep the marriage contract they both had signed and, at the very least, for his equal rights to their house.

Ten years earlier, in the movie *Kramer v. Kramer*, the divorcing couple fought for custody of their child. It's a mark of our age of materialism that, in *War of the Roses*, the couple fought for possession of the house, and custody of the children was irrelevant.

The movie is so busy with the physical and emotional confrontation between the Roses that one scarcely has time to ask why Mrs. Rose wants a divorce. The only motive one can reasonably deduce from the script is that Mrs. Rose succumbed to the disease of women's liberation. Feminist ideology teaches a woman to rank her own self-fulfillment above every other value, including solemn promises, husband, and children. Mrs. Rose suddenly decided that she would be more personally fulfilled if she lived alone and ran a little catering business making liver pâté under her own name.

The popularity of *War of the Roses* among moviegoers was probably due primarily to the fact that it touched a tender nerve in contemporary society. Some people are beginning to lament the fallout from the fundamental change in our divorce law that swept through fifty state legislatures during the 1970s, starting with trendy California in 1969 and ending with Illinois in 1984.

The feminists argued that easy, no-fault divorce would spell liberation for women. What it really did was to enable one spouse to terminate a marriage contract without the consent of the other, and virtually without penalty. Divorce "reform" laws eliminated "fault," supposedly in order to prevent bitterness. As the Kramers and the Roses confirm, bitterness does not go away: it just takes other forms.

At the peak of the women's liberation movement in January 1975, Barbara Walters confidently proclaimed in a three-hour NBC television special called *Of Women and Men* that wives should be liberated from their menial role and from the prison of a home. We were entering a new era of "serial marriages," she claimed, which means a succession of temporary roommates, without commitment or responsibility.

Probably more women than men have been hurt by this change because more men than women have the opportunity to exchange a spouse of twenty years for a younger model. But plenty of men have been hurt, too, not so much by wives who seek a new, more successful husband, but by wives who want to go it alone, while manipulating old traditions to hang on to custody of the children and the house.

Current figures show that more than 60 percent of second marriages end in divorce, but fortunately, we are beginning to see the divorce rate inching down: 1989 rates are down four percent from 1988. One newspaper has even called trying to work things out and stay hitched the "contemporary thing."

Psychologists are trying to figure out why. Perhaps the baby boomers are maturing out of the Me generation. Perhaps the fear of AIDS and other sexually transmitted diseases is persuading couples to stay together. Perhaps the post-divorce statistics are having a chilling effect on the rush to divorce.

Psychologist Dr. Diane Medved started to write a book to help people with decision making about the "morally neutral" option of divorce. When she faced the reality of her data, she found herself compelled to write *The Case Against Divorce.* That case is powerful, indeed.

1990

Macho Victims

The whole idea of painting a lawyer as a "victim" of words spoken in the workplace shows how out of touch with the real world the feminists are. The American people have a big warm heart and unlimited empathy for victims and underdogs. We send donations to victims of earthquakes and volcanoes. At ball games, we cheer for the team that is behind. But lawyers are not on the American people's list of people we feel sorry for.

Which was more ridiculous: trying to pass off attorney Anita Hill as a "victim" of some bad words in the workplace or depending on Senator Ted Kennedy (D-MA) to carry the flag of righteous indignation against sexual harassment? As an EEOC lawyer, Anita Hill knew exactly how to cope with sexual harassment, if she had ever suffered any from Clarence Thomas or anyone else.

The very nature of being a lawyer is to thrive in a hostile environment. A lawyer complaining about this is like a doctor complaining about working in a bloody environment. The nature of being a doctor is to see blood almost every day, often in traumatic circumstances. A doctor who can't take the sight of blood and a lawyer who can't take a hostile environment are in the wrong professions.

In the 1970s, the feminists painted women as helpless victims of an oppressive male-dominated society. The National Organization for Women ran spot announcements on television stations and ads in magazines and newspapers showing a darling, curly-headed child. The caption under the picture explained: "This normal, healthy child was born with a handicap. She was born female." The starting assumption of the women's liberation movement is that somebody—it isn't clear who, God or the establishment or a conspiracy of male chauvinist pigs—dealt women a foul blow by making them female, and it's up to society to remedy centuries of oppression. Feminists learned early that playing the role of victim assures easy access to the media.

By the 1980s, the feminists were trying to have it both ways. At the same time that they cover themselves with victim status, they claim they are so macho that they can do anything a man can do. The macho feminist is illustrated by *Thelma and Louise*, a movie that is important only because the feminists and their media friends have written so much favorable commentary about it. *Time* magazine made it a cover story!

To save you the trouble of going to see this depressing movie, here is a summary.

Thelma and Louise are a couple of macho feminists, tough and gun toting, riding the highways as good buddies. All men in the movie are slobs and bullies who victimize women—and that's the rationale for Thelma and Louise behaving the way they do. Their attitude toward men is illustrated by their stuffing a policeman in the trunk of the car and slamming it shut; it's clear that all men deserve to be humiliated because they are marked with the collective guilt of their gender.

At the end of this movie, the macho feminists demonstrate their liberation from men by driving off a cliff together in a suicide pact. Their final decision was made freely, without orders from any man, proving that they are truly liberated at last. Death frees the macho-feminist buddies from having to suffer the fate of living in a male-dominated world.

1991

The Feminist War against Marriage

The war on marriage that the feminists in academia are waging hit me when I received the Winter issue of my alma mater's alumnae magazine, the *Radcliffe Quarterly*. In all of fifty-two pages, under the heading "Scenes from the Family," the editors didn't include any discussion of a successful family based on a man and a woman honoring their solemn promises "to have and to hold . . . for better, for worse . . . till death do us part."

Instead, the feature article laid down the feminist line that a woman's identity disappears in marriage and that "marriage is bad for you, at least if you're female." Without any shame, the author admitted that she acquired her husband by breaking up another marriage that had lasted fifteen years and produced three children. She argued, "Instead of getting married for life, men and women (in whatever combination suits their sexual orientation) should sign up for a seven-year hitch." They may "reenlist" for another seven, but after that the marriage is "over." Another article described a "marriage" of lesbians in San Francisco. Still another extolled the wonderful life of a child born out of wedlock, and yet another explained divorce as "a significant life event that confronts individuals with the opportunity to change."

The New York–based Institute for American Values made a study of twenty post-1994 college social science textbooks used in eight thousand college courses. Called *Closed Hearts, Closed Minds*, the report concludes that most of these textbooks give a pessimistic, if not downright hostile, view of marriage, emphasizing marital failures rather than its joys and benefits.

College textbooks view marriage as especially bleak for women. The textbooks are inordinately preoccupied with domestic violence and divorce, and view marriage as archaic and oppressive, not just occasionally, but inherently. Some textbooks are larded with anti-family rhetoric. *Changing Families* by Judy Root Aulette focuses on battering, marital rape and divorce, with no mention of any benefits of marriage.

The textbooks give the impression that children don't need two parents and aren't harmed by divorce. They omit all the evidence that children in single-parent homes are far more at risk than children in two-parent homes. *Cutting Loose: Why Women Who End Their Marriages Do So Well* by Ashton Applewhite is an example of the new genre of books attacking marriage as a bad deal for women. The author dumped her husband after reading feminist Susan Faludi's *Backlash*. Applewhite seeks social approval for her walkout by encouraging middle-aged women to find independence by doing likewise. She gives advice on how to deal with lawyers, manipulate child custody arrangements, and find new relationships.

The publication of another new book, *On Our Own: Unmarried Motherhood in America* by Melissa Luddtke, attracted Hillary Rodham

Clinton, Maryland lieutenant governor Kathleen Kennedy Townsend and Senator Ted Kennedy to a book party at the home of PBS journalist Ellen Hume. Mrs. Clinton was thanked for her assistance as a "reader of the book in progress."

When the sexual revolution and the feminist revolution blasted into America's social consciousness in the late 1960s and 1970s, the voices raised against them came primarily from older women. Now we are starting to see acute bitterness from the generation that believed the liberationist lies and have discovered that, contrary to feminist ideology, women, indeed, have a biological clock.

The Independent Women's Forum's *Women's Quarterly* (Autumn 1997) is guaranteed to enrage the feminists. Called "Let's Face It, Girls: The Sexual Revolution Was a Mistake," it levels a broadside attack on the feminists for teaching young women that liberation and fulfillment come from romping around like men in casual sex while building their all-important careers. They are angry because they discovered too late that the cost of uncommitted sexual relationships is that "the window for getting married and having children is way smaller than one can possibly foresee at age 25."

So, we hear the anguish of babyless fortyish women frustrated by their inability to get pregnant, spending their money and tears on chemicals and on clinics dispensing procedures with high failure rates. They've even realized that a lot of female infertility comes from sexually transmitted diseases, and that's a high price to pay for those dead-end serial relationships.

In the *Women's Quarterly*, Carolyn Graglia exposes the consequences of the foolish feminist notion that men and women are equal in their sexual desires. This myth, which is contrary to all human experience, has deprived women of the social support they need to refuse to engage in casual sex.

Far from being empowered in their relations with men, this myth has caused women to lose control over ordinary relationships. Adult, educated women are now demanding that the government (or plaintiff attorneys) protect them from date rape and sexual harassment in situations that, in the pre-feminist era, unsophisticated high school girls could handle with confidence, knowing that a "No" would be respected.

1997

G. I. Jane: Feminist Role Model

G.I. Jane, directed by Ridley Scott, is a fitting sequel to his 1991 movie *Thelma and Louise*. Both films idealize the foul-mouthed, gun-toting woman who triumphs over the perceived discriminations perpetrated by an unfair male-dominated society.

Thelma and Louise freed themselves from an oppressive patriarchal society by driving their car off a cliff. Their double suicide proved they were liberated because they made that fatal decision independent of male coercion.

G. I. Jane (Demi Moore) proves she is a liberated woman by getting herself beaten to a bloody pulp, almost raped, and subjected to extreme bodily harassment. To the feminists, this is okay because her goal is to be treated just like men. This is the kind of equality the feminist movement has always sought (and why they remain a ridiculous subset of the left wing of the Democratic Party, far outside of the mainstream). The feminists' legal oracle in the years before Ruth Bader Ginsburg emerged, Yale Law School professor Thomas I. Emerson, described the goal of gender equality in the *Yale Law Journal* (April 1971): "As between brutalizing our young men and brutalizing our young women, there is little to choose."

The movie *G. I. Jane* was apparently designed to make Americans believe the myth that women can perform in combat just like men, even in the toughest branch of the services, the Navy SEALs. But the movie really doesn't help the feminist cause because the villain is a loud-mouthed Texas female senator (supposedly modeled on Representative Patricia Schroeder and former Texas governor Ann Richards), whose sport is to humiliate military officers for not fully integrating women into combat jobs. In order to keep her Senate seat, she spikes G. I. Jane's career in the SEALs by falsely accusing her of lesbianism.

G. I. Jane proves that women can take a beating as well as a man, but so what? The movie shows that she lacks the upper body strength to pull herself out of the water into a boat, a rather elementary test for anyone seeking to be a Navy SEAL. The pretense that G. I. Jane could do everything the SEALs do is a Hollywood fiction created with trick photography, makeup, and a stand-in for the star. It's all as make-believe as the scene where her SEAL commander talks to her in the shower and somehow doesn't notice that she's nude.

But more important than the dishonesty of it all is what the feminists are doing to America and to the relationship of men and women. When G. I. Jane is being beaten and almost raped in the movie, we can see the horror in the faces of the SEALs who watch, and their contempt for the master chief who performs this training exercise. They joined the Navy to become real men, and now are trained to be passive while watching a woman beaten and raped! It's called sensitivity training to desensitize men about the abuse and mistreatment of women.

Training civilized young men to suppress any inclinations to be protective and courteous toward women is not merely wrong and stupid, it is evil and wicked. We have no respect for the men who participate in programming men to treat women as though they are men.

Civilization is on the chopping block. The feminists have not given us progress for women; they are turning men into the stereotype of the caveman who drags his woman by her hair.

1997

Who's Home Alone Now?

America's massive news gathering apparatus and round-the-clock coverage should leave us saturated with news. Yet two liberal-leaning authors have tackled a subject consistently off-limits in public debate.

Sylvia Hewlett, in her much publicized book *Creating a Life*, breathlessly reveals what she calls a "well-kept secret," namely, that "at midlife, between a third and half of all high-achieving women in America do not have children," and most of them did not choose to be childless. Bernard Goldberg, in his best-selling book *Bias*, tells us that "the most important story you never saw on TV" is "the terrible things that are happening to America's children" because "mothers have opted for work outside of the house over taking care of their children at home."

These social commentaries are two sides of the same coin. The feminist movement, which flowered in the 1970s, persuaded young women to opt for a career in "a man's world," and whether they ended up with or without a child, they don't relish suggestions that they were mistaken in their priorities.

Hewlett's book is a compilation of depressing interviews with women who broke business barriers and achieved enormous career success, now earning six-figure incomes, but are not happy. They confide in Hewlett how they yearn for a baby, enduring expensive and humiliating medical procedures trying to get pregnant, or traveling to the ends of the earth to adopt.

Goldberg's book, which is an exposé of the biases of the media elite, describes how female media executives who do have children drop them off every morning in daycare or leave them with a nanny, and then are fiercely hostile to any criticism of the plight of their children. The feminists have made it taboo for the media to report or debate the social costs of the fact that millions of American children have been left to fend for themselves, "with dire consequences."

Goldberg says that these feminists have so completely intimidated media elites that all the TV anchormen routinely dismiss any negative news about daycare with their favorite epithet, "controversial," and even tough Sam Donaldson "turns into a sniveling wimp when it comes to challenging feminists." Feminists react to any discussion about the troubles of latchkey kids or about daycare's diseases and behavior problems as though it were a personal attack on the mothers as well as on the feminist movement.

A *New York Times* front-page article labeled Hewlett's book "the publishing world's mystery of the year" because it's been a total flop in the marketplace after receiving unprecedented free publicity. Why is anybody surprised? Even *Oprah, 60 Minutes,* the covers of *Time* and *New York* magazines, and the morning and evening television shows can't make women buy a book that rubs salt in the wound opened by the central feminist mistake.

While Goldberg worries about the plight of home-alone children, Hewlett is busy portraying career-minded women as victims. She thinks that when 49 percent of $100,000-a-year women executives, but only 19 percent of men executives, are childless, that proves hard-hearted employers and government have discriminated against women during their childbearing years.

Hewlett thinks she has made a sensational discovery that women after age forty are less fertile than they were in their twenties. Our oppressive male-dominated American society has forced women into a "cruel trade-off": if they focus on their careers in their youth, it's extremely difficult to get pregnant after age forty.

Hewlett's solution for the problems of the successful career women is preferential treatment (not equality!) by both employers and government. She wants employers to give every working parent a "time bank" of six months of paid leave to be taken at the employee's option until each child reaches age eighteen, plus a Mommy Track of reduced working hours without diminished pay and promotions.

Hewlett thinks European countries are much better for women, especially Sweden, where mothers can limit their workday to six hours until each child is eight years old. She doesn't tell us that few Swedish women earn $100,000 a year.

Like a typical feminist, Hewlett is full of plans for more government spending and regulation. She wants even small companies to be forced to give women paid medical leave, tax incentives for companies that give women paid time off, and legislation to prevent employers from requiring longer hours of work.

Goldberg shows how the media elite "have taken sides." Instead of anyone saying on television that kids would do better if a parent were home after school, we get so-called experts calling for more quality daycare and legislation to enable employed mothers to continue working out of the home and spend less time with their children.

2002

III

Questioning a Woman's Place

O how full of briers is this working-day world!

As You Like It

What's Wrong with Equal Rights for Women?

Of all the classes of people who ever lived, the American woman is the most privileged. We have the most rights and rewards, and the fewest duties. Our unique status is the result of a fortunate combination of circumstances.

We have the immense good fortune to live in a civilization that respects the family as the basic unit of society. This respect is part and parcel of our laws and customs. It is based on the fact of life—which no legislation or agitation can erase—that women have babies and men don't.

If you don't like this fundamental difference, you will have to take up your complaint with God because He created us this way. The fact that women, not men, have babies is not the fault of selfish and domineering men, or the establishment, or any clique of conspirators who want to oppress women. It's simply the way God made us.

Our Judeo-Christian civilization has developed the law and custom that, since women bear the physical consequences of the sex act, men must be required to pay in other ways. These laws and customs decree that a man must carry his share by physical protection and financial support of his children and of the woman who bears his children, and also by a code of behavior that benefits and protects both the woman and the children.

This is accomplished by the institution of the family. Our respect for the family as the basic unit of society, which is ingrained in the laws and customs of our Judeo-Christian civilization, is the greatest single achievement in the history of women's rights. It assures a woman the most precious and important right of all—the right to keep her own baby and to be supported and protected in the enjoyment of watching her baby grow and develop.

The institution of the family is advantageous for women for many reasons. After all, what do we want out of life? To love and be loved? Mankind has not discovered a better nest for a lifetime of reciprocal love. A sense of achievement? A man may search thirty to forty years for accomplishment in his profession. A woman can enjoy real achievement when she is young by having a baby. She can have the satisfaction of doing a job well—and being recognized for it.

Do we want financial security? We are fortunate to have the great legacy of Moses, the Ten Commandments, especially "Honor thy father and thy mother that thy days may be long upon the land." Children are a woman's best social security—her best guarantee of social benefits such as old age pension, unemployment compensation, worker's compensation, and sick leave. The family gives a woman the physical, financial, and emotional security of the home for all her life.

The second reason why American women are a privileged group is that we are the beneficiaries of a tradition of special respect for women that dates from the Christian Age of Chivalry. The honor and respect paid to Mary, the Mother of Christ, resulted in all women, in effect, being put on a pedestal.

This respect for women is not just the lip service that politicians pay to God, Motherhood, and the Flag. It is not—as some agitators seem to think—just a matter of opening doors for women, seeing that they are seated first, carrying their bundles, and helping them in and out of automobiles. Such good manners are merely the superficial evidences of a total attitude toward women that expresses itself in many more tangible ways, such as money.

In other civilizations, such as the African and the American Indian, the men strut around wearing feathers and beads, and hunting and fishing (great sport for men!), while the women do all the hard, tiresome drudgery, including the tilling of the soil (if any is done), the hewing of wood, the making of fires, the carrying of water, as well as the cooking, sewing, and caring for babies.

This is not the American way because we were lucky enough to inherit the traditions of the Age of Chivalry. In America, a man's first significant purchase (after a car) is a diamond for his bride, and the largest financial investment of his life is a home for her to live in. American husbands work hours of overtime to keep their wives in fashion, and to pay premiums on their life insurance policies to provide for their widow's comfort (benefits in which the husband can never share).

In the states that follow the English common law, a wife has a dower right in her husband's real estate which he cannot take away from her during life or by his will. A man cannot dispose of his real estate without his wife's signature. Any sale is subject to her one-third interest.

Women fare even better in the states that follow the Spanish and French community property laws, such as California, Arizona, Texas, and Louisiana. The philosophy of the Spanish and French law is that a wife's work in the home is just as valuable as a husband's work at his job. In community-property states, a wife owns one-half of all the property and income her husband earns during the marriage, and he cannot take it away from her.

In Illinois, as a result of agitation by "equal rights" fanatics, the real-estate dower laws were repealed as of January 1, 1972. This means that in Illinois a husband can now sell the family home, spend the money on his girlfriend or gamble it away, and his faithful wife of thirty years cannot stop him. "Equal rights" fanatics have also deprived women in Illinois and in some other states of most of their basic common-law rights to recover damages for breach of promise to marry, seduction, criminal conversation, and alienation of affections.

The third reason why American women are so well off is that the American free enterprise system has produced remarkable inventors who have lifted the backbreaking "women's work" from our shoulders.

In other countries and in other eras, it was truly said that "Man may work from sun up to sun down, but woman's work is never done." Women labored every waking hour—preparing food on wood-burning stoves, making flour, baking bread in stone ovens, spinning yarn, making clothes, making soap, doing the laundry by hand, heating irons, making candles for light and fires for warmth, and trying to nurse their babies through illnesses without medical care.

The real liberation of women from that drudgery is the American free enterprise system, which stimulated inventive geniuses to pursue their talents—and we all reap the profits. The great heroes of women's liberation are not the straggly haired women on television talk shows and picket lines, but Thomas Edison, who brought the miracle of electricity to our homes to give light and to run all those labor-saving devices—the equivalent, perhaps, of a half-dozen household servants. Or Elias Howe who gave us the sewing machine that resulted in such an abundance of readymade clothing. Or Clarence Birdseye, who invented the process for freezing foods. Or Henry Ford, who mass produced the automobile so it is within the price range of almost every American.

A major occupation of women in other countries is doing their daily shopping for food, which requires carrying their own containers and standing in line at dozens of small shops. They buy only small portions because they can't carry very much and have no refrigerator or freezer to keep a surplus anyway. Our American free enterprise system has given us the gigantic food and packaging industry and beautiful supermarkets, which provide an endless variety of foods, prepackaged for easy carrying and a minimum of waiting. In America, women have freedom from the slavery of standing in line for daily food.

Household duties have been reduced to only a few hours a day, leaving the American woman with plenty of time to moonlight. She can take a full- or part-time paying job, or she can indulge to her heart's content in a tremendous selection of interesting educational or cultural or homemaking or volunteer activities.

It's time to set the record straight. The claim that American women are downtrodden and unfairly treated is the fraud of the century. The truth is that American women never had it so good. Why should we lower ourselves to "equal rights" when we already have the status of special privilege?

This famous article, published in the Phyllis Schlafly Report *of February 1972, launched the movement to defeat the Equal Rights Amendment.*

1972

Social Security Is Pro-Woman

Social Security benefits paid to dependent wives and widows have been part of the Social Security system for more than forty years but are now under attack from the feminist movement.

Dependent wives as a class are the greatest financial asset the Social Security system has. Since Social Security is a pay-as-we-go system (today's benefits are paid from today's taxes and tomorrow's benefits will be paid from tomorrow's taxes), the Social Security retirement benefits that will be received by today's workers are wholly dependent on tomorrow's crop of young workers paying into the system.

The paramount reason for the future financial problems facing Social Security is the dramatic decline in the American birth rate over the last few years. The U.S. birth rate is now below population maintenance level.

By bearing and nurturing six children, who have grown into educated citizens who will pay decades upon decades of taxes into the Social Security system, I have done vastly more financially for the Social Security system than any worker who pays taxes into the system all his or her life. In the normal course of events, my four sons can be expected to pay taxes into the Social Security system for forty to fifty years each, and my two daughters for at least twenty to thirty years each. That is many times the financial value of a male or female worker who pays taxes into the system all his or her life.

In addition to this financial contribution to the Social Security system made by the dependent wife and mother, the benefits to society from her career lifestyle are tremendous and real, even though they are difficult to calculate in dollars. When a wife and mother spends her time in the home rearing children who are moral, law abiding, industrious, educated, emotionally well adjusted, and capable of forming strong families of their own, she makes the greatest of all contributions to a healthy society and to the future of our nation.

The dependent wife and mother who cares for her own children in her own home performs the most socially necessary role in our society. The future of America depends on our next generation being morally, psychologically, intellectually, and physically strong.

Our public and tax policy should encourage strong families and should encourage mothers to care for their own children. It would be a tragic mistake for Congress ever to adopt any public or tax policy that encourages mothers to assign child care to others and enter the labor force. Such a policy would clearly be anti-family and against the best interests of our nation. What is particularly relevant here is that such a policy would deal a fatal blow to the long-term financial integrity of our Social Security system and to its ability to serve our national needs.

For more than forty years, the payment of Social Security benefits to dependent wives and widows has been the official and tangible recognition of the value of their lifestyle to their families, to society, and to the financial solvency of the system. The wife's benefit today performs exactly the same necessary function as it did in the 1930s.

But a few aggressive groups of women, with good jobs plus the ability to speak and write, have ganged up to ask Congress to take away the dependent wife's and widow's benefits. I use the expression "ganged up" because that's exactly what it is. The list of the four hundred persons who gave advice to the Social Security Administration in connection with its 1979 publication *Social Security and the Changing Roles of Men and Women* included most radical feminist leaders—but not a single dependent wife.

Changing Roles proposed three alternative plans for the radical restructuring of Social Security, all of which would eliminate the current dependent wife's benefit. Under Options 1 and 2, the traditional family's benefits would be cut up to 19 percent. Under Option 3, the husband of the dependent wife would be forced to pay double Social Security taxes in order for his dependent wife to receive the same benefits she gets now.

When these proposals were presented to the public in hearings all across the United States in 1979, they simply didn't sell. The public reacted with indignation to this attempt to punish the dependent wife and the traditional family.

The dependent wife's benefit is not a welfare payment and never has been. The dependent wife's benefit represents our forty-year public policy of recognizing the value to society and to Social Security of the wife/mother in the home. The real welfare benefits in Social Security are the weighted benefits paid to low-income workers who do not pay nearly enough taxes to justify the retirement benefits they receive.

The fact that millions of wives have entered the labor force is no argument at all for taking away benefits from those who remain in the home! A dependent wife needs her benefit today for exactly the same reasons that the dependent wife's benefit was put into the system forty years ago. The movement of so many wives out of the home into the labor force makes it more important than ever before that public policy encourage mothers to stay in their homes and care for their children.

A typical feminist complaint against the wife's benefit is that "it isn't fair" for a dependent wife to receive as large a Social Security benefit as the employed woman. This argument depends on your scale of values. The feminists believe that, by definition, the dependent wife isn't worth much because she isn't paid in cash wages.

On the traditional scale of values, however, the dependent wife is worth just as much as the employed wife. If she nurtures two children to adulthood, she is worth a great deal more to the long-term financial integrity of Social Security. She is worth much, much more if she raises more than two children to adulthood.

The feminists have no legitimate complaint because, in fact, female workers are treated exactly like male workers—which is what the feminists have been asking for. Because of Supreme Court decisions and statutory changes, there is no sex discrimination in Social Security. Actually, the female worker gets significantly more for her tax dollar than the male worker because she lives longer.

It is in the best long-term interests of female workers as well as male workers for public policy to encourage the dependent wife to care for her own children rather than to induce her to enter the labor force. Economists agree that when women enter the labor force, they have fewer children than they otherwise would have, and the elimination of the wife's benefit would cause an increase in the number of wives seeking employment. The social and economic costs of artificially inducing more millions of wives into the labor market could be tremendous.

To eliminate the dependent wife's benefit would strike a mortal blow to women's economic ability to choose a traditional family lifestyle because it would impose financial penalties on it. But eliminating the dependent wife's benefit would not give the employed woman any increased benefit. Why, then, is a little group of highly educated employed women trying so hard to wipe out the dependent wife who is in her nursery or kitchen and may not have the skills to defend herself?

Motivation is a difficult question, but after reading the literature on the subject, I conclude there are two reasons: (1) the belief that it is a social good to move all or most wives and mothers into the labor force (and to assign child care to professionals in daycare centers), and (2) envy that the Social Security system values the dependent wife as much as the employed woman.

The feminist movement is trying to make the dependent wife obsolete, but she is not obsolete. Babies in the 1980s are no different from babies in the 1930s: they need mother care just as much. We should applaud and encourage the wife who chooses to give her children full-time care. That decision involves significant financial sacrifice since families with dependent wives have a family income about one-third lower, on the average, than when the wife is in the labor force.

The proposal to eliminate the wife's and widow's benefits should be identified as what it is: a radical feminist proposal to punish the woman who chooses to be a dependent wife so she can care for and nurture her own children; an anti-family proposal which would put such financial penalties on the traditional family lifestyle that it would tend to drive it out of existence; a financially costly proposal which would further reduce the birth rate and tend to bankrupt Social Security; an economically risky proposal that would increase unemployment; and a foolish proposal that would result in the high social costs of neglected and institutionalized children.

The Social Security system is beautifully and wisely designed to accommodate women's different careers and lifestyles. The dependent wife's benefit serves those in the 1980s who make homemaking their primary career just as it served wives in the 1930s.

Testimony to the U.S. House Ways and Means Committee, Subcommittee on Social Security, March 6, 1981.

1981

Do Women Get Equal Pay for Equal Work?

Over the past year, a deceitful propaganda campaign has been orchestrated by the feminist movement to convince the American people that, when women take a paying job, they receive only 59 cents for every dollar paid to a man doing the same work. As it is used by the feminists, the 59-cent figure is a lie, and worse. It is part of the feminists' denigration of the role of motherhood. The 59-cent slogan is designed to eliminate the role of motherhood by changing us into a society in which women are harnessed into the labor force both full-time and for a lifetime.

Equal pay for equal work is the law of our land today. It is positively required by the Equal Employment Opportunity Act of 1972 and by many other federal statutes and executive orders. The Equal Employment Opportunity Commission is its aggressive enforcement agency and has wrung multi-million dollar settlements against the largest companies in our land, such as the $38 million settlement imposed on AT&T.

I have never met anyone who opposes equal pay for equal work. It is the most non-controversial concept in the country today. So why, then, do feminists keep talking about it? Because they want you to believe that it should mean something that it doesn't mean at all.

Equal pay for equal work does not mean that the nurse should he paid the same as the doctor, or that the secretary should be paid the same as her boss, even if she works just as hard and thinks she is just as smart. Equal pay for equal work does not mean that the woman who has been on the job two years must be paid the same as a man who has been in his job for twenty years. Nor does it mean that a secretary must be paid the same as a plumber even if she has spent more years in school, or that the woman who works in an office or at a retail store must be paid equally with the man who works in a mine or in construction work.

Equal pay for equal work means that the man and woman must be paid equally if they are doing the same job with the same experience for the same number of hours in the same type of industry in the same part of the country. That is the law today, and it has been very aggressively enforced by the Equal Employment Opportunity Commission.

Those who are carrying on the campaign to perpetrate the 59-cent fraud obviously are not talking about violations of the Equal Employment Opportunity Act. They offer no suggestions for changing it. So where did they get the 59-cent figure? This figure is the average wage paid to all women compared to the average wage paid to all men. Such a comparison doesn't prove anything at all about sex discrimination or the fairness of the wage anyone in particular is paid for any job.

We certainly don't want a society in which the average wage paid to all women equals the average wage paid to all men, because that society would have eliminated the role of motherhood. The career of motherhood is not recorded or compensated in cash wages in government statistics, but that doesn't make it any less valuable. It is the most socially useful role of all.

We don't even want a society in which the average wage paid to all employed women equals the average wage paid to all employed men, because that would be a society in which wives and mothers would be working in paid employment all their lives for as many years and hours a week as men. Most wives do not do this now and don't want to do it. By working fewer hours in the paid labor force, wives and mothers can give more time to their families and to the role of motherhood.

We want a society in which the average man earns more than the average woman so that his earnings can fulfill his provider role in providing a home and support for his wife who is nurturing and mothering their children. We certainly don't want feminist pressure groups to change public policy in order to force us into a society in which all women are locked into the work force for a lifetime, because that would mean forfeiting their precious years and hours as a mother.

When we average the wages of *all* women and compare them to the average wages of *all* men, the pay cannot and should not be equal because the work is not equal. The average man has far more work experience and seniority on his present job. The average woman has been in her present job only half as long as the average man. The average woman has more career interruptions; she is eleven times more likely to leave her job than the average man.

The average woman does not work as many hours per week as the average man. Most wives do not work full-time in paid employment; even if the statistics call it "full-time," that does not mean forty hours a week, twelve months a year. Many women prefer and take part-time jobs. The new concept called "job sharing" is proving very attractive to wives compelled to enter the labor force. Many more men than women work overtime for premium pay; most women refuse overtime work, if they can, and resent it very much when they are "forced over" (the factory term for involuntary overtime).

Included in the figures for the average man are millions of men who do dangerous, heavy jobs which women cannot do, for which most women are unsuited, and which they wouldn't take if they were offered three times the pay. These include such jobs as miners, steel and iron workers, high-line electricians, lumberjacks, salvage divers, concrete finishers, millwrights, high explosive handlers, roofers, jackhammer operators, steeplejacks, tree trimmers, longshoremen, movers, and railroad and truck crews. The men in such jobs can and do receive good pay, and they deserve it. The *Wall Street Journal* of April 14, 1981, described the job of an Arctic driller—a real he-man job. It is absolutely unjust to think that the average woman should receive equal pay for the cleaner, safer, less demanding, less dangerous jobs that women prefer.

The average woman (not all women, of course) voluntarily declines the added responsibility, long hours, and lifetime commitment required for the high-paying positions in the professional and business world.

The *Wall Street Journal* reported on March 18, 1981, that the earnings of male and female physicians differ because the average woman doctor sees forty fewer patients per week than the average male doctor, and women choose the lower-earning specialties such as pediatrics and psychiatry over the more lucrative fields, such as surgery, chosen by men. Women come out of law schools with high grades, but many are unwilling to work the long hours, nights, and weekends that are typical of the life of a young lawyer trying to build a career and make partner.

Crain's Chicago Business of October 13, 1980, reported an interview with a woman who heads an executive search firm. She found that "more women are starting to turn down job offers . . . because they refuse to make the same kind of commitment to their careers that a typical male executive would make." She gave many specific examples from her firm's experience of women who passed up good promotions because they were not willing to make the personal and family sacrifices needed to move up the corporate ladder. Wives customarily decline a position that requires a move to another city and will resign a position to accompany a husband's career move to another city. This is because keeping the family together is more important to most wives than career advancement.

The average man today has more years of education and more education in more highly paid specialties. This is why comparisons are irrelevant between young men and women today even if they have the same number of years of higher education. My daughter graduated from Princeton with honors in economics; my son graduated from Princeton with honors in electrical engineering. The statistics report them as having the same number of years in college, but the differential between the starting salaries of those two specialties is thousands of dollars per year. That is not sex discrimination, but the marketplace's recognition of the fact that electrical engineers are more in demand in our society today. Nobody discriminated against my daughter; she chose not to take engineering.

The reason women are in jobs that are less demanding, with shorter hours and less pay, is not sex discrimination but career choice. The overwhelming majority of American women make the career choice to give priority to homemaking, motherhood, and the maintenance of an intact family. Even women who do not make homemaking and motherhood a full-time, lifetime occupation nevertheless devote enough of their life to it that they cannot and do not give full-time, lifetime attention to an employment career, as men do.

It is not the job of Congress to try to change women's voluntary career choices by legislative, financial, or tax inducements. The future of our nation depends on children who grow up to be good citizens, and the best way of achieving that goal is to have emotionally stable, intact families. It is wrong for the Congress to continue to give public forums only to the narrow little minority of feminists who have themselves rejected motherhood as women's role and are trying to label motherhood as an obsolete stereotype.

These problems should not involve a battle between homemakers and working women. Homemakers work very hard, and millions of them are in the labor force today. Employed women have homes also, and they work hard at homemaking. Nearly all women will be in the labor force for some years of their lives.

Testimony to the U.S. Senate Committee on Labor and Human Resources, April 21, 1981.

1981

Women's Studies v. Academic Freedom

The American Civil Liberties Union certainly gets involved in unusual cases. Its latest is a suit in a California court designed to assure that

women's studies courses at state universities can teach feminism and lesbianism to the exclusion of traditional values. That's the real issue in a
suit filed by the ACLU Foundation of Southern California against California State University at Long Beach, its Board of Trustees and officers.

The plaintiffs are an unusual bunch. One is identified as an expert
on "Feminist Theory," another an expert in "Lesbianism," another an
expert on "Women and Racism," another an expert on "Women and
Mental Health," and another an expert on "Women and History." The
complaint states that the plaintiff faculty members are "experts in the
feminist discipline, methodology, and process which is an essential re-
quirement for teaching in a program of Feminist Studies. In addition
all plaintiffs . . . are feminists."

The complaint starts off by defending women's studies courses, and
then, by a semantic sleight-of-hand trick, slips into calling them feminist studies. The lawsuit is designed to equate the one with the other.

The women's studies program at California State University in Long
Beach started in 1970 as something to benefit all women. The female
faculty converted it to a program to promote radical feminist-lesbian
goals and values to the exclusion of traditional women's goals and values. The complaint by the ACLU admits that "its focus was to be the feminist discipline."

The controversy started when some churchgoing women enrolled
in women's studies courses at California State University at Long Beach.
When they found out what was taught in "Women's Studies 101: Women
and Their Bodies," and what was the assigned reading, they went into
shock. The women complained to university officials that "Women and
Their Bodies" was pro-lesbian; that the texts and recommended books
were "inappropriate, pornographic, and pure filth"; and that the women's
studies program was not balanced because it failed to offer courses that
espouse traditional American values. Several women who had taken
women's studies courses filed affidavits in which they stated that they
had been shown x-rated and pro-homosexual films in class, that the

teacher had a foul mouth, and that classroom activities and homework included sexual activities.

The textbooks and recommended reading for the women's studies courses included *Sapphistry: The Book of Lesbian Sexuality* by Pat Califia, *Sex For Women Who Want to Have Fun and Loving Relationships With Equals* by Carmen Kerr, and *Lesbianism and the Women's Movement* edited by Nancy Myron and Charlotte Bunch. The books are so pornographic that they are not quotable in this article. With explicit prose and pictures, they advise women how to become lesbians and to engage in every type of perverted sex, including group sex, orgies, bestiality, sadomasochism, and bondage.

The thirty-page ACLU complaint attempts to wrap these courses in the sacred mantle of the First Amendment, due process, equal protection, and academic freedom. In addition, the complaint charges that terminating the feminist-lesbian courses was sex discrimination in violation of Title IX of the Education Amendments of 1972.

As a result of the uproar, the California State Senate Finance Committee introduced a resolution ordering the University Chancellor to find out if any of the courses offered by the California State University System allowed credit for engaging in "sexual behavior," and if so, the University was to be penalized one million dollars. Then, a California Assembly-Senate Conference Committee adopted, as part of the state budget, a resolution providing that no funds could be used to support causes "which offer academic credit for engaging in sexual experiences."

It's time taxpayers found out what is going on at some universities in the name of academic freedom and women's studies—and how traditional moral and family values are censored out of the curriculum.

1983

What Do Smith Women Want?

"What Do Women Want?—Feminism and its Future" was the title of a sixteen-page article by Barbara Grizzuti-Harrison in the October 1981 *Harper's* magazine. It is important reading for anyone who seeks to understand modern trends among women.

Harrison posed some profound sociological questions about women's hopes and ambitions, and then spent a week on the campus of Smith College seeking the answers from the young, elite feminists there. She chose Smith, the country's largest privately endowed all-women's college, as a microcosm of the best feminism has to offer in terms of education and career aspirations.

This report is not about my views on Smith, as I have never been there. This is a review of Harrison's commentary about Smith. Harrison's article is sympathetic to feminism and never challenges its assumption that its goals are the goals of all women.

Harrison tells us that Smith College, which was undisturbed by the turbulent 1960s, is today "no longer quite so ladylike." "There are still Friday afternoon teas," she says, "but few people are shocked and even fewer surprised when they become the occasion for 'lesbian workshops.'"

Smith women have rejected the career of homemaking. "In seven days on campus," Harrison writes, "not once did I see a woman wearing an engagement ring. . . . I had yet to meet a student who thought of motherhood as a vocation." The figures record the change: in the class of 1960, 61 percent of graduates said they wanted to be homemakers; in the class of 1970, 15 percent said they would be homemakers; in the class of 1980, not even one percent chose homemaking.

Harrison refers repeatedly to the lesbian presence on campus. She tells of the lesbian residences, the two hundred who came to a lesbian dance, the cult of anti-male separatism, and the talk of "dismantling the family which they no longer see as a functioning unit." She is not judg-mental, often using the euphemism "women-identified women" instead of "lesbians."

Harrison asked Smith president Jill Ker Conway whether "the re-portedly large number of 'women-identified women' in the Valley, and their claim to an exclusive culture, had any effect on the Smith popula-tion." After a long pause, Conway replied, "I don't define it as a prob-lem because I think it's a private and personal preference with which the college should have no prying concern."

But Smith does, indeed, exert powerful pressures about personal careers. The one message the students receive loud and clear is that "if you're not the head of a corporation, you're not a successful woman." Only among a few students did Harrison detect a yearning to have what their mothers had *in addition to* a preferred place in the corporate world. As one student asked, "Why *can't* we have it all?"

Harrison wonders who among Smith alumnae might serve as role-models for young women who want to have it all? Alum Gloria Steinem has neither husband nor children; alum Betty Friedan is without hus-band. Alum Nancy Reagan is one of the most admired women in the world, according to national polls, but feminists will not accept her as a role model.

Harrison calls it a "paradox" that one has to go back before the birth of the feminist movement to find a famous Smith graduate who com-bined a successful marriage, six children, and a career of outstanding achievement: Anne Morrow Lindbergh.

A week at Smith left the author weary of "sexual politics." The most intense campus conversations involved whether women's studies should be a separate department. She did not find out what women want; she did not even find out what feminists want. Harrison ended her article "with hope and sorrow so intimately braided I cannot tell them apart." It is easy to see why she is sorrowful at what she learned at Smith. But her article gives no clue as to where one could find hope for the future at Smith College, since all respect for the role of wife and mother has been censored out of the academic and social life on the campus.

1983

Women and the Law

When Ronald Reagan announces even minimal cuts in federal funds for education, a chorus of anguished, orchestrated yelps goes up on cue from the media and academia. We are given tear-jerking rhetoric about worthy students who will be forced to abandon college and look for a job in the cruel world. A good antidote for the bleeding hearts about education cuts would be to read the registration book for the Fourteenth National Conference on Women and the Law held in Washington, D.C., April 7-10, 1983.

The second page of this booklet explains that it cost "hundreds of thousands of dollars to prepare and plan this Conference," which was sponsored by seven area law schools: American, Antioch, Catholic, George Mason, George Washington, Georgetown, and Howard.

The financial impetus came originally from Antioch Law School, which was founded with federal funding about a decade ago. A new law school is about the last thing in the world for which federal funds can be justified, but Antioch was apparently started specifically to train left-wing legal activists at the taxpayers' expense.

The conference had 214 workshops. No words of mine can describe them nearly so well as the following direct quotations from the registration book:

"Lesbian as Mother: Custody Issues. Overview and tactical approach to child custody issues, as they pertain to lesbian mothers. Litigation strategy for practitioners representing lesbian mothers in custody battles will also be presented."

"Career Options for Lesbians: Traditional and Non-Traditional Legal Spheres. Roundtable discussion led by panelists representative of employment options available to lesbians pursuing careers in law. Options appraised will include law firms, teaching positions, and starting law collectives, among others."

"Legal Challenges to Discrimination Against Lesbians. General overview of the law regarding discrimination against lesbians in civil, criminal, and employment contexts, including: right to privacy; universities and other public forums; civil service and private employment."

"Surviving Law School as a Lesbian. Brief presentations followed by open discussion. Topics to be addressed include: the pros and cons of being *out* to one's school community; coming out as a lesbian after starting law school; the process of finding supportive environments. Workshop open to women only."

"Lesbians and Motherhood—In That Order! Artificial Insemination and Adoption. Examination of considerations to be made by lesbians who choose to become mothers; legal ramifications of the choice. Topics include: artificial insemination—anonymous vs. known donor; adoption; enforceable documents concerning partners' legal relationship."

"The Politics of Women's Sexuality. Facilitated discussion of the personal/political ramifications of women's choices of sexual relationships (lesbian, heterosexual, bisexual, celibate): exploration of myths about different sexual orientations; homophobia. Workshop open to women only."

"Lesbians and Elected Office: Can You Do Both? Presentation by lesbians who have held or are holding elected offices. Topics to include: factors surrounding a decision to run for local, state, or national office; campaign strategies; lesbianism, polling and the media; and can an *out* lesbian really be elected?"

"Stay the Curse: A Feminist Critique of Reaganomics. Appraisal of the 'New Federalism,' budget cuts, regulatory destruction, and supply-side economics, as they affect women, particularly disabled women. Consideration of the use of international law to attack the policies of the Reagan Administration."

"Prostitution Issues. Workshop will address the relationships between prostitutes' rights, abortion/reproductive rights and lesbian rights. Panelists will also discuss the current state of the law, and the social and economic consequences of decriminalization versus legalization of prostitution."

"Genitalia and the Constitution. Panel discussion of the importance placed on anatomical differences between women and men in constitutional doctrine."

It is an offense against women, decency, and common sense to teach such courses with taxpayer or university funds. State legislators, university trustees, taxpayers, and parents should look carefully at what is being taught in the name of women's studies courses and what is being done with the funding given to women's centers.

1983

Comparable Worth Is Not Pay Equity

The Comparable Worth bill is touted as a bill to promote pay equity. Equity means justice, but what is justice when it comes to setting wages?

Clearly, there must be something mighty just and fair about the American economic system, which has provided higher wages and more of the good things of life to more people than any nation in the history of the world. The free market, which allows most economic decisions to be made freely by individuals and unions of individuals, has produced an American standard of living that is the envy of the world.

The method of wage setting that produced the highest wages for the most people is the system that allows wages to be determined by freedom of choice: what is an individual willing to work for, and what is an employer willing to pay? The result is what is called market wages.

Our society has made a few slight modifications to this system. Prior to the current generation, society's notion of pay equity was generally understood to include giving the job preference, the higher pay, and the promotion to the father who is supporting a family. He was perceived to need the wage more than other men or women.

Some twenty years ago, the American society codified into federal law the consensus that equity in wage setting includes the concept that an individual should receive "equal pay for equal work" as determined by looking at two or more persons doing substantially equal work. Since then, there has been no apparent dissent from this principle. Now, however, a bill called Comparable Worth comes along seeking to engage in wage setting by the subjective opinions of anonymous persons who will decide job "worth."

This is an even more intangible will-o'-the-wisp than "pay equity," and even less able to produce consensus or equity. How can we agree on what you or I are "worth" in dollars and cents? Who are the unnamed persons who can fulfill the bill's assumption that "job evaluation techniques" can be "equitable"? Are they the same job evaluators as those in the State of Washington case who decided that laundry workers are "worth" the same wage as truck drivers and should be paid equally?

The estimated $1 billion judgment levied against the taxpayers of the State of Washington by the judge who decided that case, *American Federation of State, County, and Municipal Employees (*AFSCME*) v. State of Washington*, was based on a job evaluation that called for wages to be paid according to the following points allegedly describing job "worth": laundry worker 96, truck driver 97, librarian 353, carpenter 197, nurse 573, chemist 277. The evaluation concluded that (female) laundry workers should be paid the same as (male) truck drivers, and that (female) librarians and nurses should be paid about twice as much as (male) carpenters and chemists.

Do the sponsors of the Comparable Worth bill really think that the American people will accept as "equitable" a job evaluation that comes up with such subjective opinions? Once you divorce wage setting from prevailing market rates, every determination of job "worth"—being a matter of subjective opinion—will result in a dispute, and most of those disputes will end up in the courts. That's the inevitable scenario of artificial wage setting. That's why the federal judge, who rejected the Denver nurses' demand that they be paid equally with tree-trimmers, said that the Comparable Worth theory "is pregnant with the possibility of disrupting the entire economic system of the United States."

Comparable Worth is basically a conspiracy theory of jobs. It asserts that (a) a massive societal (male) conspiracy has segregated (or ghettoized) women into particular occupations by excluding them from others, and then (b) devalued the "women's jobs" by paying them lower wages than other occupations held primarily by men. No evidence has been produced to prove these assumptions.

For two decades, women have been free to go into any occupation; there are even three thousand female coal miners today. But most women continue to choose traditional, rather than nontraditional, jobs. The pay gap between men and women is not due to discrimination; it is due primarily to the fact that men and women get married. The average married woman spends only 35 percent of her potential working years in the labor force, and this has a dramatic effect on her earning power. Most married men are motivated to work harder in the labor force to provide for their families; most married women are motivated to spend more effort on the daily care and nurturing of their children.

That's why most women choose occupations that allow repeated entry and exit from the labor force, part-time work or shorter hours, transfer to another city in order to accompany their husbands, and pleasanter and less risky work environments. Comparable Worth is an attempt to force employers, taxpayers, and consumers to pay women as though they had not made those career choices.

Since the essence of the Comparable Worth notion is a comparing of jobs held mostly by women with jobs held mostly by men, if women's jobs are allegedly underpaid, then which men's jobs are overpaid? The occupations alleged to be overpaid are truck drivers, construction and highway workers, electricians, plumbers, mechanics, maintenance and repair men, policemen and firefighters. The Comparable Worth notion asserts that it is unfair for blue-collar men to be paid more than pink-collar women.

The true answer to the pay differential is to have open access to all occupations so that women are not barred from any. There is nothing equitable about forcing workers who do unpleasant, risky, outdoor work to subsidize those who do clean, safe, indoor work.

Testimony to the Compensation and Employee Benefits Subcommittee, House Post Office and Civil Service Committee, April 4, 1984.

1984

Trying to Measure the Unmeasurable

We oppose the concept called Comparable Worth for two principal reasons: (a) it's unfair to men, and (b) it's unfair to women.

The Comparable Worth advocates are trying to freeze the wages of blue-collar men while forcing employers to raise the wages of some white- and pink-collar women above marketplace rates. According to the Comparable Worth rationale, blue-collar men are overpaid and their wages should be frozen until white- and pink-collar women have their wages artificially raised to the same level. The proof that this is what Comparable Worth is really all about is in both the rhetoric and the statistics of its advocates.

I've been debating feminists and listening to their arguments for more than a decade. It is impossible to overlook their rhetoric of envy. I've heard feminist leaders say hundreds of times, "It isn't fair that the man with a high school education earns more money than the woman who graduated from college or nursing or secretarial school."

That complaint means that the feminists believe that truck drivers, electricians, plumbers, mechanics, highway workers, maintenance men, policemen, and firemen earn more money than feminists think they are worth. And how do the feminists judge "worth"? By paper credentials instead of by apprenticeship and hard work, and by ignoring physical risk and unpleasant working conditions.

So the feminists have devised the slogan "Comparable Worth" to make the blue-collar man feel guilty for earning more money than women with paper credentials, and to trick him into accepting a government-enforced wage freeze while available funds are used to raise the wages of some women.

Statistical proof that the aim of Comparable Worth is to reduce the relative earning power of blue-collar men is abundantly available in the job evaluations commissioned and approved by the Comparable Worth advocates. You can prove this to yourself by making a job-by-job examination of any study or evaluation made with the approval of Comparable Worth advocates; it is always an elaborate scheme to devalue the blue-collar man.

For example, look at the evaluation used in the famous case called AFSCME *v. State of Washington*. Evaluator Willis determined that the electricians and truck drivers were overvalued by the state and that their "worth" was really far less than the "worth" of a registered nurse. More precisely, Willis produced an evaluation chart on which the registered nurse was worth 573 points, whereas the electrician was worth only 193 points (one-third of the nurse), while the truck driver was worth only 97 points (one-sixth of the nurse).

The federal court accepted the Willis evaluation as though it were some kind of divine law (refusing to listen to the Richard Jeanneret PAQ evaluation that produced very different estimates of worth). How do jobs get certain points? The evaluator invents them, that's how. The Comparable Worth advocates hire an evaluator under a contract in which he or she is obligated (a) to ignore all marketplace factors and (b) to produce a point scheme to "prove" discrimination against women.

One of the techniques by which this is done is the devaluing of the physical and working-condition factors so important in blue-collar jobs. This devaluation of blue-collar jobs is an inevitable result of integrating white-collar and blue-collar jobs in the same evaluation. If federal white-collar and blue-collar pay classifications were integrated, blue-collar employees would be tremendously devalued because the federal white-collar pay system accords less than 5 percent of the possible points to "physical demands" and "working environment" combined.

Comparable Worth advocates and evaluators join in a chorus to claim that it's so "scientific" because "worth" is based on education, training, skills, experience, effort, responsibility, and working conditions. The fact is that, once you throw out marketplace factors, the evaluation is completely subjective and wholly reflective of the bias of the evaluator.

The Willis evaluation determined that the "mental demands" on a nurse are worth 122 points, whereas the mental demands on an electrician are worth only thirty points, and the mental demands on a truck driver are worth only ten points. That's the view of the pro-feminist evaluator. For a contrary view, ask the electrician and the truck driver about the worth of the mental demands made on them.

Comparable Worth evaluations must be recognized as a racket to get people with your own biases on the evaluation team, or to saddle the evaluator with a contract that binds him to produce the results you predetermine.

Not only is the Comparable Worth concept wholly subjective, but it is also wholly arbitrary. It proposes to raise only some women's pay at the expense of men and other women. Only those jobs where 70 percent or more of the employees are female would be eligible for Comparable Worth raises. This was made clear in a devastating analysis of the Wisconsin governor's evaluation, made by the Wisconsin Association of Manufacturers & Commerce.

The Wisconsin Governor's Task Force Study lists the job called Institution Aide as having a "c-w gap" of $5,132. But the employees in this position would not get a c-w raise because only 67 percent of the 116 employees are women, and Institution Aide cannot be designated a "women's job" unless it meets the 70 percent test.

Now suppose that the state needs two more Institution Aides. If it hires two women, it will cross the 70 percent threshold. The state will then have to give all Institution Aides a raise, and it will therefore cost the state $595,000 to hire two women. The personnel manager can easily manipulate the system, depending on whether he is pro-feminist or pro-budget-cutting.

Or, look at the position called Nursing Assistant 3. Because it has 70 percent women, all 104 employees would be scheduled to get a raise of $3,626 to close the c-w gap. If the personnel manager simply hires one male or fires two females, he can avoid c-w raises for all and save $377,136 in his budget.

The entire concept of Comparable Worth hangs on comparisons between male-dominated jobs and female-dominated jobs, so it is impossible to escape the arbitrary nature of the 70 percent rule.

Comparable Worth is also unfair to women because its effect is to squeeze lower-skilled women out of the job market altogether. The respected economist June O'Neill has written lengthy treatises to show how and why this is the result.

That's not the only way Comparable Worth is unfair to women. It also hurts the women who have moved into nontraditional jobs. When the Illinois nurses sued the State of Illinois, claiming they should be paid equally with the (mostly male) electricians and stationary engineers, eleven female state employees in nontraditional jobs tried to enter the lawsuit as intervenors. They all work in a job classification called Correctional Officer, a euphemism for Prison Guard. The evaluation said that these "male-dominated" jobs are not "worth" as much as they are now paid. Illinois was paying prison guards $145 a month more than entry-level secretaries, but the Comparable Worth evaluation gave secretaries twelve more Comparable Worth points than prison guards.

The women prison guards claimed that the present system of compensation properly rewards them for their special skills, performance of particularly difficult, dangerous, and unpleasant work, their willingness to challenge stereotypes and perform nontraditional jobs, and the nondiscriminatory market forces of supply and demand. Put another way, the state has found that it must pay more to hire prison guards than office personnel because of the risks on the job and the unpleasant work.

Ask yourself: how many women would be willing to be a prison guard if the pay were the same or less than the pay of a secretary?

Women flood into the so-called traditional women's jobs by the millions. If the pay is raised for those jobs above market rates, even more women will seek those jobs and abandon plans to go into nontraditional lines of work. At the same time, businesses will eliminate jobs in order to cut costs, and low-skilled women will be laid off. That's why Clarence Pendleton says that Comparable Worth for women is as self-defeating as saying, twenty years ago, that the way to improve the economic lot of blacks would be to raise the pay of red caps.

Since Comparable Worth has become a controversial issue, the pro-feminist bias of the media has produced a pro–Comparable Worth bias on most television programs.

So it was with particular interest that I discovered a confidential and copyrighted memorandum on Comparable Worth distributed by the legal department of the National Association of Broadcasters for the benefit of its television and radio station members. This memorandum warns stations to "think very carefully before undertaking any formal study of the relationship between the 'value' or 'difficulty' of the positions held by their employees and the salaries they receive." Be sure to consult your lawyer, the memorandum says. "If an employer's only motive is to protect itself against the hazards of new theories of wage discrimination like Comparable Worth, it is fair to say that a job evaluation study is far more likely to be a burden than a boon."

That's good advice, not only for television and radio broadcasters, but for any employer, including federal and state governments.

Testimony to the Compensation & Employee Benefits Subcommittee, House Post Office and Civil Service Committee, May 30, 1985.

1985

The UN Women's Conference in Nairobi

The notion of American women attending a conference with women from countries all over the world to discuss their common problems is so ridiculous that it could only happen in a comedy cartoon or in the United Nations. American women are trying to get out of their kitchens, while the fondest dream of women in foreign countries would be to have an American-style kitchen. The conveniences American women take for granted are unattainable luxuries to women in other lands.

Call the roll of the great gifts that our private enterprise system has produced to liberate women from traditional women's work—the supermarket, frozen foods, ready-made clothes, washers, dryers, refrigerators, deep freezes, dishwashers, garbage disposals, sewing machines, and the telephone. We can even enjoy such additional extravagances as electric beaters, meat grinders, orange juice squeezers, ice cream freezers, hair dryers, and paper diapers.

In Africa, women do most or all of the hard work. They carry the water and firewood (on their heads), till the fields, and build the houses. The men use their energies for hunting, fishing, and fighting in tribal wars.

In Africa, men show their manhood by how many children they produce by many different wives. That's quite different from America where a man shows his manhood by getting a job and bringing home his paycheck every week to support his family.

In the Soviet Union and European communist countries, the women work two jobs, one in the labor force and one to keep the household functioning. Standing in line for the privilege of buying a head of cabbage consumes hours of every woman's week. The average woman has eight abortions without anesthetics, while the average man is anesthetized most of the time with vodka.

In America, a man can bring his girlfriend or wife such treats as candy or flowers. In the Soviet Union, a special gift most appreciated by women is a roll of toilet paper.

In Communist China, a woman faces compulsory abortion if she dares to conceive a second child. If she persists in having her baby, she and her family are punished by a cutoff of food and housing allowances.

The status of women in Muslim countries is so many centuries behind the modern world that it is hard for Americans to visualize. Nevertheless, the Iranian delegates at the UN conference weren't complaining: they hung a Khomeini poster on a tree to show their loyalty to their leader.

The best friend women ever had is the American private enterprise system, made possible by the economic freedom guaranteed in the U.S. Constitution. It has made American women the most fortunate class of people who ever lived on the face of the earth, and we should count our blessings every day.

When the two thousand U.S. feminists attending the Non-Governmental Forum in Nairobi berated the American delegation for failing to support their radical agenda (topped by government-funded abortions and Comparable Worth), Maureen Reagan aptly responded, "How fortunate they have the right to do that. Many delegates here don't have that right."

The UN Decade for Women pursued a bitter and divisive trail from Mexico City in 1975 to Copenhagen in 1980 and then Nairobi in 1985. They didn't dare meet in the United States: if they had, most of the delegates would have thought they had died and gone to heaven, and they would never have returned to their native countries.

The Nairobi conference reminded many people of the International Women's Year Conference held in Houston in November 1977, which was the U.S. offshoot of the UN Decade for Women. None of these conferences proved that women want the feminist agenda, but only that feminists, liberals, and socialists are skillful in getting their hands on government, UN, foundation, university, and organization funds with which to promote their own agenda.

1985

☺

Why the Equal Rights Amendment Failed

The Equal Rights Amendment (ERA) to the United States Constitution was presented to the American public as something to benefit women: "Put women in the U.S. Constitution," and lift women out of their so-called "second-class citizenship." However, in thousands of debates, ERA advocates were unable to show any way that ERA would benefit women or end any discrimination against them. The fact is that women already enjoy every constitutional right that men enjoy and have enjoyed equal employment opportunity since 1964.

In the short term, clever advertising and packaging can sell a worthless product; but in the long term, the American people cannot be fooled. ERA's biggest defect was that it had nothing to offer American women.

On the other hand, the opponents of ERA, were able to show many harms that ERA would cause.

1. ERA would take away legal rights that women possessed—it would not confer any new rights on women.

a) ERA would take away women's traditional exemption from conscription and from military combat duty. The classic "sex discriminatory" laws are those that say "male citizens of age 18" must register for the draft and those that exempt women from military combat assignment. The ERA advocates tried to get around this argument by asking the Supreme Court to hold that the Fourteenth Amendment already requires women to be drafted, but they lost in 1981 in *Rostker v. Goldberg*, when the Supreme Court upheld the traditional exemption of women from the draft under our present Constitution.

b) ERA would take away the traditional benefits in the law for wives, widows, and mothers. ERA would make unconstitutional the laws, which used to exist in every state, that impose on a husband the obligation to support his wife.

2. ERA would take away important rights and powers of the states and confer these on other branches of government that are farther removed from the people.

a) ERA would give enormous power to the federal courts to decide the definitions of the words in ERA, "sex" and "equality of rights." It is irresponsible to leave the courts to decide such sensitive, emotional, and important issues as whether or not the language applies to abortion or homosexual rights.

b) Section 2 of ERA would give vast new powers to the federal government that now belong to the states. ERA would give Congress the power to legislate on all those areas of law that include traditional differences of treatment on account of sex: marriage, property laws, divorce and alimony, child custody, adoptions, abortion, homosexual laws, sex crimes, private and public schools, prison regulations, and insurance. ERA would thus result in a massive redistribution of powers in our federal system.

3. ERA would take away rights from women students, upset many customs and practices, and bring government intrusion into private schools.

a) ERA would force all schools and colleges, and all the programs and athletics they conduct, to be fully coeducational and sex-integrated. ERA would make unconstitutional all the current exceptions in Title IX which allow for single-sex schools and colleges and for separate treatment of the sexes for certain activities. ERA would mean the end of single-sex colleges and force the sex integration of fraternities, sororities, Boy Scouts, Girl Scouts, YMCA, YWCA, Boys State and Girls State conducted by the American Legion, not to mention mother-daughter and father-son school events.

b) ERA would risk the income tax exemption of all private schools and colleges that make any difference of treatment between males and females, even though no public monies are involved. ERA is a statement of public policy that would apply the same rules to sex that we now observe on race, and it is clear that no school that makes any racial distinctions may enjoy tax exemption.

4. ERA would put abortion rights into the U.S. Constitution and make abortion funding a new constitutional right. *Roe v. Wade* in 1973 legalized abortion, but the fight to make abortion funding a constitutional right was lost in *Harris v. McRae* in 1980. The abortionists then looked to ERA to force taxpayer funding. The American Civil Liberties Union filed briefs in abortion cases in Hawaii, Massachusetts, Pennsylvania, and Connecticut arguing that, since abortion is a medical procedure performed only on women, it is "sex discrimination" within the meaning of a state ERA to deny tax funding for abortions. The Connecticut Superior Court ruled on April 19, 1986, that the Connecticut state ERA

requires abortion funding. Those who oppose tax funding of abortions demand that ERA be amended to prevent this effect, but ERA advocates want ERA only so long as it includes abortion funding.

5. ERA would put "gay rights" into the U.S. Constitution because the word in the Amendment is "sex," not "women." Eminent authorities have stated that ERA would legalize the granting of marriage licenses to same-sex couples and generally implement the gay and lesbian agenda. These authorities include the *Yale Law Journal*, the leading textbook on sex discrimination used in U.S. law schools, Harvard law professor Paul Freund, and Senator Sam J. Ervin Jr.

6. In the final years of the ERA battle, two new arguments appeared. Both were advanced by the ERA advocates, but they quickly became arguments in the hands of the ERA opponents.

a) ERA would require "unisex insurance," that is, would prohibit insurance companies from charging lower rates for women, even though actuarial data clearly show that women, as a group, are entitled to lower rates both for automobile accident insurance and life insurance. This is because women drivers have fewer accidents and women live longer than men. Most people found it a peculiar argument that women's rights should include the "right" to pay higher insurance rates.

b) ERA would eliminate veterans' preferences. This conclusion rests on the same type of legal argument as the abortion funding argument: that is, since most veterans are men, it is "sex discriminatory" to give preferences to veterans. Naturally, this argument was not acceptable to the veterans, and their national organizations lobbied against ERA.

Congress passed ERA and sent it to the states on March 22, 1972, with a seven-year time limit for ratification. When it became clear that ERA could not win ratification by the necessary three-fourths of the states, Congress voted a time extension of three years, three months, and eight days. After ten years of national debate, which was heated and dramatic at state capitols, ERA died on June 30, 1982. At its peak, thirty-five states had ratified ERA, but five of those rescinded their ratification, so the final count was thirty out of the thirty-eight needed.

1986

Postscript: On November 25, 1998, New Mexico's state Supreme Court held that New Mexico's state Equal Rights Amendment requires the state to pay for elective abortions under the Medicaid program. *N.M. Right to Choose/*NARAL *v. Johnson* (975 P.2d 841, 1998). In 1993, Hawaii's state Supreme Court ruled that the denial of marriage licenses to same-sex couples was unconstitutional under Hawaii's state Equal Rights Amendment. *Baehr v. Lewin* (852 P.2d 44, 1993). The court remanded the case for trial. On December 3, 1996, the Hawaii trial court in *Baehr v. Miike* (Haw. Cir. Ct., Civ. No. 91-1394) enjoined the denial of marriage licenses to same-sex couples, ruling that the state statute allowing only heterosexual marriage was unconstitutional. To undo the damage done by adding ERA to the Hawaii constitution, Hawaii voters passed a constitutional amendment on November 3, 1998, stating that "the legislature shall have the power to reserve marriage to opposite-sex couples."

The Intelligent Candidate's Guide to the Women's Vote

Eager political candidates all over the country are preparing their campaigns for public office. As they select their campaign issues and labor over their position papers, at some point their staffs raise the question, "How can we get the women's vote?"

If you ask the wrong question, you will get the wrong answer, and that's the wrong question. There isn't any "women's vote" any more than there is a "men's vote." A candidate who asks such silly questions is on the road to defeat.

The notion that candidates can get the women's vote by pandering to the so-called "women's issues" went down the drain in the 1984 election. In early 1984, National Organization for Women president and pro-abortion activist Eleanor Smeal wrote a book called *Why and How Women Will Elect the Next President*. Women *did* elect the next President, and his name was Ronald Reagan.

Such false concepts as "the women's vote" and "the women's movement" are based on the 1984 media myth called the "gender gap." This was a bogeywoman created by the feminists and the media in order to defeat targeted candidates by generating diversionary news stories that forced them to talk about non-issues instead of real issues. Like the Wizard of Oz, the gender gap was a phony and was buried (along with most feminist candidates) under the 1984 Reagan landslide.

The first thing any candidate must learn is the semantics of the subject. Feminist is an antonym for feminine, not a synonym. Feminine is an adjective that can be applied to pro-family women of any age or party, but not to those who call themselves feminists. A feminist will hiss and boo you if you use the terms "girl" or "lady"; a lady will not. In fact, a lady probably will never hiss or boo at all.

The feminists define women's rights as a woman's right to tax-paid abortion on demand, any sexual activity in or out of marriage, easy divorce, government subsidies for the cost of daycare, affirmative action (the government forcing an employer to hire a quota of women in preference to better qualified men), and Comparable Worth (the government raising some women's wages so they will equal the pay of entirely different traditionally male jobs for which women never even applied).

To the feminine or pro-family woman, women's rights means equal opportunity in education and employment, an end to the discriminations against the full-time homemaker that exist today in the income tax system and the Individual Retirement Accounts, and the opportunity to live in a free American economy made prosperous by lower taxes and a growing number of private-sector jobs.

Here is a list of dos and don'ts for candidates who want to prepare themselves for traps laid by feminist reporters.

1. Don't talk about "women's issues" and "women's concerns" unless you know what you are talking about and have cleansed your statement of words that may have a different meaning to you and to your audience (such as "women's rights" or "Comparable Worth").

2. Don't be cute, funny, personal, patronizing, or sarcastic in referring to women. You might offend some women. Even if what you say isn't offensive, feminists might take offense because they have no sense of humor.

3. Don't flatter women's appearance. That offends feminists.

4. Don't use profanity or tell off-color jokes. This offends feminine women.

5. Don't think you can please both kinds of women by offering some pledge to both. Both sides will conclude you can be manipulated by pressure.

6. Don't appoint a women's committee to advise you. This simply provides an opportunity for feminists to stage media events and make unreasonable demands.

7. Don't respond to attacks by feminists. This gives them a chance to have public tantrums and attract more media by attacking you again.

8. Don't use "Ms." to address any woman, orally or on paper, unless you know that the individual woman prefers that salutation. Married women work hard for the *r* in their *Mrs.* and they don't appreciate your taking it away.

9. Don't use expressions that some women find obnoxious. Don't call any woman a "women's libber"; call her a feminist. Don't call any woman a "non-working wife"; call her a full-time homemaker or career

homemaker. Don't call any woman a "working wife" because that implies that other wives are not working; call her an employed wife.

10. Don't ask women to "get together and decide what they want." Have you asked Ronald Reagan and Walter Mondale to "get together and decide what they want"?

1986

Sexist Software

I recently bought a personal computer along with an assortment of software. I discovered that one of the software programs will search material on the word processor, identify "sexist" words, and instruct the operator how to purge all sexist words and substitute different words. When the right keys are pushed, the program prints out its long list of sexist words followed by the gender-neutral word with which it should be replaced.

According to this software, we may no longer talk about businessmen, firemen, newsboys, mailmen or doormen; they must now be business persons, firepersons, paper carriers, postal carriers, or doorpersons. Longshoremen are out; they must now be dock workers. Horsemen and horsewomen are intolerable; they must be called equestrians.

Sportsmanship is out! It must be fair play. Salesmanship must be replaced by sales ability, chairmanship by chairpersonship. Mankind must be written as humanity. We may not say lady, gentleman, man, or woman; we must say person or people. Boy and girl must be replaced by child; never mind that those words don't have the same meanings. Unable to supply synonyms for such plainly sexist words as he, she, his, and her, the software curtly orders the typist to "revise."

Man-made must be replaced by artificial, spokesman by representative. Yet those word substitutions simply do not have the same meaning. Diplomat is to replace statesman, even though all statesmen are not diplomats and all diplomats certainly are not statesmen.

Some words apparently give such trauma to the software program that it bluntly spits out the instruction "avoid." These censored words are macho, manliness, manly, ladylike, gentlemanly, and manpower.

Now we're getting into real trouble. The software states that groomsman must be replaced by groom. But the groom is the guy who gets the bride, and the groomsman is the male friend who helps get the lucky fellow to the church without losing the wedding ring. The groomsman would be quite surprised to learn that he is a substitute for the groom.

But that's not the bridegroom's only problem. The software insists that stableman be replaced by groom. So now we have the bridegroom, his attendant, and the fellow who readies the horse for the getaway all answering to the same non-sexist name: groom.

Repairman and craftsman become repairperson and craftsperson. Manhours becomes personhours. But handyman? The computer must have choked on handyperson and tells us to "rephrase." A busboy is a clearer. The next time you dine in a restaurant, ask the waitress (excuse me, server) to have the clearer remove your dishes.

At least five years ago, the Bureau of Feminist Censorship persuaded big publishers to issue Censorship Guidelines prohibiting the allegedly "sexist" words, phrases, and pictures from use in textbooks. These attempts have not been able to overcome the American people's devotion to the English language.

Will the computer succeed in reprogramming our language to conform to feminist guidelines? It's not likely, since the lesson of all advertising is that you sell your product best with smiles—and smiles are contrary to feminist ideology.

1986

Why Affirmative Action for Women Is Wrong

Seventy years ago women were denied the right to vote in about half of the states. Do you think that women today should be given two votes to remedy those years when women could not vote at all?

Most people would say that's a silly question. But a "yes" answer would be equivalent to the U.S. Supreme Court's 1987 decision in *Johnson v. Transportation Agency, Santa Clara County, California*, which upheld affirmative action for women.

This was a case where a woman was hired over an admittedly better-qualified man for a job in the transportation agency of Santa Clara County, California. The employer, a state agency, gave preference to a woman to erase a "manifest imbalance in traditionally segregated job categories."

The six-to-three decision was written by Justice William J. Brennan Jr., a long time advocate of the most extreme feminist ideology. In his 1973 majority opinion in *Frontiero v. Richardson*, Brennan wrote that American women were discriminated against by an attitude of "romantic paternalism which, in practical effect, put women, not on a pedestal, but in a cage."

"A cage"? That's what he said. Presumably the cage to which Brennan referred was the home. In the same paragraph, he held up for ridicule and disdain a quotation from a nineteenth century Supreme Court decision that "the paramount destiny and mission of women are to fulfill the noble and benign offices of wife and mother. This is the law of the Creator."

Surely "cage" must have been a slip of the pen. But no, when you read further in the *Frontiero* opinion, you find Justice Brennan lacing his fantasies about societal oppression of women with echoes of the radical feminist writers. Continuing, Brennan wrote: "although blacks were guaranteed the right to vote in 1870, women were denied even that right" until the Nineteenth Amendment. (Brennan should have fact-checked his decisions: women voted in half the states prior to the Nineteenth Amendment.) Brennan concluded that "classifications based upon sex, like classifications based upon race, alienage, or national origin, are inherently suspect."

In the post-feminist era, Brennan's extravagant rhetoric is no longer fashionable, but he didn't get the message. Whereas in 1972 he used such rhetoric to say that any difference of treatment on account of sex was unacceptable, in 1987 he used similar rhetoric to conclude that job hiring must be done on account of sex. So we've come full circle. What was forbidden a decade ago is now mandatory. The trouble with this convoluted reasoning is that it avoids the fundamental issues involved in affirmative action.

The first reason why affirmative action is wrong is that the woman receiving the benefit is not a woman who was ever discriminated against. The benefits are not targeted for the victims. Nobody should be entitled to receive a remedy for an injury suffered by someone else.

The second reason why affirmative action is wrong is that it is based on a theory of group rights as opposed to the American tradition of individual rights. Women are not a monolithic, cohesive group in which a grievance suffered by one woman should translate into a right or a remedy granted to another woman.

The third reason why affirmative action is wrong is that compliance is judged on quotas. As a rose by any other name smells just as sweet, quotas concealed by euphemisms, such as numerical indicators, goals, timetables, statistical balance, and curing underrepresentation, smell just as bad.

The fourth reason why affirmative action is wrong is that it is based on the feminist notion that men and women are fungible, that there is no difference between the behavior of women and men in the labor force, and that anything less than a fifty-fifty male-female distribution in all job categories is proof that the employer discriminated against women.

This is false. Despite decades of equal employment opportunity statutes and aggressive enforcement, the majority of women still avoid occupations that require physical strength, risky and unpleasant working conditions, or sixty-hour work weeks.

The fifth reason why affirmative action is wrong is that it is an open invitation to blackmail and extortion. When an employer is served with a lawsuit on behalf of a woman he didn't hire or promote or award a contract to, the employer's lawyer will tell him it's cheaper to pay off the woman than to defend the case. In the $20 million lawsuit waged against Sears by the Equal Employment Opportunity Commission, the government was never able to produce a single woman who had been discriminated against.

The sixth reason why affirmative action is wrong is that it is demeaning to women. Women should be willing to compete equally with men on the basis of equal opportunity and should neither expect nor accept preferential treatment.

The seventh reason why affirmative action is wrong is that it creates resentment and animosity in the workplace. Since the system is fundamentally unjust, it produces contempt for the hypocrisy of pretending that injustice is justice. Personnel managers play the numbers game, snicker, and say, "I'll hire a black woman because she qualifies in two quotas."

That's not social justice. That's not stopping discrimination. That's reverse discrimination. During President Reagan's 1980 campaign, he said: "We must not allow this noble concept of equal opportunity to be distorted into federal guidelines or quotas which require race, ethnicity, or sex—rather than ability and qualifications—to be the principal factor in hiring or education. Increasing discrimination against some people in order to reduce it against others does not end discrimination."

1987

Yes, Virginia, There Is a Difference

We had a mouse in our house this week. The women screamed, and the men disposed of the mouse. Despite fifteen years of women's lib teaching us that men and women are really the same, it seems that there are persistent differences, and one of them reveals itself whenever a mouse arrives unannounced.

Of course, only women have functioning breasts and wombs and bear babies. But those are not the only differences. Only men have an Adam's apple that sticks out. Who knows why! We're just made that way. Colorblindness has a sex difference: ten times as many men as women are colorblind. Stutterers divide by gender: five times as many stutterers are men.

High heels distort our awareness of the big difference in height between men and women. In bare feet, the average man is six inches taller than the average woman. The difference in average weight between men and women is not only thirty pounds but also a difference in the weight they want to be. Rich men are fatter than poor men, but rich women are thinner than poor women. Dieters are 80 percent female and, you guessed it, 93 percent of those who suffer from anorexia are women.

Women's life expectancy is seven years longer than men's. That's why life insurance costs women less per year: they'll be paying seven years longer before they die. Twice as many men as women die accidentally.

Fifteen years of gender-neutral teaching have not erased the fact that young men are the risk-taking segment of society. That's why automobile accident insurance rates are much higher for young men under age twenty-five than for young women. After men take the big plunge of marriage, their yen for other risks seems to wane and their automobile accident insurance rates decline.

Six times as many men as women are injured at work. Is that because men are clumsier than women? Not likely. It's because most women are simply not willing to take the jobs where they risk bodily injury or death. We depend on the men to do risky jobs and protect us!

Since 1964, federal laws have guaranteed women open access to every type of job, but 99 percent of plumbers are still men. Are we prisoners of obsolete stereotypes? Hardly. Even high wages can't lure many women to this most essential trade. On the other hand, 97 percent of daycare workers are women. No one dares admit there is a biological maternal instinct, but the statistic can't be disputed.

The gender difference is not just in physical labor jobs. Despite the crying need in industry for engineers and the good pay they receive, 96 percent of engineers are men. A new college graduate in electrical engineering can walk into a job paying thousands of dollars a year more than a new graduate in liberal arts, which most women choose. The Education Amendments of 1972 guaranteed women's entry into any professional school of their choice, but still, last year 88 percent of the PH.D.s in mathematics and science were awarded to men.

My husband tried to talk all our six children into attending engineering school. He argued that you get more for your education dollar in engineering school and, anyway, you learn things that are true instead of so many false things taught in liberal arts that you have to unlearn later. So, our four sons graduated in engineering, but the two daughters rejected their father's advice. One daughter chose journalism: upon college graduation she went to work at less than one-half the pay any B.S.E.E. graduate could get. That was not sex discrimination: it was career choice.

When it comes to spending money, however, women write the checks in two-thirds of the households whether they are employed outside of the home or not.

1987

Feminists Want to Have It Both Ways

For the last twenty years, the feminists have been demanding that women be treated just like men. They demand to be "one of the boys." They insist on admission to all-men's clubs and the right to get off the elevator on the clubs' forbidden floors. They want to walk into men's locker rooms where male athletes are wearing only their birthday suits.

Led by Representative Patricia Schroeder (D-CO) and that great spokesman for women's rights Senator Ted Kennedy (D-MA), the feminists demand assignment to high-risk military combat jobs. The feminists filed suit to gain entry to Virginia Military Institute, where men shave their heads and are called Brother Rat. The feminists brought discrimination suits against fire departments all over the country, demanding to be hook-and-ladder firepersons sleeping in the firehouses along side of men.

Among the "sexist" laws which the feminists expunged from the state statute books were the laws that forbade men to use obscene language in the presence of a woman. In the new era of feminism, women must be given their right to hear dirty jokes and vulgar language just like men. We've come a long way since the days of Golda Meir, who rejected feminism and said that no man ever told a dirty story in her presence.

The feminists want to make all federal and state laws gender neutral. They want to force us all to conform to their agenda based on the unnatural ideology that there is no difference between men and women.

The feminists have had considerable success with their goals, due in part to the failure of men to understand that the feminists' goal is not fairness or equality of opportunity, but a gender-neutral society with feminists exercising the power. As feminist author Robin Morgan told a Phil Donahue audience, "We are becoming the men we once wanted to marry."

At the same time, feminists want to play the role of victim. Anita Hill was the epitome of the phony pose adopted by the feminists when it serves their purposes of taking power: "poor little me," the injured ingenue, the damsel in distress who cries for Big Brother Federal Government to defend her from the wolves in the workplace—not merely from what they might do, but even from what they might say.

Because it suited their goals, the feminists—through Anita Hill—put on a crybaby act and told us that, because men are in positions of power in the workplace, women are afraid to say "no" to any man. The whole assumption is patronizing—and, indeed, sexist—because it implies that women can't handle uncomfortable situations without the help of government.

Anita Hill was not a helpless or vulnerable teenager at the time of any alleged impropriety by Clarence Thomas. She was a Yale Law School graduate. According to the testimony of her office associates, Anita was known to her co-workers as tough, aggressive, unyielding, patronizing, and one who "wouldn't take anything from anyone." They described her as opinionated, arrogant, and quite capable of telling off any man.

Any woman who is smart enough and tough enough to graduate from law school should be perfectly capable of telling a man to button his lip, keep his hands off, get lost, bug off, or just plain "no."

1991

Code Name: Glass Ceiling

It isn't just minorities who seek affirmative action quotas. Feminists seek quotas, too, and they have invented their own code word to promote this objective: Glass Ceiling. This phrase has become the latest fad in Washington, D.C., where words are the chief manufactured product.

The feminists allege that there is an invisible or glass "ceiling" which women bump into on their way up the career ladder and which denies them promotions into high-paying jobs. No one can see this Glass Ceiling except the feminists—hence the artfulness of the term.

Glass Ceiling is a semantic tool to achieve two goals: (a) to make businessmen feel guilty for not moving over and giving their executive positions to career women, and (b) to intimidate business executives into establishing formal or informal affirmative action quotas for women in senior management. Feminists plan to accomplish these objectives by setting up a government commission so they can pursue their campaign at taxpayers' expense.

The feminists are promoting legislation to set up a Glass Ceiling Commission of feminists to use taxpayers' funds to conduct studies and research to "prove" the "findings" they have already specified. These findings assert that women are "significantly underrepresented in executive management and senior decision making positions in business" and that this is caused by "artificial barriers."

Did you think that the demolition of the Iron Curtain and the liberation of Eastern Europe mean that the threat from George Orwell's Big Brother is gone forever? Don't be too sure. The feminists are planning on passing Glass Ceiling legislation to empower Big Sister to do Orwellian snooping on private businesses. The Big Sisters on the Glass Ceiling Commission will investigate to find out "the manner in which business fills executive management and senior decision making positions." The tax-funded feminists on the warpath will "encourage American companies to modify practices and policies" in order to promote the "upward mobility" of women into top jobs and will be glad to provide specific guidance on how they should do this.

Just because there is a small percentage of women in senior management does not prove discrimination. It proves instead that the majority of women have made other choices—usually family choices—

rather than devoting themselves to the corporate world for sixty to eighty hours a week.

Equal pay for equal work has been the law since 1963; the Civil Rights Act has been applied to women since 1964; the Equal Employment Opportunity Commission has aggressively promoted equal employment opportunity for women since 1972. If systematic evidence of discrimination exists, the lawyers would be lining up plaintiffs for lucrative class action cases under existing anti-discrimination laws.

We've had twenty years' experience with tax-funded commissions run by the feminists, most notably the 1977 Commission on International Women's Year chaired by Bella Abzug, to which a muddle-headed Congress gave $5 million of the taxpayers' money. The feminists always use such commissions as platforms to pursue their radical agenda.

Businessmen in senior decision making positions who are supporting a wife and family should not let the Glass Ceiling brigade make them feel guilty when they refuse to acquiesce in this ploy. You can bet that a Glass Ceiling Commission will not tolerate any representation in behalf of the wives of the men who would be the losers in a system of affirmative action quotas for executive women.

1991

Ruth Bader Ginsburg's Feminist Worldview

How does it happen that a Supreme Court nominee whose only experience in private law practice was seven years as general counsel to the ACLU came to be praised by almost everyone as a "moderate" and a "centrist"? This just proves how easily men are fooled by a skirt. They have concluded that Ruth Bader Ginsburg is "moderate" because she isn't a loud-mouthed, frizzy-haired, bra-burning street demonstrator.

In fact, Ginsburg's writings betray her as a radical, doctrinaire feminist, far out of the mainstream. She shares the chip-on-the-shoulder, radical feminist view that American women have endured centuries of oppression and mistreatment from men. That's why, in her legal writings, she identifies with feminist Sarah Grimke's statement, "All I ask of our brethren is that they take their feet off our necks." In a speech published by the Phi Beta Kappa *Key Reporter* in 1974, Ginsburg called for affirmative action hiring quotas for career women. Using the police as an example, she said, "affirmative action is called for in this situation."

On the other hand, she considered it a setback for her version of women's rights when the Supreme Court, in *Kahn v. Shevin* (1974), upheld a Florida property tax exemption for widows. Ginsburg disdains what she calls "traditional sex roles" and demands strict gender neutrality (except, of course, for quota hiring of career women).

Ginsburg's real claim to her status as the premier feminist lawyer was her success in winning the 1973 Supreme Court case *Frontiero v. Richardson*, which she unabashedly praised as an "activist" decision. She obviously shares the view of Justice William Brennan's opinion that American men, "in practical effect, put women, not on a pedestal, but in a cage," and that "throughout much of the nineteenth century the position of women in our society was, in many respects, comparable to that of blacks under the pre–Civil War slave codes."

Anyone who thinks that American women in the nineteenth century were treated like slaves, and in the twentieth century were kept in a "cage," has a worldview that is downright dangerous for a Supreme Court justice.

Ginsburg passed President Clinton's self-proclaimed litmus test for appointment to the Supreme Court: she is "pro-choice." But that's not all: she wants to write taxpayer funding of abortions into the U.S. Constitution, something that 72 percent of Americans oppose and even the pro-abortion, pro–*Roe v. Wade* Supreme Court refused to do.

It has been considered settled law since the Supreme Court decisions in a trilogy of cases in 1977 (*Beal v. Doe, Maher v. Roe*, and *Poelker v. Doe*) that the Constitution does not compel states to pay for abortions. These cases were followed by the 1980 Supreme Court decision of *Harris v. McRae* upholding the Hyde Amendment's ban on spending taxpayers' money for abortions. The Court ruled that "it simply does not follow that a woman's freedom of choice [to have an abortion] carries with it a constitutional entitlement to the financial resources to avail herself of the full range of protected choices."

Ginsburg planted herself firmly in opposition to this settled law. In a 1980 book entitled *Constitutional Government in America*, Ginsburg endorsed taxpayer funding of abortions as a constitutional right and condemned the Court's rulings.

"This was the year the women lost," Ginsburg wrote in her analysis of the 1977 cases. "Most unsettling of the losses are the decisions on access by the poor to elective abortions." Criticizing the six-to-three majority in the funding cases, Ginsburg asserted that "restrictions on public funding and access to public hospitals for poor women" were a retreat from *Roe v. Wade*, as well as a "stunning curtailment" of women's rights.

Ruth Bader Ginsburg is a longtime advocate of the extremist feminist notion that any differentiation whatsoever on account of gender should be unconstitutional. Her radical views are made clear in a book called *Sex Bias in the U.S. Code*, which she co-authored in 1977 with another feminist, Brenda Feigen-Fasteau, for which they were paid with federal funds under Contract No. CR3AK010.

Sex Bias in the U.S. Code, published by the U.S. Commission on Civil Rights, was the source of the claim widely made in the 1970s that eight hundred federal laws "discriminated" on account of sex. The 230-page book identified those laws and recommended specific changes demanded by the feminist movement to conform to the "equality principle" and promote ratification of the Equal Rights Amendment (ERA), for which Ginsburg was a fervent advocate. Fortunately, the ERA died in 1982.

Sex Bias in the U.S. Code is a handbook that describes how the feminists want to change our laws, our institutions, and our attitudes and convert America into a gender-free society. It clearly shows that the feminists are not trying to redress any legitimate grievances women might have but want to change human nature, social mores, and relationships between men and women—and want to do that by changing our laws. Despite the noisy complaints of the feminists about the oppression of women, a combing of federal laws by Ruth Bader Ginsburg, then a Columbia University Law School professor, and her staff under a federal grant of tax dollars, unearthed no federal laws that harm women!

Sex Bias in the U.S. Code was forthright in targeting the traditional family concept of husband as breadwinner and wife as homemaker. "Congress and the President," Ginsburg wrote in this volume, "should direct their attention to the concept that pervades the Code: that the adult world is (and should be) divided into two classes—independent men, whose primary responsibility is to win bread for a family, and dependent women, whose primary responsibility is to care for children and household. This concept must be eliminated from the code if it is to reflect the equality principle."

In further definition of the equality principle, Ginsburg stated, "The increasingly common two-earner family pattern should impel development of a comprehensive program of government-supported child care." It is fundamental to feminist dogma that one of the proofs of the oppression of women is that society expects mothers to care for their babies, and this burden must be lifted by government-provided daycare.

Ginsburg was vehement in her desire to abolish any legal preference or protection that women might have. She advocated getting rid of laws against statutory rape as "discriminatory on their face" and the Mann Act because it was "meant to protect weak women from bad men." At the same time, she demanded gender-based preferences for women, even in the military. Such is the feminist notion of equality.

Ginsburg's *Sex Bias in the U.S. Code* embraced gender neutrality even to the extremes of demanding that the word "manmade" be replaced with "artificial," "mankind" with "humanity," "manpower" with "human resources," "midshipman" with midshipperson," and "he" and "she" with "he/she." To paraphrase a feminist obscenity, the feminists are obsessed with pronoun envy.

Finally, who but an embittered feminist could have said what Ruth Bader Ginsburg said when she stood beside President Clinton in the Rose Garden the day of her nomination for the Supreme Court. She wished that her mother had "lived in an age when daughters are cherished as much as sons." Where in the world has Ginsburg been living? In China? In India? Her statement was an insult to American parents who do, indeed, cherish their daughters as much as their sons.

1993

∞

Feminism's Fundamental Defects

Feminism is incompatible with the truth. It's based on the lie that American women are oppressed and mistreated, whereas American women are in fact the most fortunate class of people who ever lived.

Feminism is incompatible with human nature. The premise of the feminists is that God goofed in making us in two different sexes, and our laws should remedy His mistake. They've taken on the impossible task of changing human nature and the eternal differences between men and women. Despite feminist attempts to deny it, women do have a biological clock that influences them. I went to law school after I was fifty years old, but I'm glad I didn't have my six children after I was fifty.

Feminism is incompatible with common sense. The rejection of the family flies in the face of all human experience. The family is the proven best way for men and women to live together on this earth. A family provides people who care about us, a nest and a shelter from which we can face life's challenges. The family is the original and best department of health, education, and welfare.

Feminism is incompatible with marriage and motherhood. Women's lib raised false expectations that young women could "have it all" right now. But while the feminists rejected motherhood, not many men changed their attitudes, and babies didn't change at all. A *Wall Street Journal* study showed that 52 percent of successful women are divorced or unmarried, compared with only 5 percent of men.

Feminism is incompatible with personal happiness. Its technique of identifying and exaggerating grievances produces a chip-on-the-shoulder attitude toward life as well as a disdain for traditional values and roles. Feminist Anne Taylor Fleming, in her book *Motherhood Deferred*, describes herself as part of the sisterhood of the infertile, a lonesome, babyless baby boomer now completely consumed by the longing for a child of her own. She wrote that she's tempted to roll down the window and shout out loud, "Hey, hey, Gloria, Germaine, Kate. Tell us how does it feel to have ended up without babies, children, flesh of your flesh. Was your ideology worth the empty womb?" This cry comes from a woman who, twenty years earlier, proudly asserted her feminism, with all its cruel condescension of homemakers, and said in a CBS debate against me, "If I were pregnant now, I'd go out and have an abortion."

Feminism is incompatible with the private enterprise system because feminists propose government as the solution to every problem. The feminists claim they want to be independent of men, that they never want to defer to a husband or be financially dependent on a husband. But the feminists who proclaim their liberation from men always run to Big Brother Government as a replacement.

Need a job? Big Brother will get you an affirmative action quota position. You don't meet the physical requirements? Big Brother will gender norm the test results and give you a higher score. Not satisfied with your salary? The Comparable Worth commission will order your employer to give you a raise. Want a promotion? The Glass Ceiling commission will force your employer to give it to you.

Need time off to tend to a sick child? The Family Leave commission will arrange it for you. Need a babysitter for your child? A federally funded daycare center will relieve you of the burden of caring for your child. Need an abortion? Universal healthcare will pay for it.

Want to punish your boss for some remarks you didn't like? The Sexual Harassment gestapo will give him a hard time. Not getting along with your husband? The Legal Services Corporation will arrange a divorce. Want to punish your husband? The Violence Against Women agency will give you free housing while you accuse your husband of spousal rape, and the local prosecutor will believe your story without corroboration.

Faith, commitment, hard work, family, children, and grandchildren still offer the most fulfillment, as well as our reach into the future. Feminism is no substitute for traditional marriage. Liberation is no substitute for fidelity. Political Correctness is no substitute for chivalry. Careers are no substitute for children and grandchildren.

1994

Feminists Try to Stamp Out the Radical Truth

August 26, 1995 was the seventy-fifth anniversary of the ratification of the Nineteenth Amendment to the United States Constitution, the women's suffrage amendment, which forbade any state thereafter to deny women the right to vote. August 26 is an anniversary worth celebrating and honoring with a U.S. postage stamp.

But the feminists turned this anniversary into propaganda for radical feminist goals and revisionist history. They got the United States

Postal Service (which is supposed to be non-political) to issue a postage stamp giving equal billing to both the August 26 anniversary and
the radical demonstration in Springfield, Illinois on May 16, 1976 in
support of the failed Equal Rights Amendment (ERA).

That 1976 gathering of radical feminists had absolutely nothing to
do with women's suffrage. It happened fifty-six years after all American women had the right to vote. Contrary to the Postal Service's news
release issued with feminist Representatives Patricia Schroeder (D-CO)
and Nita Lowey (D-NY) looking on, the 1976 demonstration was not a
"milestone." It was not a significant event, it did not establish or reverse
any law or policy, it did not change anything at all. The cause for which
the demonstrators marched was a total failure. That event should not
be honored on a U.S. postage stamp.

The May 16, 1976, demonstrators included large numbers of lesbian
activists, socialists, government employees, unkempt radicals, and college students who were encouraged to come to Springfield, Illinois, on
subsidized buses from campuses all over the country. The May 16 demonstration was the first of many pro-ERA demonstrations at the Illinois
State Capitol, which became more radical with each passing year. By
1982, the demonstrators had become downright bizarre. For weeks, a
"chain gang" of pro-ERAers chained themselves to the door of the Senate Chamber on the third floor so that Senators had to step over them
to go into the session.

On June 25, 1982, ERA supporters went to the slaughterhouse, got
plastic bags of pigs' blood, and used it to deface the flags and to write
on the marble floor the names of the legislators they hated the most.
Despite the many pro-ERA demonstrations in Illinois, the Illinois legislature never ratified ERA, although it was forced to vote on ERA every
year for eleven years (1972-1982).

It is unfortunate that the U.S. Postal Service honored a pro-ERA
demonstration in Springfield along with the commemoration of the

women's suffrage amendment. This was a blatant attempt by liberal-feminist revisionists to rewrite history in order to advance their agenda.

1995

Feminist Assault on Reasonableness

Twenty years after women began attending law schools in greater numbers, feminists are turning up as law school professors, law review writers, state legislators, congressional staffers, prosecutors, law clerks, and even judges. It's splendid to have women in all those positions, but large numbers of feminists are causing ominous dislocations in basic concepts of American law and justice. An excellent policy analysis on "feminist jurisprudence" by the Cato Institute, dated June 19, 1996, explains why.

The feminist goal is not fair treatment for women, but the redistribution of power from the "dominant" class (the male patriarchal system) to the "subordinate" class (nominally women, but actually only the feminists who play by rules they have invented). Feminists have peddled the fiction that men are engaged in a vast conspiracy against women, that something like 85 percent of employed women are sexually harassed in the workplace, and that something on the order of 50 to 70 percent of wives are beaten by their husbands.

Feminists want to establish the rule that offenses against women should be defined (not objectively, but subjectively) on the basis of how the woman *felt* instead of what the defendant *did*.

Before the feminist movement burst on the scene in the 1970s, there were literally hundreds of laws that gave advantages or protections to women based on society's commonsense recognition of the facts of life and human nature. These included the prohibition against statutory rape, the Mann Act, the obligation of the husband to support his wife and provide her with a home, special protections for widows (for example, one state gave widows a little property tax exemption, another prescribed triple penalties against anyone who cheated a widow), and laws that made it a misdemeanor to use obscene or profane language in the presence of a woman.

The premier feminist lawyer in the 1970s, Ruth Bader Ginsburg, then a professor at Columbia University Law School, argued that all such differences of treatment based on gender were sex discriminatory and should be abolished. She won several Supreme Court cases on that theory. In state after state, as well as in Congress, feminist lawyers were able to persuade legislators to gender neutralize their laws.

In the 1990s, the feminists no longer even pay lip service to a gender-equality goal (except, of course, when it suits their purposes). Their goals are the feminization and subordination of men, and their tactics are to cry "victimization" and "conspiracy." They have launched an attack on basic precepts: equality under the law, judicial neutrality, a defendant is innocent until proven guilty, conviction requires proof beyond a reasonable doubt, and guilt or liability should be judged according to the traditional "reasonable man" theory.

Female plaintiffs had always been able to sue for offensive sexual actions in the workplace by using the common law remedies of tort and contract. Feminists reject these remedies because they want sexual harassment cases to be based on their nutty notion of a male conspiracy to victimize women, or their newly invented legal theory that a "hostile work environment" is a form of "sex discrimination" prohibited by Title VII of the Civil Rights Act.

The U.S. Supreme Court adopted this feminist theory in the 1986 case of *Meritor Savings Bank v. Vinson*, where the Court even went so far as to say that "'voluntariness' in the sense of consent" is not a defense. This notion was invented by Michigan Law School professor Catharine Mackinnon, who was reported to have boasted, "What the decision means is that we made this law up from the beginning, and now we've won." That's exactly what happened.

In a 1991 Jacksonville, Florida, case, a federal district court found an employer guilty of a "hostile work environment" even though there was no evidence of sexual language or demands directed at the plaintiff who claimed she felt sexually harassed. The other female workers said they did not feel sexually harassed, but the judge said that their testimony merely provided "additional evidence of victimization." In order to accommodate their claim that 85 percent of employed women are sexually harassed, the feminists have defined it so broadly that it is trivialized to include behavior that is merely annoying.

A 1991 Ninth Circuit Court of Appeals decision replaced the common law "reasonable man" standard with a "reasonable woman" test, embracing the 1990s feminist notion that men and women can't see the same events in the same way. The court declared that the old common law standard "systematically ignores the experiences of women."

Nevertheless, the feminists go even further. They are now demanding the "unreasonable woman" rule. They want the victim rather than the law to define the offense.

Remember, the feminists repealed the old laws making it a misdemeanor to speak "any obscene, profane, indecent, vulgar, suggestive or immoral message" to a woman or girl. Now the feminists are trying to enforce rules that any man's words can be punished if a woman subjectively doesn't like them. They argue that it can be just as actionable for a man to call a woman "honey" or "baby" as to call her a "bitch."

The feminists are actively promoting college speech codes to prohibit what they call discriminatory or harassing speech. Jokes are not allowed because feminists have no sense of humor. Nearly four hundred colleges and universities adopted these anti–First Amendment speech regulations, about a third of which target "advocacy of offensive or outrageous viewpoints or biased ideas."

The feminists even push the Catharine Mackinnon fantasy that all heterosexual sex should be considered rape unless an affirmative, sober, explicit verbal consent can be proved. They want to establish a license for women to kill their allegedly abusive spouses. They would have us believe that killing a man in his sleep can be excused as self-defense.

More lawyers, scholars, and academics are badly needed to speak up and expose the feminist foolishness for what it is: a scurrilous attack on our Bill of Rights.

1996

Feminists Have Global Goals, Too

Did you think that those United Nations conferences held in Cairo, Beijing, and Istanbul were just consciousness-raising sessions where the feminists in the Clinton Administration could commiserate with females from 189 countries about how badly women are treated by the male patriarchal society? Well, think again. When we give the feminists a tax-paid junket to cultivate their grievances, you can bet they will use that opportunity to cook up a lot of mischief.

Did you think that, in our constitutional government, "all legislative powers" are vested in the Congress, where laws, to be valid, must be passed by a majority in both Houses? Think again. The feminists have devised a sneaky way to bypass the constitutional process, achieve what they want by "consensus" at a UN conference, and then use the federal bureaucracy to implement their policies as though they were law.

In May 1996, the Clinton Administration set up the President's Interagency Council on Women chaired by those two longtime friends and co-conspirators in feminist activism, Hillary Rodham Clinton and HHS secretary Donna Shalala. Its mission is to "follow up on U.S. commitments made at the UN Fourth World Conference on Women, Beijing, September 4-15, 1995." On September 28, 1996, the President's Interagency Council held a national conference via satellite to report on the "progress" made toward Beijing's "Platform for Action."

Soon after the feminists returned from China in 1995, UN ambassador Madeleine Albright, who was the U.S. delegation chair in Beijing, spelled out the goals in a document called "Bring Beijing Home." These included "family responsibilities must be shared" (obviously, the government should force husbands to do the dishes and the diapers) and, of course, assuring abortion rights. Albright announced that Beijing had produced "an international women's movement of activists, advocates and advisors to the nations of the world." U.S. taxpayers paid one-third of the $14 million bill for the gab session.

The Beijing commitments are being implemented through a federal entity composed of high-level representatives from thirty federal agencies. It holds monthly meetings, engages in outreach activities, conducts local seminars, and uses a White House address.

The longtime feminist goal called Comparable Worth is a major goal of this President's Interagency Council. The feminists think it's unfair that jobs held mostly by men, such as plumber and prison guard, have higher pay than clerical jobs held mostly by women. The feminists allege that paper credentials are "worth" more than unpleasant or dangerous working conditions. Although nobody is stopping more women from becoming plumbers and prison guards, the feminists argue that "pay equity" requires freezing the wages of male-dominated jobs in order to increase the wages of the jobs women prefer.

Another "top priority" of this group is ratification of the United Nations Convention on the Elimination of All Forms of Discrimination Against Women. Only radical feminists could believe the silliness that the lot of American women would be improved by allowing a UN agency to define our rights.

Domestic violence is another major item on the Beijing agenda. This will encourage the feminists to demand that the $1.6 billion voted by Congress for the Violence Against Women Act be channeled to their friends as feminist pork.

The National Education Association produced a video on the Beijing Conference called "Cornerstone for the Future" featuring (surprise, surprise) Hillary Rodham Clinton. Designed to promote discussions in middle schools about women as victims who need more government services, the video was launched by Mrs. Clinton at a middle school in Fairfax County, Virginia.

The behind-the-scenes activist coordinating this agenda was Bella Abzug, the former congresswoman who is head of the Women's Environment and Development Organization, which (as expected) is a recipient of U.S. taxpayer grants. At Feminist Expo '96, organized by former National Organization for Women head Eleanor Smeal and held in Washington, D.C., Abzug boasted: "You made a contract with the world's women, and that has to be enforced. And how does it get enforced? By politics, by political action."

Abzug is an experienced activist. In addition to her twelve-point "Contract with American Women" that includes demands for Comparable Worth and affirmative action, she boasts that work is under way to promote her platform in high schools, colleges and universities through courses and seminars on Beijing's notion of "gender equity."

If she runs out of U.S. taxpayer grants, Abzug can call on the United Nations Development Fund for Women, whose literature announces that it is working with governments to transform Beijing's 362 paragraphs into "national strategic plans and programs."

1996

A Lousy Way to Run a Company

The Sisters of St. Francis in Philadelphia used their ownership of a little stock to engage in feminist mischief making. They demanded that a Silicon Valley company called Cypress Semiconductor select its board of directors on the basis of racial and gender diversity. CEO T. J. Rodgers wrote back with the put-down the nuns deserved. He rejected their arguments as "not only unsound, but even immoral." He admonished them that Cypress's board of directors "is not a ceremonial watchdog, but a critical management function."

The nuns had tried to lay a guilt trip on Cypress by suggesting that it lacks corporate "morality" and Christianity by failing to appoint a board of directors with "equality of sexes, races, and ethnic groups." Rodgers didn't hedge in his response. "I am unaware," he said, "of any Christian requirements for corporate boards; your views seem more accurately described as 'politically correct,' than 'Christian.'" Rodgers explained that, contrary to the nuns' argument, "a woman's view on how to run our semiconductor company does not help us, unless that woman has an advanced technical degree and experience as a CEO."

Sounds like common sense, doesn't it? "I believe," he said, "that placing arbitrary racial or gender quotas on corporate boards is fundamentally wrong." Then, Rodgers went on to argue that the nuns' presumptuous requirements for corporate boards are "immoral," which he defined as "causing harm to people." He pointed out how all the retirees whose pension funds invest in Cypress would suffer if Cypress were run on anything other than a profit-making basis.

Since the letter from the nuns was so sanctimonious that it did not allow for any possibility that a CEO could be moral if he disagreed with their position, Rodgers told the sisters to "get down from your moral high horse." He reiterated that "choosing a board of directors based on race and gender is a lousy way to run a company. We will never be pressured into it. We simply cannot allow arbitrary rules to be forced on us by organizations that lack business expertise."

Rodgers obviously warmed up to the challenge from the nuns' do-good busybodyism. "The political pressure to be what is euphemized as a 'responsible corporation' today," he said, "is so great that it literally

threatens the well-being of every American." He cited a *Fortune* magazine report showing that the so-called "ethical mutual funds" that invest according to a social-issues agenda, which control $639 billion in
investments, produced an 18.2 percent return in the last 12 months, while
the S&P 500 returned 27.2 percent. Thus, the investors in the "ethical
funds" lost 9 percent of $639 billion, or $57.5 billion in one year, because
they invested on a social-issues basis!

Rodgers concluded by stating that he stands for "personal and economic freedom, for free minds and free markets, a position irrevocably
in opposition to the immoral attempt by coercive utopians to mandate
even more government control over America's economy."

May his tribe increase, and may his forthright statement embolden
other CEOs to speak up, too.

1996

The United Nations Treaty on Women

President Clinton called a special news conference in 1997 to announce
that he finds it "an embarrassment" that the U.S. Senate has not ratified
the United Nations Convention on the Elimination of All Forms of
Discrimination Against Women. He said that, although 130 other nations have ratified this treaty, the United States hasn't, and "there is no
excuse for this situation to continue."

A treaty to enforce uniform rules for us and other nations, under
the supervision of UN busybody bureaucrats, can only diminish the rights
and benefits now enjoyed by American women. Ratification of this UN
Treaty on Discrimination Against Women would be craven kowtow-
ing to the radical feminists, exceeded only by its unlimited capacity for
legal mischief. It would be a massive interference with U.S. laws as well
as with our balance of powers between federal and state governments.

Article 1 purports to abolish discrimination against women "in the political, economic, social, cultural, civil or any other field." Private relationships should be none of our government's business, much less the business of the United Nations.

Article 2 reiterates that the treaty would "eliminate discrimination against women by any person, organization or enterprise," including "customs and practices." No human behavior is beyond the purview of this impudent UN document. The treaty would mandate the longtime feminist goal of total sexual integration in the military. It would turn over to the UN all decisions regarding military personnel, including the assignment of women to ground combat.

Article 3 would require us to pass new federal laws not only in political but also in "social, economic and cultural fields."

Article 5 would require us "to modify the social and cultural patterns of conduct of men and women" and to give assurances that we are following UN dictates about "family education."

Article 10 would make it a federal responsibility to ensure "the elimination of any stereotyped concept of the roles of men and women at all levels and in all forms of education . . . by the revision of textbooks . . . and teaching methods." Unable to persuade Americans voluntarily to go along with their censorship attempts, the feminists are trying to get the UN to do this job for them.

Article 11 would chain us to the feminist goal that wages should be paid on subjective notions of "equal value" rather than on objective standards of equal work. It would also require the federal government to establish "a network of child-care facilities."

Article 16 would require us to allow women "to decide freely and responsibly on the number and spacing of their children." In feminist theory, this means that the United States would have to allow abortions at any time for any reason. On the other hand, this language does not protect Chinese women victimized by their government's policy of forced abortions. China asserts that a woman is not "responsible" if she bears more than one child.

Article 16 also levels a broadside attack on state's rights. It would obligate the federal government to take over all family law, including marriage, divorce, child custody, and property.

To monitor the "progress" made under this treaty, Article 17 sets up a Committee on the Elimination of Discrimination Against Women consisting of twenty-three "experts." No doubt that means such "experts" in feminist ideology as Hillary Rodham Clinton and Barbara Boxer.

The State Department memo that explains the treaty, which was written by the late Edmund S. Muskie, candidly admits that it applies "to private organizations and areas of personal conduct not covered by U.S. law." It also admits that the treaty completely fails to take into account "the division of authority between the state and federal governments in the United States."

President Jimmy Carter signed this terrible treaty in 1980, and ever since the Senate has had the good judgment to refuse to ratify it. We trust the Senate will retain its sanity on this issue, despite Mr. Clinton's embarrassment.

1997

Paula Jones and Anita Hill

I cannot resist pondering the fix that Paula Jones put the feminists into, and the feminists' contortions in their vain effort to defend their ideology and the president they love. It remains to be seen whether Bill Clinton will be convicted of sexual improprieties while governor of Arkansas, but Jones certainly has convicted the feminists of hypocrisy and double standards. Even the liberal media are laughing at them.

The funny thing is, the feminists did it to themselves. As the old saying goes, they made their bed and now they have to lie in it. They invented the current use of "sexual harassment." There is nothing in Title VII, the employment law, that defines or prohibits sexual harassment. Sexual harassment is judge-made law, and the feminists are responsible for its widespread use.

Without the feminists' campaign against sexual harassment that began with Anita Hill, and their claim that it is a pervasive problem, there would be no Paula Jones lawsuit. And without Paula Jones's lawsuit, we would never have known about Monica, Kathleen, Dolly, Clinton's perjury, Clinton's obstruction of justice, and the intimidation of Clinton's bimbos who didn't keep their mouths shut.

The feminists are claiming that Paula Jones and her backers just want to "undo the 1992 election": they just can't stand it that Clinton won. Oh, really? The Anita Hill hearing was all about trying to undo George Bush's victory in the 1988 election by denying him his right to name a conservative justice to the Supreme Court.

Now the feminists are saying Paula Jones shouldn't be believed because she "waited too long." But how long is too long? How can Paula's two-year wait be "too long" when Anita Hill waited ten years? Paula's charges were not, like Anita Hill's charges, a last-minute ambush to prevent her target from achieving high office.

The classic model of sexual harassment, according to feminist ideologues, is the Big Boss asking sexual favors of a female subordinate. In feminist dogma, this "power relationship" automatically creates such a hostile work environment that the Big Boss need not threaten the woman in order to be guilty of the sin of sexual harassment. That's exactly the model of Bill Clinton and Paula Jones, a minimum-wage clerk with limited education, just two months on the job, being summoned by His Honor the Governor, and even escorted to His Presence by the state police. Anita Hill, on the other hand, was a lawyer who knew her rights and who could not have been fired from her civil service job.

The feminists allege that Paula Jones should be disbelieved because her case was assisted by some of Bill Clinton's enemies. Well, well! Anita Hill was surrounded, promoted, and coached by feminists and liberals who had identifiably political motives to block the confirmation of Clarence Thomas. Anybody who attended the Thomas confirmation hearings would have seen the whole assortment of feminists and liberals clustered around her, including the National Organization for Women, the National Abortion Rights League, and the staffs of Senators Ted Kennedy and Howard Metzenbaum.

When it comes to sexual allegations that cannot be positively proved one way or the other because there are no eyewitnesses, most people decide what is credible based on a pattern of behavior. In Clarence Thomas's case, despite all the investigative efforts of the liberal media and the liberal Senate staff, no "second woman" was unearthed to come forward with similar charges.

On the other hand, Paula's charges have credibility because of Clinton's pattern of behavior. As Pat Buchanan wrote: "Paula Jones may not have gotten her day in court, but she got her pound of flesh." Clinton will go into the history books as an embarrassment to our nation.

1998

Violence against Women

The federal government's insatiable demand for more power was slowed down by the Supreme Court in *United States v. Morrison.* The Supreme Court just said no and properly invalidated a key provision in the 1994 Violence Against Women Act (VAWA).

At issue was whether the federal government can regulate aspects of marriage and domestic relations, which have always been within the exclusive domain of the states. Radical feminists and their allies in the media sought to transfer this power to the federal level, where they can more easily apply political pressure. Such a fundamental transfer in power from the states to the federal government should require a constitutional amendment. But after Clinton won the presidency and control of Congress in 1992, those seeking federal control over domestic relations tried a more direct approach.

Senator Joe Biden (D-DE) included in the VAWA a little noticed provision to undermine local control over domestic issues. He piggybacked on media sensationalism about the 1991 Navy Tailhook convention. That provision, section 13981, gave federal courts unprecedented power over domestic relations. If this provision had been upheld by the Supreme Court, there would be no constitutional limitation on federal expansion in this area. It would have been a giant step towards a takeover of marriage and domestic relations law by the federal government.

VAWA also included a provision awarding attorney's fees, thereby creating a bonanza for contingency-fee attorneys seeking to intimidate defendants with allegations of rape and even spousal rape. While states place sensible time limits on such accusations to assure prompt and fair investigation of the facts, VAWA allowed attorneys to make allegations up to four years afterwards.

No one is helped, least of all women, when a criminal victim turns to a contingency-fee attorney rather than to local police. If the allegations are true, only the local police can stop the perpetrator from continuing to harm the victim. If the allegations are embellishments, no one benefits from the spectacle of a federal court, years later, trying to separate fact from fiction. A cadre of gold-digging attorneys traipsing to federal court would likely make the problem worse.

Finally, in Virginia, a courageous federal judge stood up to the pressure and defended the fundamental principle that local domestic relations disputes should be addressed promptly by local authorities.

When *U.S. v. Morrison* reached the Supreme Court, sixty-seven liberal and feminist organizations filed amicus curiae briefs in an attempt to preserve this federal intrusion. It was the feminists' most important case, and they were determined to win it. Attorneys were salivating at the opportunity to apply VAWA to many of the million-plus domestic breakups that occur each year, which could easily have translated into a new billion-dollar industry for lawyers.

Fortunately, the Supreme Court, in a straightforward decision, confirmed that Congress cannot do what the Constitution did not give it authority to do.

The media and VAWA supporters persistently concealed the fact that the defendants in *U.S. v. Morrison* were blacks who had been exonerated by the criminal justice system, yet were later subjected to civil allegations unsupported by an independent investigation. Their victory in this case, after years of being smeared, was a triumph of justice.

2000

IV

A Gender-Neutral Military?

They shall yet belie thy happy years
That say thou art a man. Diana's lip
Is not more smooth and rubious; thy small pipe
Is as the maiden's organ, shrill and sound,
And all is semblative a woman's part.

Twelfth Night

Women Should Not Serve in Combat

The push to repeal the laws that exempt women from military combat duty must be the strangest of all aberrations indulged in by what has become known as the women's liberation or feminist movement. The very idea of women serving in military combat is so unnatural that it almost sounds like a death wish for our species.

Last Sunday's newspapers carried a front-page picture of a man expressing the disgust of the average American with the humiliation of our nation by the radicals in Iran. The man held up a large sign that said, "Kick me, I'm an American." Yet, here we are at a House committee hearing at which representatives of the women's liberation movement are, in essence, saying, "Kick me, I'm a woman. I want to be sent into war where I can be shot at and captured just like a man." Some men seem willing to let that happen.

Has our nation sunk so low that we are willing to send our daughters into battle? Is chivalry completely dead? Breathes there a man with soul so dead that he will not rise up and defend his wife, his sweetheart, his mother, or his daughter, against those who want to wound or capture them, whoever they may be?

There is no evidence in all history for the proposition that the assignment of women to military combat jobs is the way to promote national security, improve combat readiness, or win wars. Indeed, the entire experience of recorded history teaches us that battles are *not* won by coed armies or coed navies. Even Hitler and the Japanese, when they ran short of manpower, found it more efficient to use underage and overage men in combat than to use female troops. Of the thousands of books written about World War ii, no one ever wrote that Hitler or the Japanese should have solved their manpower shortage problem by using women in combat.

Every country that has experimented with women in combat has abandoned the idea. Israel used women in combat for a few weeks in the war of 1948 but never did so in later military operations. Women are now treated very differently from men in the Israeli armed forces. They serve only about half as long; they are housed in separate barracks; they have an automatic exemption if they marry or have a baby. Israel has a smaller percentage of women in its armed forces than the United States.

The Soviet Union used some female troops in World War ii but has since abandoned this altogether. Women make up less than one percent of Soviet troops today. There must be a reason for the unanimous verdict of history that the armed forces demand different roles for men and women.

The first reason is that women, on the average, have only 60 percent of the physical strength of men. This truism, so self-evident to those with eyes to see, has been confirmed by many studies. However, under pressure from the feminist movement, much of this evidence is not allowed to see the light of day or, if it does, is couched in apologetic terms. For example, a report by the Comptroller General of the United States called *Job Opportunities for Women in the Military: Progress and Problems* surveyed the actual experience of enlisted women placed on military jobs formerly reserved for men. The Comptroller General said, "If as the Air Force Surgeon General has concluded, females are only 60 percent as strong as males, it seems there are some jobs that males, on the average, can do better than females."

As I travel around the country, I do many radio call-in programs. Everywhere I go, I hear the same complaint from men in the U.S. Armed Services: the women are getting the same pay and have the same rank as the men, but they are not doing the equal work, and the male soldiers must do part of the women's jobs for them. This situation is not just and is destructive of morale and good personnel relations.

Sex-neutral treatment of men and women in the military is just as unfair to women as it is to men. If you interview the women who are army privates or navy sailors, you get a different story from that of the officers who must toe the administration line.

The second reason for the unanimous verdict of history that the armed forces demand different roles for men and women is that women get pregnant and men do not. That particular sex-role stereotype has become a tremendous problem in the military today. Why should anyone be surprised? When young men and women in the age group of eighteen to twenty-five are required to live in close proximity, often doing unpleasant tasks and suffering from loneliness away from home, the inevitable happens. News stories report that the pregnancy rate is about 15 percent among servicewomen. Another 5 percent have had their babies and brought them back to the post. The rape rate is also said to be about twice what it is in civilian life.

Yet we are told that the armed services cannot discharge a woman who becomes pregnant because that would be "sex discrimination" unless the services also discharge the father of the baby! And it would be obviously impossible for the armed services to discharge every man who fathers a baby. The services are required to ignore the obvious fact that pregnancy keeps a woman from doing her job in a way that fatherhood does not interfere with a man's performance on the job.

How did we get into our present situation, in which our military officers are issuing maternity uniforms, opening nurseries on army posts, and pretending that women can do anything that men can do? For the answer to that, we must look at two of the false dogmas of the women's liberation movement.

The first false dogma is that there really is no difference between the sexes (except those obvious ones we need not discuss) and that all those other differences you think you see are not inherent but are due merely to sex-role stereotyping which can and must be erased by sex-neutral education, laws, and changed attitudes. The sex-neutral dogma is variously called gender free, unisex, or the elimination of sexism from our society and attitudes.

Neither Congress nor the military will ever be able to cope with the problems and demands raised by the feminists until we realize that the feminists look upon the military as a vehicle to achieve the gender-free goals of the women's liberation movement—not as an instrument to defend the United States of America. Since the armed services are an institution where people must obey orders, it is the perfect vehicle to enforce the sex-neutral goals of the feminist movement. Feminists also look upon the armed services as a giant social welfare program, designed to provide upward social mobility for minorities which, according to their peculiar definitions, include women.

The national security of the United States, justice to the majority of young men and women, respect for the wishes of the great majority of the American people, and rational behavior all demand that we continue to structure the armed services of our nation on the commonsense premise that there must be different roles for men and women in the military. We cannot allow those values to be upset and disoriented by the strident demands of a few over-draft-age feminists who have high-level affirmative-action jobs in the Pentagon, or by the handful of high-ranking women officers who seek greater recognition at the expense of their sisters who will have to march in the combat infantry.

It is interesting that the desire of women for sex-neutral treatment in the military is usually in inverse proportion to their rank. A few of them have delusions of grandeur that women must be accepted as armchair generals and admirals, but the price that our own daughters will have to pay in the ranks, in case of another war or a reinstated draft, is far too high, as is the price of reduced combat readiness.

The second false dogma of the women's liberation movement is that we must be neutral between morality and immorality, and between the institution of the family and alternative lifestyles. As the national conference on International Women's Year at Houston in 1977 proved, the feminists demand that government policy accord the same dignity to lesbians and prostitutes as to wives, to illegitimate births as to legitimate, to abortions as to live births, and that we support immoral and anti-family practices with public funds. In deference to feminists, the armed services are now supporting and maintaining servicewomen who engage in immoral practices and bring their babies back to the posts. We must stop this public funding of immorality.

The purpose of the armed services is to defend the United States of America—not to create a tax-funded haven for sexually active young men and women, nor is it to serve as a giant social welfare institution. The need for combat-ready troops and a stronger national defense has never been greater in our country's history. The very idea of ordering women into combat jobs would send a message to the world that we have reduced the strength of our troops to the physical strength of the average female. It would be a sign of weakness because it would tell the world we do not have enough men willing to defend America.

I urge Congress to reject all demands to repeal the laws that exempt servicewomen from combat jobs. I urge Congress to maintain and reinforce the time-tested rule that there must be different roles for men and women in the United States armed services. Anything less than that will waste the valuable energies of our military officers on the exhausting task of coping with the escalating demands of a few feminist spokesmen who do not speak for anyone but their own narrow group. The first priority of the armed services should be to rebuild the military strength and the combat effectiveness of the United States.

Testimony to the House Armed Services Committee, Military Personnel Subcommittee, November 16, 1979.

1979

The Feminization of the U.S. Military

The same week that Middle East terrorists and the hostage problem dominated the news, the *New York Times* featured a front-page story headlined "West Point Picks Woman to Lead Cadet Corps." The position of first captain of the Corps of Cadets, the academy's highest honor, puts her in charge of overseeing virtually all aspects of life for the 4,400 West Point cadets.

The picture showed a casual, T-shirted, straggly-haired twenty-year-old girl. What do you suppose the bad guys of the world—the terrorists, the Soviets, the Chinese thugs, Qaddafi, or Castro—think when they see this image of the one selected to lead West Point seniors?

West Point's superintendent, General Dave R. Palmer, said, "She does not have the position because she's a woman." He is correct, but not the way he meant it. She has this honor because he is a wimp who toadies to the feminists who are constantly breathing down his neck and demanding more "career opportunities."

The *Times* article tried to reassure its readers that she deserves this position of leadership over all other West Point cadets, 90 percent of whom are men, by saying she has "a strong academic record, played soccer and competed in cross-country skiing." And one more qualification: she "worked as a speechwriter in the Pentagon." As Queen Victoria would have said, "We are not amused."

The superintendent who made this newsworthy choice must think his mission is to train young people to be paper pushers in the Pentagon in a peacetime military, while keeping fit with athletics (but not the really tough men's sports). But if that's all West Pointers are being trained for, the cadets can go to any state university at one-twentieth the cost to the taxpayers.

When General Douglas MacArthur, hero of three wars and the most distinguished cadet who ever graduated from West Point, delivered his great "Duty, Honor, Country" commencement speech there on May 12, 1962, he gave it to them straight. "Your mission remains fixed, determined, inviolable. It is to win our wars. Everything else in your professional career is but corollary to this vital dedication. . . . You are the ones who are trained to fight." MacArthur continued, "Yours is the profession of arms, the will to win, the sure knowledge that in war there is no substitute for victory, that if you lose, the nation will be destroyed."

Times and weapons have changed, but the mission of West Point graduates is—or should be—the same as it ever was. This is not a mission for girls (even if they excel at skiing and speechwriting), but a mission for real men.

As MacArthur said, West Point must graduate men who, whether they are "slogging ankle deep through mire of shell-pocked roads, . . . blue-lipped, covered with sludge and mud, chilled by the wind and rain," or, on the other side of the globe, in "the filth of dirty foxholes, the stench of ghostly trenches, the slime of dripping dugouts," in "the loneliness and utter desolation of jungle trails," can be relied on to muster the strength and courage to kill the enemy.

Can we believe that this 112-pound, five-foot-four-inch girl can do that—and in addition lead troops of men to risk death under such circumstances? You have to be kidding!

The official excuse for this catering to the feminists is that the baby boomers are now past military age, causing a shortfall of men who will volunteer for the all-volunteer services. But the real reason there is a shortfall of male volunteers is not demographics: it is the feminization of the military. Men are attracted to serve in the military because of its intensely masculine character. The qualities that make them courageous soldiers—aggressiveness, risk taking, and enjoyment of body-contact competition—are conspicuously absent in women.

Fighting wars is a mission that requires tough, tenacious, and courageous men to endure the most primitive and uncivilized circumstances and pain in order to survive in combat against enemies who are just as tough, tenacious, and courageous, and probably vicious and sadistic, too. The armies and navies of every potential enemy are exclusively male, and no women diminish their combat readiness.

Pretending that women can perform equally with men in tasks that require those attributes is not only dishonest, it corrupts the system. It discourages men from enlisting, and it demoralizes servicemen and keeps them from developing those skills that produce Douglas MacArthurs and George Pattons in our country's hour of need.

1989

Sending Mothers to War

The newspaper photographs of soldier mothers tearfully saying goodbye to their babies as they departed to serve in the Gulf War shocked Americans who had not realized that this is what the ideology of feminism demands. The U.S. armed services even shipped out breastfeeding mothers of infants only a few weeks old.

How uncivilized has our nation become! No national emergency required this inhumane sacrifice. No cause in the Middle East justified this shame to our nation.

In a speech at the Pentagon last fall, President George Bush said that he sent our forces to the Middle East in order to defend "our way of life." Sending moms to battle isn't the "way of life" for any Americans except feminists who are over military and childbearing age and haven't any daughters.

Who created the asinine rule that mothers of newborns are "fully deployable"? It surely wasn't Congress or the American people. The Pentagon made its own rule, and it is up to the Pentagon to dig itself out of this hole. U.S. law specifically excludes not just mothers but all women from military combat duty. When the Carter administration tried to repeal these laws, Congress held hearings and said to forget it.

But the feminists didn't give up, since combat duty has always been the cutting edge of their goal to transform America into a fully gender-neutral society. Militant feminists in the Pentagon, and in the tax-funded special-interest lobby called DACOWITS (Defense Advisory Committee on Women in the Services), nagged the military until so many "combat-related," "combat-support," and "combat-zone" positions were filled by women that the distinction became blurred.

The great and powerful U.S. military has been pretending there is no difference between men and women, even if they are mothers, and that giving birth to a baby is only a temporary disability, like breaking a leg. To carry on this pretense, official U.S. military policy has ignored common sense, family integrity, and American culture.

The deception appeared to be satisfactory in the peacetime military, when women were pursuing their career opportunities and upward social mobility, as the feminists like to say. But then along came a war with real bullets and, as summarized in a recent headline, "For women near the front lines, there's no such thing as non-combat duty."

The U.S. military deliberately chose to ignore the babies who are the chief victims of this silly pretense. It's embarrassing to see these big tough officers, with their chests full of medals, complaining, "Those women signed up voluntarily and filed forms stating that, in case they were deployed, they had arranged for a 'care provider' for the child left behind." It's now obvious that this procedure was a sham.

Twenty-year-old girls didn't comprehend how their world would change if a baby came into their lives and we had a shooting war at the same time. Older officers should have known better; yet they allowed those young women to live in the dreamworld of believing that having a baby is compatible with military service, and that military service has nothing to do with war.

One new mother ordered by our military to ship out for the Gulf said she felt she had to go because she made a commitment and "there are times when we're mothers and times when we're soldiers." As if they are equally important! The truth is that there is only one job in the world she can do better than anyone else, and that is to be a mother to her own baby. There are a million men in America who could do her job in the Gulf.

The men in the Pentagon and the armed services have brought this embarrassment on our nation because they allowed themselves to be henpecked by the militant feminists. The whole idea of men sending women, including mothers, out to fight the enemy is uncivilized, degrading, barbaric, and embarrassing. It's contrary to our culture, to our respect for men and women, and to our belief in the importance of the family and motherhood.

And furthermore, no one respects a man who would let a woman do his fighting for him.

1991

The Pregnancy Problem

The proposal to assign women to combat duty in the U.S. armed services is based on the feminist ideology that there isn't any difference between men and women—that men and women are fungible in all occupations, even in the most demanding, vicious, and dangerous occupation of military combat.

So, how does the military deal with the problem that women get pregnant and men do not? When a servicewoman gets pregnant, she is given the option of resigning immediately (escaping from the remainder of her term of enlistment) or having limited duty during pregnancy, receiving full medical benefits, receiving paid maternity leave ranging from six weeks to a couple of months, and promising to accept deployment then to anywhere in the world.

It costs $1 million, more or less, depending on the type of aircraft, to train a pilot in the U.S. armed services. When war comes and there is some nasty fighting to do, every female pilot would have the option to say: "Pardon me, fellas. I'm taking nine months off from flying in order to be pregnant, and then a couple of months more to recuperate. You guys go ahead and kill off the enemy, and I'll see you all in about a year."

All the female pilots won't get pregnant, but some of them will. Even if they promise, at the start of their training, not to get pregnant, some will change their minds. Based on actual experience since the sex integration of the armed services, about 10 percent of servicewomen are pregnant at any one time. The army's rate of discharge for pregnancy during Desert Shield and Desert Storm was four times the normal rate.

A few facts leaked out despite tight military news management. When the ship *Acadia* docked in San Diego, it had thirty-six pregnant crew members. When the *Yellowstone* docked, twenty of the crew were pregnant. The navy spokesman defensively protested, "These women have a right to get pregnant."

The columnist Jack Anderson reported from Saudi Arabia that doctors told him "their most frequent visitors were women asking for pregnancy tests because a positive result would be a ticket home."

This situation is not fair or just or equal. The life of a serviceperson in peacetime can be interesting, exciting, and productive. The life of a soldier in wartime can be nasty, dangerous, and fatal. Our all-volunteer army is voluntary when GI Joe and GI Jane sign up—but once they sign up, it's not supposed to be voluntary whether they take the wartime duty when it comes.

Repealing the combat-exclusion laws for women would give women expensive aircraft training in peacetime along with the choice to opt out (by pregnancy) when the nasty duty comes along. Of course, the men would get no such option.

The military women who appear on panels and on television to argue that pregnancy is not a problem are usually career women over child-bearing age with no children. Women eligible for combat assignment are in their prime childbearing years: eighteen to twenty-six years old.

There is no way out of this dilemma. We hear a constant refrain that times have changed and that public attitudes have changed. There is no change in the fact that young, healthy women are apt to get pregnant. Feminist ideology has not yet corrupted our thinking to the extent that the military would send a pregnant pilot up to engage in aerial dogfighting with the enemy.

Repealing the combat exclusion cannot by any stretch of the imagination be justified as "equal rights" or "an end to discrimination." Repealing the combat exclusion would be manifestly discriminatory against men and against those women who want to pursue a serious military career and do not become pregnant.

After a year of pregnancy and maternity leave, during which time the servicewoman receives full pay while others have been doing all or part of her work, we face the motherhood problem. Present military policy is based on the feminist notion that there isn't any difference between motherhood and fatherhood and that, after maternity leave, the new mother is fully deployable anywhere in the world. After all, she voluntarily enlisted, so she is supposed to make daycare arrangements for her baby.

It's ridiculous even to discuss women in combat until the military comes to grips with the pregnancy and motherhood questions. The present policies are contrary to combat readiness, common sense, and respect for family integrity.

1991

Affirmative Action in the Military

Repealing the combat exclusion laws so that women officers can fly planes in military combat would mean affirmative action quotas for women in an occupation in which they cannot compete equally with men. We know this would be the result because of the mountain of evidence that women are not performing equally with men in military service today.

We can thank the Virginia Military Institute (VMI) trial for providing us with proof of how affirmative action functions for female cadets at West Point. Those who sued VMI to force it to admit women and to feminize its curriculum called as their witness Colonel Patrick Toffler, a West Point spokesman, who was supposed to testify that sex integration is a success at the U.S. Military Academy. During five hours of cross examination under oath, he revealed a lot of things that West Point had heretofore concealed.

Colonel Toffler admitted that West Point does not require the same physical performance of female cadets that it requires of male cadets. He admitted that West Point has dual standards for males and females; that women cadets do not pass the same physical tests as the men; and that, if they perform the same task, the women are given higher grades. Female cadets are allowed to hold leadership positions based on their padded scores.

Colonel Toffler admitted that the training has been changed— "modified" he called it—to accommodate what the female cadets are physically capable of doing and so that they won't be "psychologically discouraged." For example, a number of events have been eliminated from the obstacle course "which require considerable upper-body strength," cadets now run in jogging shoes instead of in boots, a lighter-weight rifle has been substituted, judo is allowed to substitute for boxing, and the forced march carrying a heavy pack has been eliminated.

Colonel Toffler admitted that West Point has a sex-quota system for the admission of women cadets and for their assignment after graduation (for instance, to the engineers). "Those quotas have got to be met," he said. The women cadets do not compete with the men, but compete only against each other for designated female quota slots.

Colonel Toffler admitted that, to accommodate the women who cannot perform as well as the men, West Point has changed from equal training of all cadets to "comparable or equivalent training." This is the concept that, if men and women exert equivalent effort, they will be ranked as though they had achieved equal performance. Since women lack the arm strength to do pull-ups, they are required only to exert "comparable effort" to do a "flexed arm hang."

Colonel Toffler's sworn testimony proves that West Point has been engaged in a practice called "gender norming," that is, giving women higher grades on tests than men receive for similar achievement.

Colonel Toffler admitted that no free speech is permitted about the performance of women at West Point. Female cadets are allowed to correct their superiors who use such words as "chairman" instead of "chairperson," but men are not permitted to make any negative statement about women in the military. The *New York Times* reported on May 26 that it is a "career-killer" for a man to utter anything negative about the performance of women. Colonel Toffler even said that the cadets are given sensitivity training to help promote acceptance of the sex-integrated program.

1991

The *Myth of Israeli Women in Combat*

One of the feminists' false arguments used to promote repeal of the laws and regulations that exclude women from military combat duty is the assertion that women successfully fight alongside men in the Israeli army. This argument has been bolstered by pictures of Israeli female soldiers training with weapons and being taught to march and shoot.

This whole argument is a fabrication. Israel tried using women in combat in the war of 1948 but abandoned it as a bad idea and never tried it in subsequent wars. Israeli female soldiers are definitely not treated like male soldiers.

A dispatch from Jerusalem by a female reporter for the *Chicago Tribune* told it like it is, for the first time, in a metropolitan newspaper. The reality is not a gun-toting female soldier fighting alongside men, but "a bored eighteen-year-old in a stuffy office where the most exciting military task is making coffee for her male commanding officer."

Women are drafted in Israel, but men do three years of compulsory military service, while women serve only two years. Almost all men serve, but at least one-third of draft-age women receive exemptions, either because they are married or are strictly observant Jews. After active service, men spend at least one month a year on reserve duty, and in the last four years many have served two months a year. Women, except for nurses, are exempt from reserve duty.

Basic training is six months for men, only one month for women. Many say the women's training "is mostly a joke." One female soldier said, "It's a game that we imitate what the boys do, but it is irrelevant to what we do later. They teach you to shoot, take you out on marches, and then send you to be a secretary." The *Tribune* quoted one female officer saying, "A woman in the [Israeli] army is like a musician in an orchestra who is allowed to do everything but play. The army is super-sexist, and it can't be any different. The woman is always the helper."

Women are assigned to a separate Women's Corps, much like our WACs and the WAVES during World War II. The army apparently doesn't consider the Women's Corps essential: the chief of staff, General Ehud Barak, wants to eliminate it to cut the budget. More than one-third of Israeli military women work as secretaries.

The *Tribune*'s interviews discovered that "most Israelis of both sexes believe that women cannot take the pressures of war as well as men." One female soldier said, "We can't carry as much or stand up to the pressures and conditions. Whoever tells you we can, don't believe him."

She said that, at the end of her basic training, the then head of the Women's Corps told the female draftees, "The job of the woman is to bring spark and chic to the army. You should bring flowers into the office, smile and make sure your uniform is pressed." While some are not wholly pleased with the present procedures, the reporter found that "nobody suggests that women fight."

She found that "even those women who serve as instructors, then watch their trainees assume command of the tank or personnel carrier and go to war, say they would not want to fight even if the army changes its rules." One instructor said, "Sometimes I feel frustrated, but I thank God I don't have to be in a situation where I have to choose whether or not to hit a man."

The Israeli army is different from the U.S. Army in a fundamental way. In the United States, many people look on our armed services not as a commitment to go to war, but as a career opportunity offering upward social mobility. Join the service, see the world, get an education, and be all that you can be. The U.S. armed services have been pretending that they want to be an equal opportunity employer while concealing the double standards, female quotas and gender norming that have accompanied the buildup of women in the U.S. military to its approximate 10 percent figure today.

The current debate in Congress over repeal of the combat exclusion laws is a good time to expose the truth about the double standards applied to women and men in the U.S. armed services. The army test allows women three minutes more than men to do a two-mile run; men must do forty push-ups, women only sixteen. The navy test allows women three minutes more than men to do a 1.5-mile run; men must do twenty-nine push-ups, women only eleven. The Marine Corps requires men to do three pull-ups but doesn't require women to do any at all—just a sixteen-second flexed arm hang.

Israel can't afford the luxury of playing around with social experimentation, because it has the constant threat of war hanging over its head. Commenting on the sex-integration practices of the U.S. armed services, one Israeli general said, "We do not do what you do in the United States because, unfortunately, we have to take war seriously."

1991

Women Don't Belong in Combat

The issue is not whether women *can* be assigned to combat duty in the U.S. armed forces, but whether they *should* be. The question we should ask is not whether some women can perform admirably in many military situations (they can), but whether the U.S. armed services are going to rank fundamental American family values above the feminist goal of a sex-neutral society.

When we look back on the Gulf War, one of the images that are seared into our memory is that of tearful soldier-mothers saying goodbye to their two-month-old breast-feeding babies. That was a national embarrassment. How did this unnatural event happen? There was no shortage of able-bodied men to "man" those posts in the Middle East. Those unhappy cases were the result of a deliberate Pentagon policy to acquiesce in the feminist doctrine that men and women are fungible, that military assignments must be made without regard to the sex of the individual, and that the U.S. armed forces should be an instrument of social experimentation to demonstrate total sex equality.

This women-in-combat issue is not a new issue; it has been widely debated across America. It was the cutting edge of the ten-year constitutional battle that was waged across our country from 1972 to 1982 over the proposed amendment to the U. S. Constitution called the Equal Rights Amendment. ERA would have put a sex-neutral straitjacket on our society. It would have forced (among other things) precisely the result that is before you in this commission, namely, assigning women to combat.

The chief ERA theoretician, Yale Law School professor Thomas I. Emerson, laid down the official ERA line in a one-hundred-page, widely quoted article in the *Yale Law Journal* (April 1971). "As between brutal-izing our young men and brutalizing our young women," he wrote, "there is little to choose. . . .Women will serve in all kinds of units, and they will be eligible for combat duty." This military issue was the principal reason why ERA was defeated, despite immense support from impor-tant politicians and organizations, ample funding, and the universal clamor of the media.

Throughout many wars, our American culture has approved of a difference of treatment between young men and young women. Yet, all the feminist leaders without exception—and I debated scores of them—always said: Yes, women must be drafted and assigned to combat; that's what we want; that's equality! They could not sell the American people on that unnatural policy, and that's a major reason why ERA failed.

The feminists carried their demand to the U.S. Supreme Court in the 1981 case called *Rostker v. Goldberg*. The brief filed by the National Organization for Women labeled women's exemption from the mili-tary draft "blatant and harmful discrimination" and said it consigns women to a "second-class status."

The Supreme Court ruled in *Rostker v. Goldberg* that it is constitu-tional for Congress to exempt all women from the military draft and from draft registration because draft registration, conscription, and military combat are all one continuum. The Court based its decision on the fact that any military draft is for the purpose of raising combat troops. So, women can be constitutionally exempted from the draft and from draft registration *only* because they are *not* eligible for combat duty.

The Supreme Court specifically cited the statutory restrictions on the participation of women in combat in the navy and air force (10 U.S.C. 6015 and 8549) as the reason why girls are not required to be drafted.

There are many cultural, societal, family, pregnancy, and practical reasons why women should not be drafted. Women have more important things to do, such as taking care of their babies and keeping their families together. And, of course, women can serve as volunteers. But when the Supreme Court states that combat exclusion is the reason for exempting women, then that is the law of the land, and we must make our decisions in the light of that ruling.

This means that a decision to assign servicewomen to military combat does not affect volunteer servicewomen only. This decision is a life-threatening and a family-threatening danger to every girl who is draft age now or in the future. We have no crystal ball—we cannot know what the future holds in terms of war or a reinstated draft that could impose involuntary conscription on young women.

The women-in-combat decision must not be made on the basis of what is desired by volunteer servicewomen. It should be made for the welfare of the 99.8 percent of American women who have not chosen a military career. This includes women who believe that their family comes first, women who do not want to spend their childbearing years trying to do what the entire world has always considered man's work, and women who believe that mothering is more important than flying a plane or driving a tank.

American culture honors the obvious and eternal differences between men and women and expects them to be respected by the military. American women do expect their fathers, brothers, husbands, and sweethearts to defend them from the bad guys of the world, and American culture will not accept the image of men at home while women go off to fight the enemy.

Furthermore, we expect the military to adhere to a standard of honesty about the differences between male and female performance, rather than deceive the public through double standards, gender norming the tests, set-asides, and quotas, combined with intimidating allegations about "sexual harassment" against men who criticize these standards.

We hear the constant refrain that "times have changed," but there is no change whatsoever in obvious facts of human nature, such as that men and women differ in so many important ways, that healthy young women are apt to get pregnant, and that there is a profound difference between male-to-male bonding and male-to-female bonding—a factor that can make the difference between life and death on the battlefield. No matter what social changes are alleged to have taken place, the policies of our U.S. armed forces should respect the dignity and value of marriage and motherhood.

Women serve our country admirably, both on the home front and in many positions in the U.S. armed forces. But they should not be assigned to military combat.

Testimony to the Presidential Commission on the Assignment of Women in the Armed Forces, June 9, 1992.

1992

The Feminist Assault on V.M.I.

For a century and half, Virginia Military Institute (VMI) conducted a unique style of undergraduate education which graduates disciplined, honorable young men who are exemplary citizens and are ready to serve their country in time of war. It is a tough regimen that few men can endure and no women have ever tried. Ted Koppel called it "quaint," but the proof of VMI's value is the many thousands of good citizens and leaders it has graduated since 1839.

Those with common sense and experience with life can understand why women were not rushing to enroll in VMI. Most women don't like to be forced to keep their hair only one-fourth-inch long, to be called "Brother Rat," to be insulted and ordered around as VMI freshmen are, or to share common washrooms with a bunch of men. Most women don't like the lack of privacy involved in being forbidden to have a lock on your door or a curtain on your window, or having strangers enter your bedroom at any hour, day or night, or body contact sports.

You would think the Department of Justice would have enough to do, dealing with our nation's many legal and criminal problems, but on a slow day in 1990 Justice filed suit against Virginia Military Institute, charging "sex discrimination" because VMI does not admit women.

The purpose of this mischief-making lawsuit to force the all-male Virginia Military Institute to admit women wasn't about "ending sex discrimination" or "allowing women to have access to the same educational benefits that men have at VMI." It was a no-holds-barred fight to feminize VMI waged by the radical feminists and their allies in the federal government. The feminists just can't stand it that any institution in America would be permitted to train real men to manifest uniquely masculine attributes. Feminists want to gender neutralize society so they can intimidate and control men.

The feminists' longtime, self-proclaimed goal is an androgynous society. Repudiating constitutional intent, history, tradition, and human nature, they seek to forbid us, in public or private life, to recognize the differences between men and women.

Feminist strategy is straightforward: whine that women are victims of centuries of "oppression" and "stereotyping," lay a guilt trip on men, and use all the stereotypical cultural techniques that women have always used to wheedle what they want out of men. Then, use feminists on the public payroll in all three branches of government to change the laws in order to force us to conform.

So, the Supreme Court, speaking through Ruth Bader Ginsburg, ruled that it is unconstitutional for VMI to exclude women. The notion that a military institution that functioned with success, public acceptance, and significant prestige for 157 years, suddenly, one day in June 1996, could be rationally said to violate the Constitution is patently ridiculous. Black robes and Ginsburg's devious rhetoric about "scrutiny" can't make sense out of such judicial arrogance.

When VMI tried to comply and treat female cadets just like male cadets (which is what the feminists said they wanted before the Supreme Court decision), it turned out that equality wasn't what they wanted after all. Janet Reno's feminist Justice Department went to court to argue that failing to make adjustments for female recruits would amount to "discrimination" because it would discourage women from applying or lead them to drop out. Government lawyers argued that VMI must make far-reaching efforts to attract and retain female recruits and develop special training for them.

The VMI case is just one more example of the lies and double standards, the chicanery and hypocrisy, that are part and parcel of feminist strategy, tactics, and objectives.

1996

The Kelly Flinn Flimflam

Kelly Flinn, the first female B-52 pilot, was the air force's poster girl for the supposedly successful sex integration of the air force. She was the golden girl who "proved" that women in the military can "hold their own" with men. She was the answer to the Patricia Schroeder battalion in Congress who were demanding that women be put in combat jobs.

But Kelly blew it by indulging in adultery, perjury, and disobedience. She committed the particular kind of adultery (called fraternization) that cannot be tolerated in a military officer, namely, having sex with an enlisted man and then with the husband of an enlisted woman.

When the air force disciplined her, the media went into a feeding frenzy, allowing the feminists to portray her as a victim, and she became something of a feminist cause célèbre. Dick Morris, Bill Clinton's political consultant (who rose to notoriety and a lucrative book deal after a particularly gross adulterous relationship), predicted, "I think she may become a very significant feminist figure and spokesperson." Fortunately, his prediction has not come true.

The evidence against Kelly Flinn was so overwhelming that the air force had to press charges. She was not "singled out," but was treated highly preferentially compared to the sixty men whom the air force had court-martialed for adultery the previous year and the many male officers whose careers were destroyed for much lesser offenses.

The aggrieved spouse, Airman Gayla Zigo, explained in her letter to the secretary of the air force: "Less than a week after we arrived on the base, Kelly was in bed with my husband having sex. . . . In several occasions, I came home from work and found her at my house with Marc. While at my house, she was always in her flight suit flaunting the fact that she was an Academy graduate and the first female bomber pilot." Gayla's letter quoted Kelly as saying that "she wanted to settle down with someone." Gayla added, "I didn't know that that somebody was my husband."

The military is to blame for leading young women like Kelly to mistakenly believe they can do a man's job. Of course she can pilot a plane, but there's a lot more to being a military pilot than guiding the plane's controls. She tried to excuse herself on CBS's *60 Minutes* by saying, "I was only twenty-five years old and I was confused." Can we afford to have someone confused who pilots a B-52 carrying nuclear weapons?

Kelly's position required the emotional maturity and stamina to work at a base where her peers had wives but she did not. Kelly was lonesome. Her mother, whining about Kelly's predicament, said that the cad whom Kelly called her "first love" was "the first man who made her feel like a woman."

We have been endlessly told that women in the military can perform just like men. Now we learn that the top female bomber pilot really wanted to be treated like a woman. When the air force handed Kelly Flinn a written order to break off her relationship, she chose her lover over her spectacular career, telling the *New York Times*, "I figured at least I'd salvage my relationship with Marc [Zigo]."

Having lost their battle to save Kelly Flinn's air force career, the feminists then took revenge on air force general Joseph Ralston, who was nominated for chairman of the Joint Chiefs of Staff. To sabotage his appointment, the feminists dug up an old case of his adultery.

Ralston's case, however, was completely different from Kelly Flinn's (she was guilty of fraternization, disobedience, and perjury), but the difference was lost under the feminists' tirades. So we endured a public debate of several weeks on whether adultery should be a bar to promotion to high office.

Surveys of the media elite over the past decade have consistently shown that the nation's opinion makers do not believe that adultery is wrong. They would like to make it socially acceptable. The *New York Times*, for example, ridiculed the military's "antiquated adultery rules."

The Gallup Poll reports that 94 percent of Americans say adultery is wrong. The advocates of unfettered sexual activity are trying to paint those who affirm the standard of marital fidelity as hypocrites because the evidence shows "Americans do it anyway." But that doesn't mean they are hypocrites; it just means that they have sinned. Christians believe that man has a fallen nature and is prone to sin, and forgiveness starts with admitting you've done something wrong.

The sexual revolution that started in the 1960s hasn't lived up to its promise of freedom and fun forever. It has produced record rates of divorce, illegitimacy, social diseases, and messed-up lives. The culture war going on inside America has caused a great many casualties and will cause many more. Setting up a commission to write new morality rules for the military will only prolong the agony. The old rules are still valid. In the long run, there will be fewer casualties if the military leads the way to a restoration of duty, honor, and the sanctity of marriage.

1997

Can You Be All You Can Be?

The Pentagon is complaining that it's in a near crisis because recruitment numbers have taken a nosedive. The army and air force are falling far short of their targeted goals, while the navy is squeaking by only by lowering its standards and recruiting quotas. Our most experienced pilots are leaving in unprecedented numbers, and even large cash inducements cannot prevail on them to reenlist. The army is trying to entice young men to enlist by offering "signing bonuses" of thousands of dollars. That's on top of other bonuses including as much as $50,000 for college tuition. But raising the pay of our service personnel and buying them glitzier equipment won't remedy the problems.

The two major problems with the military today are (1) the assignment of U.S. military personnel to foreign conflicts that bear no relation to American national security and (2) the feminization of the military. Another problem for morale is the court-martialing of honorable servicemen for such offenses as refusing to wear a United Nations uniform or refusing to be "shot" with the experimental, controversial anthrax vaccine.

The Pentagon is blaming our affluent society, low unemployment, civilian career opportunities, the fact that the pool of young men age eighteen to twenty-two has declined, and particularly the drop in the number who have high school diplomas. The army is starting a program to pay thousands in this latter group to study for GEDs so they can qualify to enlist, which of course means that the taxpayers will pay a second time to teach recruits what they weren't taught in public schools.

Global cops and global social workers are not what the U.S. armed services are supposed to be, and Clinton's attempt to transform the mission of the military is a major reason for the falloff in recruitment and retention rates. Furthermore, contrary to administration propaganda, Clinton's peacekeeping expeditions were not nation building in Haiti, Somalia, or Bosnia, and they certainly were not humanitarian in Yugoslavia.

Secretary General Kofi Annan, in his speech this fall to the United Nations General Assembly, called for "a new commitment to intervention." His call to violate national sovereignty for phony "humanitarian" purposes flouts the UN and NATO charters, just as Clinton's war in Yugoslavia flouted the U.S. Constitution, which gives the war-making power to Congress not the President. We don't need high priced consultants and surveys to tell us why young Americans are not signing up. They don't want to serve in a foreign legion under foreign commanders for undefined and unconstitutional purposes.

House Military Personnel Subcommittee chairman Steve Buyer (R-IN) said it best: "We're fooling ourselves if we believe we can solve the problem with more GED programs or more money for ads. What we need is a change in foreign policy."

"Be All That You Can Be" was one of the most successful and memorable of all twentieth-century advertising slogans. Under the advice of consultants hired to refocus its $300 million recruitment advertising, the army is abandoning this famous slogan.

The army has ordered hundreds of new enlistees to go back to their hometown to persuade some of their old neighbors to sign up. When a *New York Times* reporter asked one of these new privates what his sales pitch is, he said he tells his old buddies that "it ain't so bad." Maybe the army will now be erecting billboards that read "Join the Army—It Ain't So Bad."

The Pentagon's new public relations consultants are supposed to research "the attitudes and habits of the young" in order to design new advertising. But the consultants are wasting their time if they start from the mind-set that our goal must be a gender-neutral military and that recruitment strategy must appeal equally to men and women.

A gender-neutral military is what the feminists have been demanding for twenty-five years, and now that the feminists are in the driver's seat of the Clinton Pentagon, we can see the folly of this goal. What the feminists really want is to give the orders, with the men cowed into submission.

Everybody with ordinary common sense knows that, under the Clinton Administration's social engineering in pursuit of a gender-neutral military, there is no way a serviceman can "be all that he can be." Coed basic training and the Pentagon's refusal to allow women to fail in tests for officer assignments mean that standards have been redefined and lowered to female achievement levels.

Gender-integrated basic training has resulted in lower standards, more injuries to women, more resentment among men, and scandalous examples of rape and sexual harassment. An official tax-funded survey found that 76 percent of male trainers and 74 percent of female trainers say that discipline has been hurt by gender-integrated training.

Real men will not be attracted to join an organization that invites them to be all that a woman can be. The 1992 Presidential Commission on the Assignment of Women in the Armed Forces found that, in the scoring of physical tests at the U.S. Naval Academy, a "B" grade for women in the 1.5 mile run is roughly equivalent to the "D" grade for men. The women's "A" grade in push-ups is the same as a "C" grade for men. In the field obstacle course, men jump over a wall two feet higher than women have to jump. That's called gender norming.

The purpose of the military is to defend Americans against the bad guys of the world. The warrior culture, with tough, all-male training, is what attracts young men into the armed services and motivates them to sacrifice personal comfort and safety while serving their country in uniform.

Dumbing down the physical and psychological requirements so that Clinton's political appointees and the medaled brass can continue to tell us that women and men are performing equally is destructive of morale for many reasons, not the least of which is that it is a lie.

Funny thing, the Marine Corps doesn't seem to suffer from these problems. It hasn't succumbed to mixed-gender basic training, and recruits of both sexes can realistically aspire to be all that they can be.

The Clintonistas' attack on morals is another personnel problem that is causing morale to suffer. This policy inflicted career-ending punishment on a serviceman with a superior record because he objected to spending forty-eight hours secluded with a female not his wife.

At Minot Air Force Base, North Dakota, the practice is to send two officers down to the base of the missile silo, where they spend twenty-four to forty-eight hours secluded in a space about the size of a school bus, with one bed and one bathroom behind a curtain. The Minot missile force has 250 men and eighty-three women, resulting in the high probability of mixed-gender two-person crews.

Lieutenant Ryan Berry, a married Catholic, objected to being so cozy for so long with a woman not his wife. He was punished by his commanding officer, who spouted the feminist mantra that equal opportunity is the air force's top priority. Lieutenant Berry's case proves that equal opportunity for women requires indiscriminate assignment that flouts common sense, the realities of human nature, the dignity of marriage, and respect for the wives at home.

1999

Women Don't Belong on Submarines

The Defense Advisory Committee on Women in the Services (DACO-WITS), a tax-funded civilian feminist lobby group that tries to set Pentagon policy, has been pushing for years to get women assigned to duty on submarines. Women on subs is a terrible idea. The navy's highest-ranking admirals are strongly opposed, but the powerful feminists in the Clinton Administration are trying to get their way by executive order.

This would be grossly unfair to submariners, whose undersea life is difficult enough. Picture, if you can, 130 people living together for six months at a time in the space of a medium-sized house. Submariners patrol the oceans in cramped quarters that lack fresh air, sunshine, and privacy. Sleeping areas and sanitary facilities are one-half to one-third smaller than surface ships, well below requirements for the other Navy ships. Each shower serves fifty enlisted submariners, compared to twenty-five on surface ships. About 40 percent of the crew must "hot bunk," meaning three sailors share two bunks in rotating shifts. Junior crew members frequently sleep on mattresses in noisy torpedo rooms.

The ship alterations necessary to accommodate women on subs would further reduce living standards or, alternatively, make it necessary to remove operational equipment. These millions of dollars would be spent just to please the civilian feminists in the Pentagon, not to improve readiness or morale.

Female sailors of childbearing age would face particular medical risks on submarines. Air in a submarine is constantly recycled and trace elements in the atmosphere, such as carbon monoxide, cannot be filtered out. Such elements are reasonably safe for adults, but toxic for an unborn child.

Faced with a pregnant sailor who fears irreversible birth defects, a submarine captain would have to choose between two unacceptable alternatives: exposing the unborn child to toxic elements at a time of greatest risk or compromising the secret mission by revealing the submarine's location. Mid-ocean evacuations, accomplished by means of a basket dangling from a helicopter, are dangerous for all concerned.

The tragic loss of Russia's *Kursk* reminds the world that submariners operate in an extremely hazardous environment more unforgiving than outer space. A submarine is no place for feminist experiments or civilian-mandated compromises that endanger innocent lives.

The push for women in combat roles in the U.S. armed services is a fantasy of the feminists who dream of armchair female generals running the Pentagon. This push is coming only from the female officers who seek their career advancement at the expense of the enlisted women who would get the heavy and dangerous work without any of the glamour of piloting planes. Repealing the combat exclusion laws would betray the enlisted women because they signed up when the law assured them they would be excluded from combat.

A 1997 RAND study called *Recent Gender Integration in the Military: Effects Upon Readiness, Cohesion and Morale* found that 79 percent of army enlisted women and 71 percent of female noncommissioned officers oppose serving in combat. Only 10 percent of female privates and corporals said that the army should treat women exactly like men. Professor Charles Moskos of Northwestern University interviewed scores of women who served in the Panama invasion, and he didn't find any enlisted women who favor repeal of the combat exclusion laws.

2000

The Special-Interest Lobby Called DACOWITS

The media are having a field day criticizing the lobbyists for Enron, but they are overlooking the most effective special-interest lobbyists ever to function in Washington. They have met with high-ranking administration officials, they directly influenced (some would say dictated) important national security policies, and they swaggered with the protocol rank of three-star generals.

They have been impudent to their critics, secretive with the media, high-handed in their demands, and dishonest in maintaining their power. Who else would have the chutzpa to surreptitiously use defense secretary Donald Rumsfeld's automatic signature pen to sign the confirmation papers of their pals selected by former defense secretary Bill Cohen before Bill Clinton left office?

If you figured out that these special-interest lobbyists are the radical feminists manning (excuse the expression) the ramparts of political correctness, you are correct. We are talking about members of the Defense Advisory Committee on Women in the Services (DACOWITS), a tax-funded lobby that has provided the radical feminists a platform to lobby to make the U.S. armed services gender neutral.

DACOWITS has demanded that women be assigned to submarines, to the crews of Multiple Launch Rocket Systems (the vehicles that launch rockets during land-combat operations), to the helicopter crews of special operations units such as the Army Rangers, and even to land combat units that directly engage the enemy.

Such policies, if ever adopted, would compromise training standards, weaken morale, worsen deployment problems, hurt recruiting and retention, and endanger the lives of the men who would have to depend on female soldiers to carry their share of the load. Such policies ignore the fact that only about 3 percent of women score as well as the average man on the Physical Fitness Test, and most women can't throw a hand grenade far enough away to keep from killing themselves.

The golden era of DACOWITS's fifty years of promoting social experimentation in the U.S. military was, of course, the pro-feminist Clinton Administration. No DACOWITS recommendation was too extreme for the Bill and Hillary White House, whose Pentagon appointee, Assistant Secretary of the Army Sara Lister, attacked the marines as "extremist." Members of DACOWITS appointed by Bill Clinton voted thirty-three to zero to demand feminist policies in the military that are opposed by combat experts.

The feminists co-opted U.S. Representative Heather Wilson (R-NM) to plead their case to Pentagon officials. In a meeting with Paul Wolfowitz, she claimed that women in the service "need to have a voice that is outside the chain of command." That argument is a fraud. DACOWITS is not a voice for "women" in the service: it's a voice only for women officers who ride roughshod over the concerns of enlisted women, the overwhelming majority of whom do not want to be assigned to military combat.

Get your hanky out to cry for the two examples Representative Wilson gave Wolfowitz of how DACOWITS is needed to help servicewomen. DACOWITS made sure that women's hygiene products are available at base stores, and DACOWITS corrected the "problem" that female pilots who gave birth to new babies were not allowed back into the cockpit as fast as women who took other types of medical leave. And DACOWITS insists that the army have an adequate supply of maternity uniforms.

DACOWITS's goal has always been careerism for female officers at the expense of combat readiness. Now that a real war is going on, this is no time to try to appease the unappeasable Clinton feminists in their perennial pursuit of an androgynous military.

The Bush administration is to be commended for allowing the old DACOWITS charter to expire on February 28, 2002, firing twenty-two Clinton administration holdovers and an even larger number of staff members, and reconstituting DACOWITS' duties under a more limited charter.

2002

V

Marriage and Motherhood

O mistress mine, where are you roaming?
O stay and hear, your true love's coming,
    That can sing both high and low.
    Trip no further, pretty sweeting.
    Journeys end in lovers meeting,
    Every wise man's son doth know.

Twelfth Night

Choosing a Career

Marriage and motherhood have always been the number-one career choice of the large majority of women. Do they still make a viable career for the modern woman? Do they represent servitude or fulfillment? Are they, as the women's liberation movement would have us believe, a relic from a bygone era, the institutionalized serfdom from which women must he freed if they are to find their own identity and self-fulfillment?

What is it that the women's liberation movement invites women to be liberated from? An objective reading of feminist literature compels the conclusion that the answer must be marriage, home, husband, family, and children—because, by definition, those are all evidences of the "second-class status" of women. Feminist literature paints marriage as slavery, the home (in Betty Friedan's words) as a "comfortable concentration camp," the husband as the oppressor, the family as an anachronism no longer relevant to woman's happiness, and children as the daily drudgery from which the modern woman must be freed in order to pursue more fulfilling careers.

Long before women's lib came along and made "housewife" a term of derision, it had its own unique dignity. The 1933 edition of the *Oxford English Dictionary* defined a housewife as "a woman (usually, a married woman) who manages or directs the affairs of her household; the mistress of a family; the wife of a householder. Often (with qualifying words), a woman who manages her household with skill and thrift, a domestic economist." A housewife is a home executive: planning, organizing, leading, coordinating, and controlling. She can set her own schedule and standards and have the freedom to engage in everything from children to civic work, from politics to gardening. What man on a job can do that? Marriage and motherhood are not for every woman, but before a young woman rejects it out of hand, she should give it fair consideration as one of her options.

What does a woman want out of life? If you want to love and be loved, marriage offers the best opportunity to achieve your goal. Men may want, or think they want, a cafeteria selection of lunch-counter sex. But most women continue to want what the old popular song calls "a Sunday kind of love." Marriage and motherhood give a woman new identity and the opportunity for all-round fulfillment as a woman.

Israeli premier Golda Meir was the outstanding career woman of her time. She achieved more in a man's world than any woman in any country—and she did it on ability, not on her looks or her legs. The Gallup Poll repeatedly identified her as the most admired woman in the world. Yet Golda Meir said that having a baby is the most fulfilling thing a woman can ever do, and she put down the women's liberationists as a bunch of "bra-burning nuts."

If young women think that there are greater career satisfactions in being elected to important positions, traveling to exciting faraway places, having executive authority over large numbers of people, winning a big lawsuit, or earning a financial fortune than there are in having a baby, they are wrong. None of those measures of career success can compare with the thrill, satisfaction, and fun of having and caring for babies and watching them respond and grow under a mother's loving care.

The joys of motherhood return late in life when grandchildren appear. Most feminist leaders, including Gloria Steinem, Germaine Greer, Kate Millett, and Simone de Beauvoir chose to be childless and will never know the thrill of being "born again" with grandchildren.

Amelia Earhart has been a longtime heroine of feminists because she lived such an independent and exciting life. Yet when her true story was dramatized on national television in October 1976, she was shown cuddling another woman's baby—and wishing it were her own.

One of the most successful writers of the twentieth century was Taylor Caldwell. When *Family Weekly* asked her if it didn't give her solid satisfaction to know that her novel *Captains and Kings* was to be seen as a nine-hour television production, she replied: "There is no solid satisfaction in any career for a woman like myself. There is no home, no true freedom, no hope, no joy, no expectation for tomorrow, no contentment. I would rather cook a meal for a man and bring him his slippers and feel myself in the protection of his arms than have all the citations and awards and honors I have received worldwide, including the Ribbon of the Legion of Honor and my property and my bank accounts."

Anne Morrow Lindbergh spoke for the majority of women when she described her own priorities in *Hour of Gold, Hour of Lead*: "The sheer fact of finding myself loved was unbelievable and changed my world, my feelings about life and myself. I was given confidence, strength, and almost a new character. The man I was to marry believed in me and what I could do, and consequently, I found I could do more than I realized, even in that mysterious outer world that fascinated me but seemed unattainable. He opened the door to 'real life.' . . . The first months of motherhood were totally normal, joyful, and satisfying and I would have been content to stay home and do nothing else but care for my baby. This was 'real life' at its most basic level."

Marriage and motherhood have their trials and tribulations, but what lifestyle doesn't? If you look upon your home as a cage, you will find yourself just as imprisoned in an office or a factory. The flight from the home is a flight from self, from responsibility, from the nature of woman, in pursuit of false hopes and fading fantasies.

If you complain about servitude to a husband, servitude to a boss will be more intolerable. Everyone in the world has a boss of some kind. It is easier for most women to achieve a harmonious working relationship with a husband than with a foreman, supervisor, or office manager.

That American women have always been fortunate was confirmed more than 150 years ago by the famous French commentator Alexis de

Tocqueville: "Although the women of the United States are confined within the narrow circle of domestic life, and their situation is in some respects one of extreme dependence, I have nowhere seen woman occupying a loftier position; and if I were asked, now that I am drawing to the close of this work, in which I have spoken of so many important things done by the Americans, to what the singular prosperity and growing strength of that people ought mainly to be attributed, I should reply: to the superiority of their women."

1977

The Cinderella Complex

The passing of Princess Grace was the occasion of hundreds of news stories and features, as well as the picture on the cover of *Time* magazine. Many of the stories (intentionally or unintentionally) conveyed the subliminal message that her life was "the last fairy tale," that her love story was unique and could never happen again.

The reason for those cynical undertones was that Princess Grace was the modern personification of the Cinderella fairy tale, which for years has been a despised target of the women's liberation movement. Princess Grace's very existence proved that an American Cinderella can marry her Prince Charming, move to his palace on the hill, and live happily ever after.

When the women's liberation movement held sway in the 1970s, one of the quirks of its ideology was a passionate debunking of the Cinderella fairy tale. That harmless children's story became a bête noire of the women's liberation movement; it was labeled a stereotype of women's oppression which must be censored out of children's books.

Feminist ideologues inveighed against the "myth" and "delusion" of Cinderella because it encouraged little girls to believe that a Prince

Charming could come along and that they would live happily ever after. Cinderella was decried as the ultimate in "sexist" childrearing.

The publication of the 1981 book *The Cinderella Complex* by Colette Dowling sent shock waves through the women's liberation movement. Written by a feminist, the author argued regretfully that most women do have a secret desire to depend on a husband who will support and defend his wife.

One day while I was in a television studio, a young woman producer accosted me with the question, "Mrs. Schlafly, do you believe in the thesis of the book *Cinderella Complex?*" I said, "Yes, I think most women would like to marry a man who will support and defend her." She replied, "I'm afraid you're right. But I'm trying to overcome that feeling."

Since the young woman was in her twenties and nice looking, I told her she didn't really need to try to overcome her Cinderella complex—her Prince Charming just might come along some day. Her heart told her I was right, but her liberated mind refused to accept it.

One thing is sure. If you make up your mind that you will never find your Prince Charming, you won't. If you decide in advance that it is impossible to live happily ever after, you won't. But it all can happen to you if you make up your mind that it can happen. I know—because it happened to me.

I found my Prince Charming in a small law office in a little town of forty thousand people in downstate Illinois, and lived happily ever after on the bluffs of the Mississippi River. Millions of other women have found their Prince Charmings in even less likely places. They have lived happily ever after because they worked to make their marriages succeed.

Princess Grace was the glamorous personification of the Cinderella fairy tale because (unlike some other Hollywood "queens") she remained true to her marriage vows. I never understood why Grace Kelly would choose European royalty when she could have had a fine American man who could have built a splendid business or professional career; but love conquers all, and to each her own.

The lesson is that happy, enduring marriages do still happen despite great obstacles of circumstances and liberation propaganda. Other women are not as beautiful as Grace Kelly, their Prince Charmings are not as rich, and their homes do not have as many rooms as a Monaco palace. But their love is just as enduring, their lives as fulfilling, and they do live happily "until death do us part."

We are indebted to Grace Kelly for providing a role model who proved on the world stage that a modern, talented woman can find fulfillment forever as a wife and mother in a traditional family.

1982

Where Have All the Mothers Gone?

Not so many mothers are at home in the afternoon any more. Those who are at home are usually "moms" to latchkey children, too. Confronted with the prospect of going home to an empty house, children will usually, if they can, gravitate to the home of a schoolmate whose mother is at home.

Indeed, so-called experts are now instructing latchkey children to do exactly that. In a latchkey course for nine-to-thirteen-year-olds, pupils are given a multiple-choice question. "You are walking home alone from school and you think a man in a car is following you. What would you do? (a) Stand still and see what he does. (b) Walk quickly home and lock yourself in the house. (c) Walk to a neighbor's home and stay there. (d) Other." The correct answer is (c), because "if you go home and lock yourself in the house, you could be followed, and there might not be anyone there to help you."

Brenda Hunter, author of *Where Have All The Mothers Gone?*, eloquently described her life as a latchkey child. "No matter how sunny the atmosphere outside, an empty house is always cold and dark and lonely. I always made a check under the bed and looked in the closets to make sure that no burglar had entered our home."

The liberated lifestyles that encourage wives and mothers to do their own thing have left children to bear burdens of loneliness, depression, and the empty home. Latchkey children are crying out for the love of moms who will subordinate their own career ambitions and desire for material things to the well-being of their children.

The U.S. Census Bureau published some interesting figures that cast light on changing socioeconomic trends and provide evidence that millions of mothers still accord a higher priority to giving mother care to their children than to material things. A special report called "Earnings in 1981 of Married-Couple Families" provides statistics on the intact family where a husband and wife are living together, which is the big majority of the American people. There are 49.6 million married couples (ninety-nine million Americans). The study did not cover the situation of the single-parent family.

Considering only the 42.2 million married couples where at least one spouse is employed, the Census Bureau figures show a vast difference in standard of living between one-paycheck families (husband-breadwinner and wife-homemaker) and two-paycheck families. In the fourteen million traditional families in which the husband is employed but the wife is not, the average earnings are $22,300.

But in the 26.3 million families where both the husband and wife are in the paid labor force, the average earnings are $28,560, and that figure shoots up to $34,560 if both spouses are employed full-time. These figures show that married couples where the wife is a full-time homemaker are living at a significantly lower income level. The disparity in standard of living is probably even greater than these figures indicate, since full-time homemakers often have more children than women who are in the labor force.

The national media and feminist spokespersons have put forth an incessant drumbeat to persuade Americans that, in this day and age, mothers "must work" and that the government "should" facilitate that lifestyle by providing daycare facilities. The Census Bureau report shows, however, that fourteen million mothers have rejected that notion and chosen the traditional role of motherhood even though it means living at a lower income level.

Millions of wives today are economizing and stretching every dollar in order to feed and clothe their families on the husband's single income so that their children can have something more precious than money can buy: the emotional security of mom at home. That's the kind of dedication to the role of motherhood that should be encouraged, not discouraged, by our tax laws and social legislation.

Yet, the federal income tax law gives preferential treatment amounting to several thousand dollars a year to the wife who chooses the paid job instead of the role of full-time mother. That's why the first step in addressing the problems of latchkey children is to give the full-time wife equality in the income tax law with the wife in the paid labor force.

1985

Big Brother Wants to Be Big Mama

"Early childhood education" is a phrase frequently heard at state capitols and education seminars. In the face of mounting public, private, and employer dismay at the failure of public elementary schools to teach children the skills and knowledge necessary to function in a modern society, the education bureaucracy is responding with the collective call, "Give us your children at an even earlier age."

"Early" means school for three- and four-year-olds. The plan is to make it voluntary today but compulsory tomorrow; start in the ghetto, then extend it. One bill introduced in the Illinois legislature even called for schools to take children "from birth to kindergarten."

"Early childhood education" was quietly inserted in the fine print of many comprehensive "education reform" packages considered in 1985, and these proposals are still very much alive. The education bureaucracy wants to get legislation in place before the American people realize what is happening, especially since there is no evidence to support this expensive and revolutionary plan of action.

Absolutely no replicable evidence shows that putting children in school at an earlier age makes them brighter, or better able to achieve academically, or better able to socialize positively with their peers as they move along in school. The evidence indicates that it saddles tots with burnout, stress, and frustrations that inhibit later learning.

The American Academy of Pediatricians has expressed concern about the dramatic increase of "stress-related" symptoms now apparent in children in the primary grades. Some schools have put in "stress" courses for first and second graders!

Tufts University learning psychologist David Elkind warns that early formal schooling is "burning out" our children. University of California's William Rohwer urges that formal schooling wait until much later. After extensive research, Dr. Rohwer concluded, "All of the learning necessary for success in high school can be accomplished in only two or three years of formal skill study."

All the learning that takes place in the first grade consumes a maximum of two hours per day. What do the children do the rest of the day in school? They learn the bad habits of their peers and catch their germs. Some recent findings show that children who attend preschool are fifteen times more likely to be sick as children at home, and fifteen times more likely to get involved in negative, aggressive acts.

Enormous evidence shows that children who spend more time with their peers than with their parents before the fifth or sixth grade will become peer dependent. They learn to knuckle under to the rivalry, ridicule, habits, manners, and values of their classmates. They are negatively socialized and become captives of social and moral trends.

Dr. Raymond Moore, nationally known advocate of not putting children in school before age eight, explains what often happens to an average child put in school too early: (a) uncertainty as he leaves the family nest for a less secure environment, (b) puzzlement at the new pressures and restrictions of the classroom, (c) frustration because his brain's learning tools cannot handle the scheduled, formal lessons and pressures, (d) nervousness, jitters, and hyperactivity that are caused by frustration, (e) failure, and (f) delinquency.

The adverse effect is far worse on the boys than the girls. The "system" requires boys to enter school at the same age as girls, even though they mature later. The entry of boys into kindergarten and first grade at the same age as girls means that many times more boys than girls will fail or become hyperactive or delinquent. In American high schools today, there are eight boys for every girl in classes for the emotionally impaired, and thirteen boys for each girl in remedial learning groups.

Early childhood education would vastly increase the harm to most children and give the boys a nearly insurmountable disadvantage. Washington state senator Sam Guess, a miller, provides an analogy appropriate to early childhood education: "When you grind green grain, you don't get flour. You get gum."

1986

A Long Leap into the Dark

Before Jimmy Carter chose his vice president in 1976, Walter Mondale was best known outside of his own state of Minnesota as co-author of the 1971 Mondale-Brademas Child Development Bill. That bill would have created a $2 billion network of federal daycare institutions for "comprehensive child development," not only custodial, purposes.

Senator Walter Mondale (D-MN) and Representative John Brademas (D-IN) told their constituents that this bill was based on the recommendation of the 1970 White House Conference on Children that "federally supported public education be made available for children at age three." The conference explained that "Day care is a powerful institution. A day care program that ministers to a child from six months to six years of age has over 8,000 hours to teach him values, fears, beliefs, and behaviors."

The Mondale-Brademas bill passed Congress under pressure from liberals and feminists, but was vetoed by President Richard Nixon. In a courageous veto message, he called it a "radical piece of legislation," "a long leap into the dark," and said it would "lead toward altering the family relationship." He said, "Good public policy requires that we enhance rather than diminish both parental authority and parental involvement with children—particularly in those decisive years when social attitudes and a conscience are formed, and religious and moral principles are first inculcated."

In 1975, Mondale and Brademas tried again to get the federal government to take over the task of raising children. Their Child and Family Services Bill of 1975 would have created a new philosophy of child rearing. The bill stated that "it is essential" that child rearing be done by a "partnership" of federal, state and local governments, parents, and community agencies.

The Child and Family Services Bill redefined "parent" as "any person who has primary day-to-day responsibility for any child." That language would have transferred the rights of fathers and mothers to federal bureaucrats, social workers, or teachers who have supervision over the children put in their care.

The *New York Times* reported that the 1975 Child and Family Services Bill was "considered by educational groups to be the opening wedge in their attempt to establish a universal education program beginning with 3-year-olds." The same news report explained that this program was supported by both the National Education Association (NEA) and the American Federation of Teachers (AFT) as "the first step toward

opening the nation's public schools to millions of additional children."
The *Times* news account, written on the occasion of a national AFT
convention in Honolulu, explained that the placement of three- and
four-year-old children in public schools "is viewed not only as a vehicle
to help teachers in a shrinking job market, but also [because] a substan-
tial portion of intelligence is permanently shaped before a child enters
kindergarten."

So there are two reasons powerful forces want to push little children into government institutions at the age of three and make the
government a "partner" in raising children: (a) to mold the "values, fears,
beliefs, and behaviors" of the children, and (b) to find jobs for unemployed teachers.

This 1975 bill was killed by a tremendous uproar at the grassroots
and an avalanche of letters to Congress. The resentment against the
Child and Family Services Bill lingered until 1980, when Mondale was
defeated in his bid for reelection as vice president and Brademas was
defeated in his bid for reelection to Congress.

A reincarnation of this same discredited proposal, called the School
Facilities Child Care Act, passed the House in May 1984 with only a
handful of congressmen on the floor. The sponsor was Representative
Geraldine Ferraro (D-NY), along with other liberals including Patricia
Schroeder (D-CO).

The Ferraro bill would have authorized $30 million per year for three
years to help community groups, local government agencies, and edu-
cators set up before- and after-school child-care programs, preferably
in the public schools. Mondale and Ferraro were hoping that public
sentiment had changed by 1984, that Americans would more easily accept the notion that childcare is not an individual or a family problem
or responsibility, but that children are a collective responsibility to be
assumed by the federal government. They were also hoping that their
federal goal could be realized by playing on the economics of the increasing percentage of mothers in the labor force and on public con-

cern about the problem called "latchkey children." Fortunately, the Mondale-Brademas-Ferraro plans failed. Most parents want to be more than mere part-time custodians of their own children in a "partnership" with the government.

The demand for the government to warehouse children isn't going away. Large numbers of women have changed their lifestyle and moved into the paid labor force, and babies are inconvenient to job schedules. But babies have stubbornly refused to change their lifestyle and adapt to an empty house. They are just as demanding as babies ever were.

When mothers look about for someone else to fulfill those demands, they find that daycare services bought for money are very expensive. The chief reason for the enormous expense is that, whereas a teacher of grade-schoolers can handle a class of twenty-five children, a care provider for preschoolers can effectively handle only three children on the average, and only two if they are infants.

Employed mothers don't want to pay the high cost of employing other persons to provide the care that the children are not getting at home. The mothers want it free or at least heavily subsidized. They want the real cost of daycare to be borne by the taxpayers or their fellow employees.

Nothing could be more unjust. Children are the moral and financial responsibility of their parents. It is grievously unfair to impose a tax burden on those who fulfill this responsibility in order to subsidize those who have chosen a lifestyle that shifts this responsibility to someone else. This means taking from lower-income traditional families who care for their own children and giving to higher income two-earner couples who don't care for their own children.

Society simply has not invented a better way of raising children than the traditional family with a father-breadwinner and a mother-home-maker. That division of labor is cost efficient, the environment is healthy, and the children thrive on the "object constancy" of the mother.

1986

The Two-Class American Society

Is the traditional family an anachronism in the 1980s? That seems to be the assumption of television and radio talk shows, lecture platforms, lifestyle sections of metropolitan newspapers, magazines, the theater and movies, public opinion surveys, and all the channels that report socio-cultural trends. This dreary message is beamed at the public, overtly and subliminally, in a thousand ways every week.

The economic side of this message is that all wives will soon be out of the home and in the paid labor force and that this trend is not only an economic necessity but a social good. We are incessantly told that a single-earner couple cannot support a family, that mothers "have to work" in order to support their families, and that the wife in the home is as extinct as the dodo.

What is presumptuously called "the women's movement" has sup-posedly "liberated" women from the drudgery of housework and given women new opportunities for careers in the paid labor force, especially in non-traditional (formerly all-male) occupations (from astronaut to coal miner).

The social side of this message is that sexual liberation has perma-nently changed moral attitudes, made every sexual activity socially re-spectable, and redefined the family to include any group of persons living together even if not related by blood, marriage, or adoption. "Alternate lifestyles" are now supposedly acceptable, including serial marriage (fre-quent changing of partners through multiple divorces), cohabitation without marriage, and homosexual and lesbian couples. Premarital sex among teenagers is asserted to be a permanent fact of life. We are not supposed to be judgmental about this but instead should free it from guilt and pregnancy by making contraceptives and abortions available without parental knowledge or consent.

Everybody, we are told, will probably be divorced at some time in life. "Single parenthood" is the modern style family. Divorce on demand must be available to any spouse without the consent of the other. Abortion on demand should be available to any woman without the consent of her spouse (or parent, if a minor).

Taxpayers are supposed to pay the financial costs of all these policies, including daycare for mothers who prefer to be in the paid labor force, separate housing and generous money payments to teenagers who have illegitimate babies, tax-paid abortions, and a variety of costly benefits to divorced wives whose husbands have been allowed to evade their support obligations.

We have the freedom to choose our own values and goals. But the frequency and intensity (often combined with ridicule and sarcasm) with which media spokespersons try to thrust these anti-family attitudes down our throats indicate their emotional demand for social acceptance of these changes in values. They seem determined to make those who live by traditional moral standards feel out of step with the times. These anti-family attitudes have established themselves as dominant in the fantasy world of communications, but they have not succeeded in the real world.

The majority of Americans still consider marriage a lifetime commitment, in sickness and in health, for richer and for poorer. They look upon marriage as the beginning of a new family in which children will bear their father's name and are entitled to faithful nurturing by their mother. A recent survey shows that among couples who marry in church and continue to attend church regularly, the divorce rate is only one in fifty.

America has become a two-class society. The class division has nothing whatsoever to do with level of income or education or job status or talent or sex or race or color or advantage of birth. It has everything to do with whether or not you have a commitment (1) to moral values (respect for God, church or synagogue, and the Ten Command-ments), (2) to family values (marital fidelity, mother care of children, and parental rights in education), and (3) to the work ethic (thrift, savings, and the right to enjoy the fruits of one's labor and improve one's economic lot in life).

The Americans who share these traditional commitments have little voice in the channels of communication today. But these Americans exist, and the more the media claim they are obsolete, the more the media lose credibility.

1986

Understanding Men

Why can't the wife pursue a career and the husband take care of the house and babies? That is one of the questions I am most frequently asked by young women when I visit college campuses. My stock answer never pleases them. "You don't have to get my permission," I reply. "All you need to do is to find a young man who wants that kind of marriage. My observation of life is that very few men are willing to play that role."

Those who seek the substantive answer to that question, or the answer to the question of why so many college women ask such a silly question, should read the book called *Men and Marriage* by George Gilder, author of the best-selling defense of private enterprise called *Wealth and Poverty*. Gilder's book also provides answers to the question I am most often asked by college men. "Why, when young women seem totally bent on a career and independence from men, is 'money . . . a good job . . . a promising career' still the first quality they look for in a man they might want to marry?" Young women say they want men to be "sensitive" and "compassionate" and share in the diapers and dishes, but most of all they want a husband to have a good income. All the Phil

Donahue-attributes he can muster will not compensate for failing to fill the role of provider.

Men and Marriage is unique; no other book addresses such fundamental questions as why men marry and why society depends on the natural and different roles of men and women—in marriage, in the family, and in society. For the past two decades, the fad of feminism has taught the falsehood that men and women, husbands and wives, fathers and mothers, are interchangeable. Gilder proves, with a wealth of sociological detail, that this is so much nonsense. Men and women have different natures, different purposes, and different functions. Civilization depends on understanding and respecting those differences.

Gilder's book is enlivened with a couple of allegories. One explains why men marry—and what often happens to them, and to society, when they don't. Another explains why the biggest profiteer of women's liberation is the successful middle-aged man who now can, without shame, put his faithful wife out to pasture and enjoy the favors of a new wife in her youthful, fertile years. The women's liberation movement has had a profound effect on our society. It has produced a high divorce rate, twenty million abortions, much androgynous mischief, and social acceptance of promiscuity and non-marital lifestyles for women and men.

The U.S. Census Bureau reported this year that 7,500,000 fathers have vanished. That's a disaster far in excess of all the battle deaths in World War II (292,131), in the Korean War (33,629), and in the Vietnam War (47,318) combined. One-fourth of American families with children are horribly disadvantaged because they have no father in the home. No amount of taxpayers' money can ever compensate for this personal and societal tragedy. Did a foreign enemy steal into our cities at night and slaughter the fathers? No, women's liberation and sexual liberation stole into the minds and hearts of a generation and "liberated" millions of men and women from marriage and its responsibilities.

Women's liberation taught young women to seek fulfillment in paid employment instead of as wives and mothers. Sexual liberation taught men and women to seek temporary pleasures instead of a monogamous, lifetime commitment. Liberation advocates forgot to warn what an awful price would be paid by the children.

Men and Marriage explains the successful relationship between a man and a woman, that wonderful nexus of mystery and intimacy, of romance and practicality. *Men and Marriage* shows why traditional marriage is essential to a stable society. The next time people suggest that it is important for young people to be taught the facts of life, tell them to learn the facts of life as taught so powerfully in George Gilder's book. It's must reading especially for young women because it explains why men are the way they are.

1986

More Work, Less Income

One of the social phenomena of the last generation is the movement of wives and mothers from the home into the paid labor force. When a wife leaves the home to take paid employment, this appears to produce more take-home pay for the family. But research shows that, in the current generation of two-earner couples with children, both spouses together now have less real income than their fathers had as a single wage-earner (when their mothers were full-time homemakers). The current generation of parents is working longer hours for less real income and much less family life than their parents had.

Despite the fact that the United States has been experiencing growth in all economic indicators for the last three years, an analysis of the economic status of the baby boomers by Phillip Longman, research director for Americans for Generational Equity, based on Census Bureau statistics, produces some disturbing conclusions. They are the first generation in history not to do better than their parents. The baby boomers are the seventy-eight million Americans who were born be-tween 1946 and 1964, a period when the U.S. birth rate shot up sharply.

Some demographers and statisticians look upon 1973 as the water-shed year when trends changed for the economic status of men. That's when men's income began to decline. Let's compare the incomes of the baby boomers and their parents. Prior to 1973, young men could expect both promotions and sharp increases in their income. Thus, between 1949 and 1959, the average income of men age twenty-five to thirty-five (the fathers of the baby boomers) rose 118 percent (from $10,800 to $23,500). Between 1959 and 1969, men age twenty-five to thirty-five saw their average income rise 108 percent (from $13,900 to $28,900).

The year 1973 marked a dramatic change. From 1973 to 1984 (eleven years), the average income of men between age twenty-five and thirty-five (the baby boomers) rose only 16 percent (from $21,200 to $24,600). These incomes are in 1984 dollars, adjusted for inflation.

Now let's look at what happened to men in the age group forty to fifty. Before 1973, men in this age group had already received their ma-jor career promotions but still could expect to see their earnings rise significantly. Thus, between 1949 and 1959, the average income of men age forty to fifty (the fathers of the baby boomers) rose 34 percent. Be-tween 1959 and 1969, the average income of men age forty to fifty rose 29 percent. Again, 1973 was the changeover year. From 1973 to 1984 (eleven years), the average income of men age 40 to 50 (the baby boomers) fell 14 percent (from $28,100 to $24,100).

Why are the baby boomers, now twenty-one to forty years old, ac-tually losing ground? It is a combination of a number of factors, espe-cially the inflation that started with the 1973 oil embargo and reached double digits under Jimmy Carter and the steep increase in taxes that resulted from bracket creep and the doubling of Social Security taxes. A third major factor was the sudden expansion of the U.S. labor force, which exceeded the demand for workers and made it unnecessary to offer higher wages. This large labor supply was created both by the large number of baby boomers and by the flooding of millions of women and millions of immigrants into the job market.

The year 1973 also marked a turning point in real family income. It fell from a high of $28,167 in 1973 to $26,433 in 1984. When their income declined, the baby boomers reacted in various ways. They postponed marriage, they had fewer children, and they had them later. Most important, millions of wives moved into the labor force, which is why real family income didn't decline even further than it did.

Meanwhile, costs of necessities were going up sharply. Energy costs for home fuel and for automobiles rose more than 50 percent. The biggest price increase was in housing. In 1949, a thirty-year-old man spent only 14 percent of his monthly income on house payments. But in 1983, a thirty-year-old man spent 44 percent of his monthly earnings for house payments. In 1974 the Equal Credit Opportunity Act went into effect and forced banks to use the income of both spouses in determining their monthly mortgage payments (which, in turn, determines the price of the house they can buy). This created the fiction that twice as much money was available for the purchase of houses, and prices rose rapidly because people could get the credit to buy more expensive homes. Many young couples feel they must have two incomes in order to make it. But their situation is even worse than they think because their combined take-home pay is likely to be less than their fathers earned alone at a similar age.

1986

What Government Should Do for Mothers

Do we believe the federal government should be concerned about the financial bind that Americans are in today when it comes to the costs of having and raising children? You bet we do. We believe that Congress has an obligation, first of all, to eliminate the current discrimination that exists against some kinds of children and their mothers and in favor of other kinds of children and their mothers.

While de facto discrimination against various groups still exists, in some areas and against some minorities, de jure discrimination (specified in the law) has been pretty much eliminated. When challenged, legal discrimination on the basis of race, creed, color, or sex can hardly ever stand up in court, and it's hard to find a lawmaker at the congressional or state level who has the temerity to propose a discriminatory bill.

There is one class of Americans, however, that still is openly and massively discriminated against. This class of Americans is made up of the sixteen million full-time homemakers. The discrimination is most blatant in the income tax law. Nobody really defends the discriminatory provisions. Public officials and media spokesmen evade the issue by not talking about it.

The income tax law discriminates against the mothers who take care of their own children and in favor of the mothers who pay someone else to take care of their children. It's so outrageous that one wonders how the lawmakers had the nerve to pass something so unfair.

You can see it for yourself on line 41 of the 1986 income tax return Form 1040, and on attachment Form 2441. If you pay someone else to take care of your children under age fifteen, you can reduce your income taxes up to $720 for the first child and up to $1,440 for two or more children. But the mother who cares for her own children? Tough for her, she is denied these tax credits.

How could this be written into federal law without a big public policy debate? One explanation might be that two-earner couples, having an average of $11,000 a year more family income to spend than the traditional breadwinner-homemaker couples, are more aggressive in demanding tax reductions and preferential treatment, while the mother who is not employed is less able to go public about her needs. Another explanation might be that the social service bureaucracy lobbied for these changes in order to create a bigger demand for government-financed daycare services.

One way to remedy this discrimination is to "universalize" the child-care credit, that is, make it universally available to all children regardless of the lifestyle of their mothers. This could be done fairly and efficiently at $500 per child for the nineteen million children under age six. Now we can hear the argument, "But that is too costly!" Too costly? Discrimination ought to have no price. When it comes to taxes, fairness is far more important than cost.

An alternate remedy for this discrimination would be to trade off the child-care credit for a $1,000 increase in the tax exemption for all children. We could increase it from $2,000 to $3,000. If the cost argument is raised again, the increased exemption could be limited to children under age fifteen, or even under age six. Actually, the children's tax exemption ought to be $5,000 if a child were to be worth as much in the income tax system today as a child was worth thirty-five years ago.

Another provision of the income tax law that discriminates against homemakers is the Individual Retirement Account (IRA). Check it for yourself on line 26 of Form 1040. If both husband and wife are employed, they can put a total of $4,000 per year into IRA accounts. But if the wife is a full-time homemaker (whom Internal Revenue falsely calls a "nonworking spouse"), the couple can put a total of only $2,250 into IRA accounts, which is a discrimination of $1,750 per year plus all the income the IRA produces for the rest of their lives.

Like any employed man or woman, the full-time homemaker will grow old and need funds in her senior years. Why is the homemaker denied an equal opportunity to save tax-free funds for retirement in IRAs?

1987

Pornography's Victims

If persons in a public place engage in sexual acts, or take off all their clothes, or relieve themselves, they will be arrested—and should be arrested. They may be in violation of several laws; at the very least, they would be a public nuisance. Those acts may be all legal and proper in private, but we do not permit them in public.

If persons in a public or private place commit rape, assault, or battery, they will be arrested—and should be arrested. Rapes, whippings, beatings, and unwanted touching of another's body are against the law, and society will and should punish the offender.

Why, then, is it not likewise against the law to show a picture of these acts? Do they become socially acceptable just because they are presented on paper or film?

Those who answer yes to those questions invoke the First Amendment to clothe their illegal acts. They cry "censorship" to intimidate anyone who wants to stop their public display of, and commercial profiting from, these illegal acts.

Now add another element to this latter question. Suppose all the persons who were the target of these illegal acts were blacks, or Jews, or Native Americans, or children. The entire array of civil rights legislation and litigation developed in the last twenty-five years would move into merciless action. Our prevailing social mores would find such recordings on paper or film socially unacceptable. Publishers, periodicals, entertainment houses, and retail establishments would not risk releasing written or filmed presentations that suggest enjoyment of violent race discrimination, even if the cry of "censorship" were raised, which it would not be.

Why, then, are these acts not likewise against the law when the group targeted for rape, assault, battering, degradation, humiliation, or other abuse is women? Can these things be socially acceptable just because women are the victims? Are the civil liberties of the abusers ranked higher than the civil rights of the abused?

America has been moving relentlessly to clean up the quality of our air and water. No matter how legal or proper or necessary your business, prevailing social mores dictate that you may not pollute the air we breathe or the water we drink. The polluter is squeezed between legal action on the one hand and social condemnation on the other. In many cases, notably the pollution that comes from bituminous coal smoke belched by industry and the tobacco smoke emitted by smokers, the social condemnation preceded the legal restrictions.

Why, then, is pollution of our minds by pictures of violence and perversions not likewise against laws and social mores? Those who defend such pollution cry "censorship" at the mere suggestion that society may try to protect itself, its families, and its children from mental and moral pollution and destructive, antisocial behavior.

Those who cry "censorship" are the $8 billion-a-year pornography industry, plus all those who are making money out of any of the acts listed above. This includes the media (especially television networks, cable companies, and metropolitan newspapers that run movie ads), the entertainment industry, the abortion clinics, the organizations financed by donations or fees from pornographers (such as the American Civil Liberties Union), and the immense array of social service providers whose careers are advanced by increasing the numbers of persons with broken lives.

Pornography produces tremendously high profits. The person who goes into the pornography business may receive a higher return on his money than on almost any other investment. Retailers usually make a higher margin on pornographic materials than on any other merchandise they sell. Pornography generates its own money to finance its own advertising, its own public relations campaign, and its own paid agents to package their perversions in the cloak of the First Amendment, conducting smear campaigns against those who oppose them, such as falsely calling them "censors."

When the Attorney General's Commission on Pornography issued its report in mid-1986, it was greeted by an avalanche of press attacks crying "censorship" and "book banning" and suggestions that the report would interfere with the First Amendment and our "right to read." Such clichés were part of a clever advertising campaign orchestrated by the pornographers.

Gray and Company, the largest public affairs firm in Washington, D.C., received a lucrative account on the basis of a six-page contract offered to the pornographers' trade association. The Gray letter spelled out two principal strategies for a gigantic advertising campaign estimated to cost $900,000. First was an attempt "to convince the American people that campaigns to ban certain books, magazines, newspapers, movies, television shows, speeches and performances threaten everyone's freedom." The Gray letter set forth plans to try to "discredit the Commission on Pornography" by using newly created "front" groups under such deceptive titles as "Americans for the Right to Read" and "The First Amendment Coalition."

Second, Gray and Company's advertising strategy called for repeating, over and over again, the claim that the opposition to pornography comes only from "a group of religious extremists whose tactics and goals are clearly not representative of mainstream America" and that these religious "extremist pressure groups" are trying to "impose their narrow moral and social agenda on the majority."

To make these two themes the framework of public discussion about pornography, Gray and Company laid out an expensive plan to use a series of news conferences, "advertorials" in major national newspapers and magazines, and spokesmen on television and radio news, public affairs programs, and talk shows. Anytime you see or hear these themes, you can bet that it is, overtly or covertly, a paid political advertisement planted by the profiteering pornographers.

But are these people really against censorship? Or is that just a cover to conceal their promotion of pornography and its profits? Indeed, those who defend pornography with cries of "censorship" are themselves the most implacable censors of all.

The Attorney General's Commission on Pornography held hearings in six large media centers between June 19, 1985, and January 22, 1986: Washington, D.C., Chicago, Houston, Los Angeles, Miami, and New York City. The subject was timely, important, and controversial. The witnesses included law enforcement officers, physicians, clinicians, psychologists, psychiatrists, social scientists, film producers, publishers, legislators, and victims. Yet, these hearings produced no network or wire service coverage of the victims. The giant news media in America closed ranks and did not report their testimonies. By the end of the hearings, the transcript ran to some three thousand pages of testimony. No one cared to publish the transcripts of these sensational testimonies and make them available to the public.

This was censorship of the worst kind because there was no alternative source of the important information which the hearings provided. This censorship allowed pornographers to propagate the notion that pornography is a "victimless crime." But pornography cannot be victimless, because its very essence demands that a victim be subordinate. One cannot be an abuser unless there is an abused. Pornography portrays the past abuse, and pornography is a tool to facilitate future abuse.

The Attorney General's Commission on Pornography for the first time gave victims a platform from which to tell their eyewitness stories. These testimonies are not pleasant or comfortable or entertaining. They are ugly and depressing. But the crimes cry out for a remedy, even though the victims are not all blameless. The testimonies of these victims prove that pornography corrupts, and absolutely uncontrolled pornography corrupts absolutely. These testimonies prove that pornography is addictive and that those who become addicted crave more bizarre and more perverted pornography and become more callous toward their victims, even if they are their wives. Pornography is the bitter enemy of a stable marriage.

Pornography changes the perceptions and attitudes of men toward women, individually and collectively, and desensitizes men so that what was once repulsive and unthinkable eventually becomes not only acceptable but desirable. What was once mere fantasy becomes reality. With the poet we say, "Truth being truth, Tell it and shame the devil."

1987

Family Violence Is Everyone's Concern

"The family and family life are central to our American heritage. The family bonds give us an anchor in the past, as well as hope for the future. It is within the family that tradition is created, individuals grow, and faith is nurtured." So said President Ronald Reagan in 1984.

Stability in millions of homes in this country is threatened by a crime that flourishes in the shadows of secrecy. For generations, family violence has been the crime no one sees, talks about, or acts upon until a tragedy occurs. While the main source of fear for most people is violent crime by strangers, some Americans find that their own family members are the source of their most intense fear. They do not have to step outside their own houses to be abused, assaulted, maimed, or killed.

Usually it is the man in the family who abuses his wife or children. The head of the household, the very one charged with providing support and safety to the family, may actually inspire anything but secure feelings. The home, instead of a haven from outside forces, becomes a prison of hopelessness and of demeaning, violent behavior. Women are pushed, punched, kicked, beaten, hit with fists, slapped, or attacked with a weapon. Some are killed. Nearly 20 percent of the murders in 1986 were committed within the family.

Women are not just victimized only once. Abuse is seldom an isolated incident. The National Crime Survey showed that, during the period from 1978 to 1982, once a woman was victimized by domestic violence, her risk of being victimized again was considerably increased, especially if the crime was not reported to the authorities. Approximately one-third of these women were victimized again within six months.

These facts and figures do not include those who refuse to report on what they perceive as a private, family problem. Law enforcement officials consider spouse abuse to be the single most underreported crime in the United States.

The effects of domestic violence make an economic impact as well. It is estimated that $3 to $5 billion a year is lost to business because of injuries from domestic violence. This figure does not even include other costs which result from this crime, such as for health care, emergency aid, and welfare.

Most Americans do not want to admit that family violence is a real and enormous problem. Somehow, our society seems to have a collective unwillingness to admit that violence within family life is a tragedy of our time. We tend to ignore the violence, or condemn the victim, or choose sides, while allowing this terrible problem to evolve into a legacy of abuse. Only when we realize that violence touches our neighbors, our friends, and even our own families will we be committed to purging it from the homes in America. Hiding the crime, or hiding from the crime, may be almost as wrong as perpetrating it.

Tom Clifford of the *Newport News (Virginia) Daily Press-Times Herald* says, "People who live in domestic violence live in a tyranny of terror." Their plight is grievous because they believe they have no place to go where they can be safe and no one to whom they can turn who will listen with an understanding heart. They wear a mantle of guilt which has been placed on them by themselves and society.

Family violence is not just a political issue. It is a pro-family issue, a man's issue, a woman's issue, a church issue, a civic issue, and a criminal issue. Family violence is everybody's issue. We must all act in ways to intervene, prevent, support, and protect the victims. It is a human rights issue for which we all must take responsibility if we want to see our way of life, and the values that make America great, continue in generations to come.

1987

Feminist Ideology and Child Care

It's too bad that the feminist movement has raised false and unrealistic expectations in young women. Feminist spokesmen regularly preach that domestic duties must be shared by husbands, that child care should be subsidized by society, and that the daily chores that make a household function, by promoting cleanliness and good eating, are too menial to be performed by college-educated women.

Feminist ideology teaches that it is demeaning to women to care for their babies, and therefore the role of motherhood should be eliminated and daycare should become a government responsibility so that women can fulfill themselves in the paid labor force.

Even worse, the feminist movement has spawned the widespread notion that it's somebody else's duty to solve women's problems. What happened to individual responsibility? What happened to the physical, financial, and emotional support that families have always given to their own members?

Most of the pressure for subsidies is coming from career women who have a comfortable income but resent paying the high costs of hired daycare. This attitude is illustrated by a recent commentary in *American Medical News* entitled "Medical organizations must meet the needs of women physicians," written by Susan Adelman MD, a pediatric surgeon in Detroit.

Dr. Susan is blunt in laying her demands on the line. "The question is," she says, "what do most women physicians want? The answer is simple: a wife." Yes, you read that correctly. Dr. Susan continues: "What all women physicians need is somebody to help with housework, with food preparation, and with day care of any children they may bear."

Dr. Susan mounts her soap box and writes with force and conviction. In order to attract women members, Dr. Susan says, the AMA and its component societies should offer women physicians domestic maid services so they won't have to clean their own homes. Local and state medical societies should offer women physicians catering services so they won't have to cook for themselves.

Dr. Susan says hospitals should offer daycare services to women physicians so they won't have to take care of their own children. She wants hospitals and other employers to enjoy the benefit of a tax advantage if they provide maid services or daycare services to women physicians over and above their salaries.

Dr. Susan is almost belligerent about hurling her demands. The time has come, she said, to tell medical societies that want women members, and hospitals that want the patients of women physicians, that the women doctors will join up only if someone provides them with the services of a wife.

In the world we live in, not many people want to be the "wife" of a woman, even if she is a doctor, a lawyer, or a corporate executive, and no matter how high a salary she earns. In the world we live in, not many husbands are willing to do half of the household chores, cooking, and child care, and hardly any are willing to do the big majority of those duties which a wife gladly does for a husband.

Our society does, indeed, face many problems, and many less fortunate Americans need a helping hand of one kind or another. But the plight of the professional or business woman who wants someone else to provide her with a maid, cook, and babysitter should not be on any list of grievances for which someone else should provide a remedy. A surgeon has the income to buy her own domestic, kitchen, and baby-sitting services. She should cut out the crybaby act and stop asking others to subsidize the career lifestyle she has chosen.

1988

A Child's Place Is in the Home

More and more research is piling up to indicate that a young child's place is in the home and there is no adequate substitute for the bonding and attachment that take place between a child and his mother. A secure attachment in infancy provides the basis for self-reliance, self-regulation, and ultimately the capacity for independence combined with the ability to develop mature adult relationships.

"The primary goal of parenting should be to give a child a lifelong sense of security—a secure base from which he can explore the world, and to which he can return, knowing he will be welcomed, nourished, comforted and reassured," according to child psychologist John Bowlby of London's Tavistock Clinic. Bowlby is one of many psychologists who emphasize the importance of what is called the "attachment theory." The child's ability to establish intimate emotional bonds throughout life, as well as his mental health and effective functioning, depend on the strength and quality of his attachment to his parents, particularly his physical and emotional contact with his mother.

Research by Mary Ainsworth at the University of Virginia, Mary Main at the University of California, and Alan Sroufe at the University of Minnesota has consistently shown that the pattern of attachment developed in infancy and early childhood is profoundly influenced by the mother's ready availability, her sensitivity to her child's signals, and her responsiveness to his need for comfort and protection.

When a child is confident that his mother is available, responsive, and helpful, he develops a pattern of secure attachment. Extensive research shows how patterns of attachment that have been developed by twelve months of age are not only highly indicative of how the child will act in nursery school, but how he will act as an adolescent, as a young adult, and as a parent.

While the scientific and medical evidence shows the importance of a mother's consistent and ready availability, it does not show the need of a perfect mother. Pediatrician and psychoanalyst Donald Winnicott, who was as influential in England as Dr. Benjamin Spock was in America, showed that the conditions for secure attachment are fulfilled with what he called "good-enough mothering."

Winnicott said that adequate "holding" of a baby is indispensable to emotional development and essential for developing the child's capacity for empathy. The child should experience his mother as a "good and happy" person and should also know that his mother sees her infant as a "good and happy" person. Later, the child internalizes and draws on these images to comfort himself when the mother is not present. These same images are a reservoir from which the child can draw as he comforts others in his adult life.

Pennsylvania State University psychologist Jay Belsky (a former advocate of daycare) concluded that recent research reveals that infant daycare is "a risk factor for the development of insecure infant-parent attachment, non-compliance and aggression." Fifty percent of the daycare children he studied developed insecure attachments to their mothers and a wide range of negative behaviors.

Of course all children's behavior problems cannot be blamed on daycare. Belsky describes what he calls the "ecology" of daycare, meaning the child's total environment, including the mother's and father's emotional attitudes and skills, the family's socioeconomic circumstances, and the behavior of the mother when reunited with her child.

Recent research by other scholars confirms that the greatest risks in non-maternal care come from the failure of mother-infant attachment, which results from frequent and prolonged separations. Daycare infants are more likely to cry, more likely to be troublemakers, more likely to withdraw and be loners, more easily influenced by their peers, less cooperative with adults, and less likely to pursue tasks to completion. While it would be wrong to conclude that daycare harms all children, it clearly adds a significant level of extra distress and conflict.

1989

Mommy Tracks and Sequential Careers

Feminists reacted in holy horror when Felice Schwartz's article in the *Harvard Management Review* of January-February 1989 started the controversy about the Mommy Track. She wrote that "maternity is biological rather than cultural" and that maternity is not simply childbirth but a continuum that continues from pregnancy through bonding and childrearing.

The feminists are offended by any term indicating that there may be a different role for men and women, and they believe women are oppressed when society expects mothers to take care of their own children. They think "role" is a dirty four-letter word.

Schwartz, a credentialed career woman, spelled out a solution to the career-motherhood dilemma. She suggested that corporations offer their management-level female executives what amounts to a mommy track instead of foolishly expecting them to perform like men with 100 percent commitment to their careers. This heretical proposal upset the feminists like the little boy's assertion that the emperor has no clothes. Congresswoman Pat Schroeder denounced it as "tragic" and other feminist spokesmen are keeping their word processors hot by writing angry letters.

Ms. Schwartz comes from a feminist perspective. She admits that

some women are "career primary" and says they should have every opportunity to rise to the top in competition with men. But a successful
corporate or professional career means so many extra hours and personal
sacrifices for women that it "requires that they remain single or at least
childless or, if they do have children, that they be satisfied to have others raise them."

Ms. Schwartz argues that the majority of women are "career-and-
family women" who could be induced to stay on the job if the company
would offer part-time work, flexible hours, job sharing, and a mommy
track with lower pay and reduced rates of advancement. She says that
"most career-and-family women are entirely willing to make that trade-
off." She says this would be smart business for corporations because it
would enable them to keep talented mothers on the job and eventually
realize their investment in them.

Meanwhile, the *American Medical News* has just published an article called "Medicine + Motherhood" featuring authentic accounts of
women doctors who successfully and happily had "sequential careers."
The article gave example after example of women who raised their children first and then went to medical school, or had their babies immediately after graduation or residency training, dropped out for ten to twenty
years, and then started a medical career.

No, they didn't earn as much money as some full-time career-primary doctors. But most sequential physicians earn more than $50,000
and some more than $70,000.

The article described the lifetime satisfaction enjoyed by these sequential women. They made comments such as, "I have had the best of
both worlds of parenthood and a medical career. . . . The time I spent
with my wonderful daughters is worth every minute of the 10-year de-
lay. . . . I would advise my daughters to have children early and pursue
a professional career later."

Now that even the *New York Times* and the *Washington Post* have
conceded that we are in the "post-feminist" era, it's time to shed some

of feminism's bias against motherhood and recognize that, despite all the media propaganda and peer pressure on young women to become career-primary just like men, that's not what the majority of women want, especially if they are past thirty.

Whether women want to be career-primary and childless, or mothers and then career women sequentially, or part-time mother/part-time careerist, is a personal choice. It's a choice that should be allowed by our laws and business practices, not be restricted by laws that require a mindless gender neutrality.

1989

The Politics of Daycare

On January 7, 1988, the *MacNeil-Lehrer NewsHour* proclaimed that "child care" was America's number-one social issue. This was the opening blast of a massive media campaign to convince the American people to support universal federally financed daycare. This promotion was not designed to help the poor and needy, but to make daycare a middle-class entitlement.

NBC's *Today Show* soon boarded the publicity train for federal babysitting by giving friendly feature interviews to Betty Friedan and Patricia Schroeder. Newspapers started printing a torrent of manufactured news about an alleged "crisis" in daycare cost and safety. The cry was for "availability, affordability, and quality," catch words that translated into a demand that the federal government build, subsidize, and regulate all daycare.

On February 21, 1988, Dan Rather presented a segment on the *CBS Evening News* promoting the notion that the federal government should finance and regulate daycare. He showed visuals of a Russian daycare center and commented with admiration, "Whatever else the Soviet

Union does, it takes care of its children. Daycare is provided for all children from two months of age."

By April of 1988, the Public Broadcasting Service had joined the chorus. PBS-TV proclaimed Federal Daycare Week and spread its message on eight programs, including *Sesame Street*. A blatantly biased one-hour "documentary" on April 13 not only tried to sell the American people on federal daycare for all children, but featured oh-so-friendly interviews with Senator Christopher Dodd and Democratic presidential candidate Michael Dukakis, without a single opposing spokesman.

Media coverage of the child-care issue in 1988 was loaded at least ten to one in favor of initiating federally funded and federally regulated daycare.

By the time Congress started to consider the legislative centerpiece of this public relations offensive, the Dodd-Kildee ABC bill, subcommittee chairmen Senator Christopher Dodd (D-CT) and Representative Dale Kildee (D-MI) felt secure enough to stack the hearings without any pretense of fairness to opposing viewpoints. At the House Education and Labor Subcommittee hearing on February 25, 1988, all twenty-two witnesses supported the bill; not one witness was permitted to testify against it. The Senate Labor and Human Resources Subcommittee hearing on March 15 was similarly staged with sixteen witnesses in favor of federal daycare and only one against it.

As a result of complaints about such bias, a few persons opposed to federal daycare bills, including Secretary of Education William Bennett, were finally permitted to testify before a Kildee subcommittee hearing on April 21. Opponents of the Dodd-Kildee bill labeled it "discriminatory" because the bill would deny all benefits to mothers who take care of their own children, while benefiting only mothers who purchase daycare from federally approved providers.

The real shocker came when a Republican congressman asked a federal daycare advocate this question at a hearing: If an employed mother arranges for her child to be cared for during the day by Grandmother or Aunt Millie (who has already raised three children of her own), don't you think that mother should have the same benefit in any federal legislation as the employed mother who puts her child in a daycare center?

The liberal panelist responded: Only if Grandmother or Aunt Millie is licensed, regulated, and has received government training. The implications of that reply rippled through Washington, and President Ronald Reagan commented that we certainly can't have any legislation that requires grandmothers to be licensed or registered.

The profoundly biased news reports to which the American people were subjected in 1988 revealed the publicity professionalism of four interest groups that joined together in a political coalition to promote large-scale federal financing of babysitting centers, federal regulation of all daycare, and the establishment of group care for infants and preschool children as the norm and a new middle-class entitlement.

The first leg in this four-legged coalition was the feminists. Their ideology has taught them that society's expectation that mothers take care of their own children is unfair and impedes women's opportunity to participate full-time in the paid labor force and thereby achieve economic equality with men.

The second group was made up of the child "developmentalists" who had been seeking an opportunity to revive the discredited recommendations of the 1970 White House Conference on Children and the failed legislative proposals of the Mondale-Brademas Comprehensive Child Development bill. The chief guru of those advocating federal regulation and control of child care is Professor Edward F. Zigler at the Yale University Bush Center in Child Development. At its tenth anniversary dinner on September 18, 1987, Zigler revealed the real plans and purposes of people such as himself whom he calls "developmentalists."

Zigler called for a federal daycare program that will cost "$75 to $100 billion a year." He said he wants the new federal daycare system to "become part of the very structure of our society," under the principle that "every child should have equal access to child care and all ethnic and socio-economic groups should be integrated as fully as possible." Zigler urged, "The child care solution must cover the child from as early in pregnancy as possible through at least the first 12 years of life." He wants children to be reared by a "partnership between parents and the children's caretakers," headquartered in the public schools.

The third component of the daycare coalition was the liberal Democrats. On a January weekend in 1988, 131 Democratic congressmen went up to the Greenbrier resort at White Sulphur Springs, West Virginia, to discuss how to win the 1988 elections. They devised a game plan to use "kids' issues" to help the Democratic congressmen reclaim constituencies they had lost to the Republicans, who had rather successfully made "family values" their rallying cry during the years of the Reagan Administration.

Stanley B. Greenberg of The Analysis Group Inc. presented an issue paper called "Kids As Politics: A Proposed Campaign Strategy for Democratic Candidates in 1988." Its theme was that engaging in political rhetoric about "kids" would provide the Democrats with "an enormous opportunity to shape the political discourse, after years of responding to a public debate controlled by the Republicans." The cold and calculating discussion of children as a means to get votes was apparent from the rhetoric used by this high-priced campaign consultant: "kids are an umbrella . . . kids are a common currency . . . kids are a common coinage." The paper urged that "Democrats must get voters to focus on their anxieties about the future and make those feelings real and effective. Kids are the best vehicle."

The fourth factor in the daycare coalition was the social service professionals, a vast army of tax-salaried people who would like to expand their ranks, their pay, and their turf. The key to doing that is to have more social problems that require more care and more counseling. It's a bureaucracy that feeds on itself.

The social service professionals integrated their network with the other three segments of the coalition to form the Child Care Action Campaign. In order to focus on their legislative objectives, they staged a conference at the Waldorf-Astoria Hotel in New York City on March 17-18, 1988. It was designed to promote a massive expansion of their tax-paid turf by stimulating support for the Dodd-Kildee ABC bill.

The headline speakers were a leading liberal Democrat, Senator Chris Dodd, and a leading feminist, Gloria Steinem, neither of whom had any children. One of the problems with the child-care issue is the number of self-appointed spokesmen cavalierly prescribing group care for babies who themselves have never had the care of even one baby, let alone ten or twenty infants at one time. Most persons advocating group care of babies haven't the foggiest idea of the immense amount of work and love required to care for an infant.

The exciting highlight of the conference was breakfast with Phil Donahue. The board of directors of the Child Care Action Campaign included the former head of the National Organization for Women, Eleanor Smeal, and current heads of other feminist organizations, the NOW Legal Defense & Education Fund, the National Women's Political Caucus, and *Ms.* magazine. The Child Care Action Campaign published a newsletter that provided advice on child care from such experts as Dr. Ruth.

The stated goal of this formidable coalition was to make daycare part of the "infrastructure" of our society. Each of the four groups in the coalition, for its own purposes, wanted to change our culture by persuading the American people to adopt and publicly finance universal group care of preschool children.

Child care poses the fundamental question of whether the giant apparatus of government will be pro-family or anti-family. Will we have lower taxes or increased taxes, more government taking over of family functions or less? The complaint is often voiced that the United States is the only Western nation that has no child-care policy. We do, indeed, need a child-care policy—one that is in harmony with American freedoms, family integrity, and economic growth. That policy should be: Cut the taxes on families with children so they can spend more of their hard-earned money with 100 percent freedom of choice.

1989

Who Is Liberated by Divorce?

Back in 1970 when the women's liberation movement was just gathering momentum, a New York University professor named Warren T. Farrell provided the rationale for why it should be supported by men. Essentially, his argument was that men should eagerly look forward to the day when they can enjoy free sex and not have to pay for it.

Farrell advocated a never-never land where a husband would no longer be "saddled with the tremendous guilt feelings" when he leaves his wife with nothing, after she has given him her best years. If a husband loses his job, he should not feel compelled to take any job to support his family, Farrell told the American Political Science Association. Farrell spoke in academic verbiage, but his message was clear.

The male millennium that Professor Farrell so eagerly sought and predicted has largely come about. The chief change in our now liberated society was the adoption of easy, no-fault divorce.

This change in our divorce laws has affected the social, economic, cultural, and legal fabric of our society more than anything else that has happened in the last two decades. One can avoid participating in or succumbing to other changes, but the changed laws and attitudes about divorce affect us all. No one can force you to have an abortion or to read pornography. If you can't pray in school, you can still pray at home, in church, and in your heart. You can escape what you deem to be intolerable situations by changing your job or your school.

But divorce—the dissolution of a solemn mutual contract in which you pledge your life, your honor, your name, your commitment, and your future—can be thrust upon you without your consent. It takes two to marry, but now one spouse can terminate the marriage without the consent of the other. The very existence of this sword of Damocles hanging over every husband and wife validates the attitude that marriage is temporary and based on self-satisfaction, rather than on commitment and responsibility.

The radical feminist movement peddled easy, no-fault divorce as liberation for women when, in fact, it was chiefly liberation for men. The feminists didn't discover their mistake until Lenore Weitzman published her landmark 1985 book, *The Divorce Revolution*, which proved that easy divorce usually means economic devastation for women.

It is also time for someone to speak up and say out loud that a large part of the human cost of divorce is paid by the children.

1990

Why Feminists Target Wives

If there ever were a book that our culture has been wanting for the last thirty years, *Domestic Tranquility* by Carolyn Graglia is it. With library shelves sagging under the weight of so many tiresome tirades by third-rate feminist writers, and college courses morphing into Oppression Studies, we've been sorely needing exactly what Carolyn Graglia has given us: a scholarly brief against feminism.

Mrs. Graglia has saved us from having to read those tedious tomes and pitiful polemics taught in women's-studies courses, which ought to be called feminist indoctrination sessions. She has woven the whinings of all those pseudointellectual feminists into a coherent exposition of their incoherent ideology, and then totally demolished their pretenses.

Mrs. Graglia correctly identifies the real target of the feminists' savage campaign. It's not equality or opportunity for women in the marketplace; it's not promoting choice of careers or lifestyles. The feminists' goal is the elimination of the role of the full-time homemaker by making it un-chic and uneconomic, indeed, downright irrational. Their goal is the elimination of the full-time homemaker by status degradation on the psychological front and financial degradation on the economic front.

Why should that be? After all, wouldn't career-seeking feminists be glad, at least after they have written affirmative action into the law, to enjoy reduced competition from other women?

Not if you understand feminist ideology. The feminists realize all too well that they cannot achieve a level playing field in the marketplace so long as their male competitors have the advantage of full-time homemaker wives who cook their meals, tend their children, make their homes a refuge from the competitive world, and motivate them to work harder to provide for their dear ones. Feminists believe that achievement of their own career goals depends on depriving their male competitors of the advantage of having wives. *Ergo*, feminists are determined to push all wives out of the home and into the labor force.

The feminist animus toward wives reminds us of a Russian fable. Boris had a goat and Ivan had none. One day the good fairy appeared and told Ivan she would grant him one wish. Ivan made his request: I want that Boris's goat should die.

Mrs. Graglia comprehensively dissects feminism in all its disguises and contradictions. She unmasks it for what it is: a vicious and relentless war against the traditional family, a take-no-prisoners war to eliminate husband breadwinners and dependent-wife homemakers. Feminist tactics include laying a guilt trip on husbands and humiliating their wives, making both unhappy with their roles.

Since feminism's goals demand that virtually all women enter the labor force, feminists seek to undermine the traditional wife's financial security and destroy her self-worth, the former by changes in our laws, the latter by name-calling. Since the mid-1960s, we have been hit in our psychological solar plexus with a chorus of epithets designed to demolish the homemaker's self-esteem. She was called a parasite because she is not working in paid employment, warned that devoting herself to childrearing is an unworthy endeavor, and taunted that she lives without using adult capability or intelligence.

As Mrs. Graglia so exquisitely explains, feminism's impact on young women, not yet old enough to experience love and romance, has been dramatic. Thousands of American women made this tragic mistake. But having made it, they feel a compelling emotional need to defend it and to justify it.

In a Washington conference in January 1989, the economist and social theorist George Gilder described how feminism persuaded women to focus on their careers in their twenties and early thirties, competing intensely with men for advancement in their jobs, and then if perhaps they decide they want to "have it all," at about age forty they can think about marriage. At that point, they discover it is much harder for a woman to get married, or at least to marry a man she wants to marry. Gilder explained that the real heart of the daycare controversy "is essentially about ratifying the feminist mistake—an attempt to give public ratification to the appalling error which millions of American women made in the 1970s and 1980s."

Look to the feminists themselves for confirmation of this feminist mistake. After turning forty, Germaine Greer, one of the icons of the fiercely independent, aggressively sexual new women, who boasted of their lovers but rejected marriage and motherhood in favor of career, wrote in the British magazine *Aura*: "I was desperate for a baby and I have the medical bills to prove it. I still have pregnancy dreams, waiting for something that will never happen."

The *New York Times* Metro editor Joyce Purnick, speaking to the graduates at a Barnard College commencement, said "Don't pretend you don't have a biological clock because you do. . . . Time moves along, and then the window closes." By the time she realized she wanted children, it was too late.

Carolyn Graglia also exposes the consequences of the feminist campaign to persuade young women to abandon modesty, virginity, and the traditional withholding of sexual favors until marriage. Feminism is a Pied Piper who led them to believe that men and women are fungible, not only in the workplace, not only in the kitchen and nursery, but also in bed. Liberation for women came to mean that women must participate in, indeed, must enjoy, casual uncommitted sex just like men. Androgynous currents in literature, entertainment, and education have disadvantaged a significant segment of young Americans so that they don't know how to attract a spouse and cultivate a mutual and enduring commitment to marriage and family. That's too bad, because they are missing out on the greatest joys of life.

Mrs. Graglia's analytical description of feminist theory and behavior is depressing. But she ends on a hopeful note. She hopes that women, like Wagner's Brunnhilde, will abandon their warrior role and awaken to life in the arms of a noble, courageous, and manly man like Siegfried, who will become "my joy, my wealth, my world, my one and all!"

Mrs. Graglia eloquently defends the notion that the career of wife and mother produces rewards that outweigh those of the workplace. She invites young women to rediscover their modesty, awaken their femininity, and enjoy the rewards of conjugal love and lifetime commitment.

Can today's young woman resist the social imperatives of the feminist movement, so fiercely reinforced by unremitting pressure from peers and media? A wise man once said, there are only two classes of people in the world: those who profit from the mistakes of others and those who insist on making their own mistakes. Every young woman should arm herself psychologically by reading George Gilder's *Men and Marriage* in order to understand men, and *Domestic Tranquility* in order to understand women. They are powerful weapons of sanity in a disorganized and uncertain world.

The traditional, pro-family woman does not need to search for her identity. She has her values in good order. She is dedicated to faith in God, service to family, and appreciation for this great country in which we are so fortunate to live. She does not seek her fulfillment at the price of taking benefits away from others, as the feminists are forever doing. We know that in America, the land of supreme opportunity, women can make whatever they want of their lives.

1998

Two Faces of Marriage Tax Reform

Repeal of the marriage tax penalty is always good for a big round of applause in the campaign speeches of political candidates. But the political bombast usually conceals the social policy that lurks behind the two approaches to reform.

The marriage tax is not verbally expressed as policy in any statute but is buried in the numbers. You can't find a section in the tax law that is labeled "marriage tax." It is a consequence of our income tax treating a married couple as only 1.67 persons instead of two whole persons.

Remedying the marriage tax is not just a matter of dollars. Ideology is at stake. Is the purpose of cutting the marriage tax to give long overdue respect to marriage as an institution fundamental to our society and to the raising of children? Or is the purpose to enable government to engage in national economic planning by using taxes to influence human behavior?

If the purpose is the former, then it follows that all married couples with the same income should be taxed equally. Congress dealt fairly with this issue by passing a bill in 2000 that would tax one-earner and two-earner married couples equally. President Clinton vetoed the bill, and it did not become law.

If, on the other hand, the plan is to give a tax break only to two-earner couples, that plan would replace the marriage penalty with a new homemaker penalty. Even politicians who don't particularly care about promoting marriage should be squeamish about discriminating against one type of married couple in favor of another.

But some influential policymakers argue that it would be an economic good for the tax law to advantage two-earner couples and disadvantage breadwinner-homemaker style couples. These economists praise giving more tax breaks to two-earner couples because that will induce married women toward greater participation in the labor force, which in turn will increase our Gross Domestic Product.

Edward McCaffery, a law professor at the University of Southern California, is favorably quoted in a Heritage Foundation analysis of the marriage penalty: "The fact that potential workers would avoid the labor force as a result of peculiarities in the tax code is a clear sign of a failure to maximize eligible resources. As a result, the nation as a whole fails to reach its economic potential, which is demonstrated by decreased earnings, output, and international competitiveness." In other words, The Economy wants wives and mothers to join the workforce in order to reach our nation's economic potential.

Alan Reynolds of the Hudson Institute wrote in *National Review* in 1999 that the U.S. economy is "running short of willing and able workers" primarily because high marginal tax rates are "driving skilled married women out of the labor force." The assumption behind this argument is that full-time homemakers are economic non-contributors, indifferent to the wants of The Economy.

Look at how the two approaches to marriage tax reform impact on a family budget. Let's say a married couple is struggling financially and needs more income to support the family, perhaps because of the birth of a child. What choices are available?

One family decides to be a two-earner couple; the wife takes a job and puts her children in daycare. Under one plan considered by Congress, this couple would get a marriage tax deduction of 10 percent of her salary up to $30,000; that would chop as much as $990 off the family's federal income tax bill (at the proposed 33 percent tax rate). In addition, this couple would qualify for the existing tax credit for child-care expenses, which is worth up to $960.

In another family, the husband moonlights at a second job so his wife can care for their children at home. This family will not qualify for either the 10 percent marriage tax deduction or the child-care credit that exists in current tax law.

Moonlighting at a second job is just one of several ways a husband can provide his children with the benefits of a full-time mother and avoid commercial daycare. The husband can work longer hours at his first job; he can make the extra effort required to get a higher-paying job; he can go to school at night to train for a higher-paying career.

The husband and wife surely work just as hard in this second family as in the first. Why should they pay up to $1,950 more in federal income taxes on the same family income? Who are the bureaucrats and politicians who presume to use the tax power to force traditional husband-breadwinner, wife-homemaker couples to subsidize two-earner couples who hire paid child care?

The marriage penalty in the tax code is an immoral policy, but it should not be remedied by giving a tax cut only to two-earner couples. That would send the radical feminist message that the government sees no value in a homemaker's work at home, that the role of a "non-working" wife and mother is less socially beneficial (or less worthy) than paid employment.

2001

A Daycare Bombshell Hits the "Village"

The advocates of "It takes a village to raise a child" are having a rough year. They are scurrying around trying to come up with arguments to refute the new study showing that children who spend most of their time in daycare are three times as likely to exhibit behavior problems in kindergarten as those who are cared for primarily by their mothers.

Children who spend more than thirty hours a week in daycare were found to be more demanding and more aggressive. They scored higher on things like fighting, cruelty, bullying, meanness, talking too much, and making demands that must be met immediately. The study found a direct correlation between time spent in daycare and a child's aggression, defiance, and disobedience. The findings held true regardless of the type or quality of daycare, the sex of the child, the family's socioeconomic status, or the quality of the mother care.

Why is anybody surprised that social science research is confirming reality? True science always verifies reality; it's only junk science that manufactures illusions based on ideologies.

The new study followed more than eleven hundred children in ten cities in every kind of daycare setting, from care with relatives and nannies to preschool and large daycare centers. The study was financed by the National Institute on Child Health and Human Development, a branch of the National Institutes of Health that produced a daycare-friendly report in 1996.

The "village" advocates are swarming all over the media with their feeble rebuttals. They argue, without evidence, that better quality daycare might produce different results, that the real problem is that employed parents are tired and stressed, and that the study hasn't undergone rigorous peer review. Of course, there are other variables, including viewing television, the divorce of parents, and the amount of father care. But this new study is the most comprehensive to date and it finds daycare wanting by a significant margin.

The new study corroborates the findings of one of its principal investigators, Dr. Jay Belsky, who shocked the child-development world with an article entitled "Infant Day Care: A Cause for Concern?" in 1986. Belsky reported on the evidence then piling up that infants who spent long hours in daycare were at risk of behavioral problems later.

At that time, the daycare industry and the "village" advocates in the child-development field were preparing to launch a national advertising campaign for federally funded, federally regulated daycare as a new middle-class entitlement. They felt threatened by this article by Belsky, then just a young associate professor at Pennsylvania State University.

So the daycare industry lowered the professional boom on the upstart professor who dared to challenge the then-prevailing feminist notion that commercial daycare was what infants really needed so that their mothers could fulfill themselves in the labor force. The word went out: Don't buy Belsky's textbook, shun him at professional meetings, label him a misogynist.

The reason the daycare issue arouses such bitter antagonism is not only that it challenges liberals who want to expand government social services by having the "village" take over raising children. The daycare issue also strikes at the heart of feminist ideology: that it is oppressive for society to expect mothers to care for their own children. Any evidence that shows commercial daycare as inferior to mother care must be destroyed and the messengers vilified.

Remarkably, Belsky didn't kowtow to the politically correct gestapo, as so many academics have done. He is now a professor at the University of London, and this time he was joined in his research by some of the most respected child-development experts.

Hillary Clinton made an attempt to peddle the notion of a daycare "crisis" as her "frontier issue" in 1997. She hosted an exclusive shindig at the White House featuring all the usual suspects of those who want the "village" to raise children, such as her friend Marian Wright Edelman of the Children's Defense Fund, but the American people turned a deaf ear to her cries of "crisis."

The conservative solution to child-care needs has always been tax credits, that is, let parents spend their own money for the child care of their choice and don't force mothers taking care of their own children to subsidize babysitters for employed moms. Fortunately, we've made some progress in legislating child credits into the income tax code.

2001

The U.N. Treaty on the Rights of the Child

The United Nations Convention on the Rights of the Child, signed in 1995 by Bill Clinton but wisely never ratified by our Senate, is a pet project of those who believe that the "village" should raise children rather than their parents, including Hillary Clinton and her buddies at the Children's Defense Fund.

If this treaty were proposed as federal legislation, it would be quickly rejected by Congress and the American people. That's because it would give the federal government unacceptably broad new powers over children, families, and schools. If we wouldn't give such powers to our own government, why would we even talk about granting such powers to a panel of foreign bureaucrats, even when they call themselves "experts"?

This UN treaty purports to give the child the right to express his own views "freely in all matters," to receive information of all kinds through "media of the child's choice," to "freedom of religion," to be protected from "interference with his or her privacy . . . or correspondence," to have access to information from national and "international sources," to use his "own language," and to have the right to "rest and leisure." These are just a few of the dozens of new "rights of the child" scattered throughout the fifty-four articles of the UN treaty, which is longer than the U.S. Constitution.

Do we really want to give every child the legal right to say anything he wants to his parents at the dinner table? To watch television ("access to the media") instead of doing homework? To escape household chores because they interfere with his UN right to "rest and leisure"? To join a cult instead of attending his parents' church? To refuse to speak English in our public schools?

Unlike our U.S. Constitution, which only mentions rights that can be enforced against the government, this UN treaty declares rights of the child against parents, the family, private institutions, and society as a whole. Since the treaty is a legal document which, if ratified, would become part of the "supreme law of the land," we can expect liberal lawyers to bring test cases to persuade activist judges to push its reach as far as they can.

Current U.S. law prohibits our own federal government from prescribing any school curriculum, but this UN treaty on the child prescribes curricula with meddlesome specificity. It calls for teaching children respect for "the principles enshrined in the Charter of the United Nations," for "the national values of . . . civilizations different from his or her own," for "tolerance" and "equality of the sexes," and for "the natural environment."

This UN treaty requires governments, to the "maximum extent of their available resources," to assure the right of every child to an "adequate standard of living," including "nutrition, clothing and housing." The treaty would require us to "ensure the development" of child-care institutions, facilities, and services. These provisions cannot be implemented without money, so will the courts require our government to impose new taxes to carry out these treaty obligations?

We are not fooled by the treaty's use of abortion euphemisms such as "her right of access to health care services," "preventive health care," "family planning education and services," "reproductive health services," and "privacy." Another treaty right, "equality of the sexes," has been repeatedly used by the feminists in U.S. courts to require states to pay for Medicaid abortions.

Of course, all these far-reaching UN treaty goals would not be complete without the establishment of a new international bureaucracy, so Article 43 sets up a committee of ten so-called "experts." There is no assurance that any American will be on this committee or that even one expert will be sensitive to American institutions and traditions.

Nothing proves the hypocrisy of this treaty more than the repeated taunts that every nation has ratified it except the United States and Somalia. Countries that have already ratified it regularly engage in child labor, slavery, mutilation, and selling girls and boys into prostitution, and we don't want to join their club.

The UN Convention on the Rights of the Child is a bad deal for Americans on every count, and we hope the United States Senate will never ratify it.

2001

Index

Phyllis Schlafly was named one of the one hundred most important women of the twentieth century by the *Ladies' Home Journal.* She is America's most articulate and successful opponent of radical feminism and led the pro-family movement to victory in a ten-year battle against the Equal Rights Amendment. She has been a national leader of the conservative movement since 1964.

Mrs. Schlafly is the author or editor of twenty books on subjects as varied as politics (*A Choice Not an Echo*), family and feminism (*The Power of the Positive Woman*), nuclear strategy (*Kissinger on the Couch*), education (*Child Abuse in the Classroom*), child care (*Who Will Rock the Cradle?*), and literacy (*First Reader* and *Turbo Reader*).

Mrs. Schlafly is a lawyer and served as a member of the Commission on the Bicentennial of the U.S. Constitution, 1985-1991, appointed by President Reagan. She has testified before more than fifty congressional and state legislative committees on constitutional, education, strategic defense, foreign policy, electronic privacy, and family issues. A Phi Beta Kappa graduate of Washington University, she received her J.D. from Washington University Law School and her Master's in Government from Harvard University.

Mrs. Schlafly is a syndicated columnist, radio commentator, has written a monthly newsletter called *The Phyllis Schlafly Report* since 1967, has lectured or debated on more than five hundred college campuses, and has appeared on nearly every national television talk show. The mother of six children, she was the 1992 Illinois Mother of the Year.

This book was designed and set into type
by Mitchell S. Muncy,
with cover art by Lee Whitmarsh,
and printed and bound
by Edwards Brothers, Inc.,
Ann Arbor, Michigan.

❦

The text face is Adobe Caslon,
designed by Carol Twombly,
based on faces cut by William Caslon, London, in the 1730s,
and issued in digital form by Adobe Systems,
Mountain View, California, in 1989.

❦

The index is by IndExpert,
Fort Worth, Texas.

❦

The paper is acid-free and is of archival quality.

32